MICHELSEN, CLIVE S.
OREGON ECO-FRIENDLY WINE
: W   LEADERS IN GREEN W
C20
3756500630 100 HE

OFFICIAL
DISCARD
Sonoma County Library

S0-CBS-926

SONOMA COUNTY

WINE LIBRARY

Oregon Eco-Friendly Wine

World leaders in Green Wine

First Edition

All rights reserved. No part of this publication may be reproduced, stored in a retrieval system, or transmitted in any form or by any means, electronic, mechanical, photocopying, recording or otherwise, without the prior written permission of the copyright owner and/or the publisher. Enquiries concerning translation into another language or distribution rights should be sent to the publisher at the below address:

JAC International AB

Box 60 220

S-216 09 LIMHAMN Sweden

www.malmo-wine-academy.com

info@malmo-wine-academy.com

© Clive Michelsen, 2008

Original Oregon Eco-Friendly Wine

Cover: Eaterine Bagdavadze

Layout: Clive Michelsen

Written by: Clive Michelsen

Edited by: Leif Sahlqvist

Printed in China

ISBN: 91-975326-4-9

EAN Code: 09789197532648

This book is dedicated to my brother

Ian Sofus Michelsen

with admiration for his ability to innovate and create!

Acknowledgements go to the following contributors:

Stephany Boettner at the Oregon Wine Board for her help and data,

Dr. Don & Margie Olson, Torii Mor Vineyard & Winery for their insight in
asking me to write this book, their assistance and friendship,

King Estate for introducing me to the IPNC, and

to all the wineries and vineyards that graciously accepted me and my camera.

Contents

Next Page Left Picture: *The author drinking a good glass of Chardonnay at King Estate.* **Center & Right Pictures:** *Looking over Villamette Valley Vineyards.*

Introduction

If you had asked me fifteen years ago about Oregon wines, I would have replied "they're good or I am not really sure." However, during the last decade Oregon winemakers and growers have marched to the forefront of the winemaking world with innovative eco-friendly programs in their vineyards and wineries; what's more, they are producing some of the world's best Pinot Noir, Pinot Gris and Pinot Blanc. These wines not only show grape typicity, elegance and finesse but they are "food-friendly". This little northwestern state offers so much more than just wine. If Oregon is the "New World's" answer to Grand Cru Burgundy—Oregonians are, without doubt, world leaders in organic, biodynamic, sustainable agriculture and low-energy friendly wineries. This eco-friendly state is leading the way for all others. Their winery designs include free-flow (gravity flow), solar power energy generating units, water recycling and energy efficient programs such as LEED (Leadership in Energy and Environmental Design). These efforts should not go unnoticed by the wine-drinking public. I can only urge you to celebrate these pioneers by buying and drinking a bottle of wine from them. Oregonians also host the second largest Blues Festival in the world (a continuous three stage, four-day, jam-packed event to raise money for the hungry), various one day open-air jazz concerts in the many parks, the Pinot Camp and the acclaimed International Pinot Noir Celebration (IPNC), an annual event that draws Pinot Noir producers from around the world to show off their wines with a myriad of activities and culinary events. June, July and August are just filled with these socially oriented activities for both family and friends. Furthermore, Portland, Oregon's largest city, boasts a thriving arts community with literally hundreds of excellent restaurants serving professionally matched wines and foods. If you haven't yet found the next best thing to utopia, you should definitely plan a trip to Oregon during the month of July and August.

Terroir is one ingredient that makes Oregon Pinot Noir so good. Naturally, it's a combination of factors. Oregon has a unique topography with two mountain ranges running north/south and an extremely rich volcanic and fertile valley in between. This valley is fed with cool Pacific winds and fog through a number of corridors to the west. The Cascade Mountain Range and five very large volcanoes (Mt. Hood, Mt. Jefferson, Mt. Rainier, Mt. Adams & Mt. Helens) which lie to the east, and the Coastal Range to the west. Over 15,000 years ago the region was extremely active with volcanoes and floods. One such flood, called the Missoula Floods (10,000 to 15,000 years ago) and originating in Montana, deposited a bed of gravel, basalt, clay, loam and silt, rock and boulders over the original volcanic and sedimentary seabed. The most common type of soil found is the volcanic red Jory soil; however, it is only found 300+ feet above the valley floor as these were above the Missoula Floods. The higher ground therefore offers very high grade soils with the old volcanic red Jory, a grape vine's dream. Sedimentary-based soil can be found below the 300 feet. The fertile soils together with the cool evenings and prevailing Pacific winds along with the morning fog and hot warm afternoons create perfect climatic conditions for grape growing. Oregon's eco-friendly programs (L.I.V.E., Sustainable Agriculture, Organic, Biodynamic, LEED, Salmon Safe, and others), many of which are voluntary, lay the foundation for good wine-making. Without good fruit you will never be able to make good wine. This is a well-known fact and prerequisite which Oregonians have embraced more than any other wine region in the world. If you talk with any of the wineries they'll mention that they are "Stewards of the Land." One thing is for

*Large Picture Right: Classic sign which is part of the skyline in downtown Portland. **Next Page:** The annual Salmon Bake at the International Pinot Noir Celebration (IPNC). The pictures shows how the Salmon is baked over an open fire, wedged between alderwood and horizontally supported by cedarwood over an open fire, served with a tradition buffet. After dinner winemakers and Pinot Noir enthusiasts from around the world meet and share their wines as they go from table to table and talk Pinot. Tickets cost $150.00 per person and are worth it!*

FLATBREAD

sure, environmentalists and critics of US environmental policy have never been to Oregon!

I would never have believed that you could drink 14 year old Pinot Noirs from Oregon? Well, let me say that I have and they were spectacular! The wines tasted were excellent, well developed, showing vibrant aromas, subtle fine tannins, superb fruit and acid balance, with excellent length. After this experience I was sold on Pinot from Oregon and began to search for a perfect music scenario that could match the experience and the anticipation of drinking a well made Pinot Noir from Oregon. I came up with a few pieces of my favorite music which might explain what I really feel. I begin with a prelude to Debussy and "La Fille aux cheveux de lin", which sets the mood for opening one of your treasured Oregon Pinot Noirs. This music only takes about 2.31 minutes. So you'll have to move with some grace and urgency. I pour the wine into a large glass and put on yet another Debussy, "Clair de Lune" (5.04 minutes) while I probe the wine's bouquets. Take small, well-refined sniffs—typical, red berry, spicy, flowery characters combined with a velvety balance and the harmony of

Picture Left: *The autumn in Willamette Valley.*

a gentle touch will emerge. The romance of tranquility will begin to emerge. Take your time and enjoy the moment! Swirl the wine a number of times, sit back, relax, and take pleasure in the aromas of a top Oregon Pinot Noir. The anticipation of tasting the characters will only enhance your willingness to relish in its taste. It's time to change to Rachmaninoff's "Rhapsody," on a Theme by Paganini, variation no. 18 (3.22). Feel the finesse, balance, smoothness, growth and depth of the wine—life, romance, friends, food and Pinot Noir. Fantastic! Savor the flavor and aftertaste with Mozart's Piano Concerto No. 20 in D Minor, K. 466 (II. Romance—9:19 minutes).

If you achieve this in your tasting you have managed to experience what the best Pinot Noirs of the "Modern World" or "New World" can produce. Burgundy's Côte de Nuits has got competition in Oregon and if they want to retain their number one position they'll have to pull a few rabbits out of their hats in the near future. Taste your way through Oregon, you will not be let down. Take your time and enjoy its bounty. Its wine, personality, people and culture will stay with you for a lifetime. Once savored, forever treasured.

Cheers,

Eco-Friendly Viticulture & Vinification

There are many programs dedicated to sustainable farming practices in Oregon. Some required as much as two years within an apprentice program after fulfilling all requirements. These programs include L.I.V.E., VINEA, Organic and Biodynamic, but it does not stop there. Other programs to reduce energy and environmental design, water recycling and clean energy also exist. Although, not all are certified, many of the vineyards and wineries practice sustainable farming and LEED on a voluntary basis by employing these practices and principles in their vineyards and wineries.

LIVE (Low Input Viticulture & Enology)
LIVE, Inc. is a sustainable agricultural program which provides growers a list of practices that are either required or prohibited. Once fulfilled, it takes three years of probation and inspections to demonstrate compliance. When successful, the applicants are certified Low Input Viticulture & Enology (L.I.V.E.). Live, Inc. provides vineyards and wineries with official recognition for their sustainable agricultural practices

that are modeled after international standards. These standards are highly regarded by winemakers and consumers worldwide. They provide assurance of fruit quality and practices used to achieve this quality. The basic goals of LIVE are to minimize off-farm inputs such as agricultural chemicals and fertilizers, and to maximize biodiversity. It is a point-based program that fluctuates based upon ecological and individual vineyard and winery practices.

LIVE, Inc. is a non-profit organization providing vineyards and wineries with official certification for using sustainable farming practices based on international standards of Integrated Pest Management. The program has 112 Certification members and 1,310 Certified Sustainable vineyard acres throughout the state of Oregon. LIVE is the first organization in the United States to be certified by the International Organization for Biological Control (IOBC), which sponsors the use of sustainable, environmentally safe, socially acceptable control methods of pests and diseases of agricultural and forestry crops. Because the LIVE certifica-

tion is so rigorous, certified vineyards automatically receive the Pacific Rivers Council's Salmon Safe certification for farming practices that restore water purity to salmon habitats. Salmon Safe, is an organization dedicated to restoring and maintaining healthy watersheds. These programs aim to provide a solution for wine grape growers that are, socially responsible, environmentally sustainable, and economically viable. For more information, visit www.liveinc.org.

VINEA
– The Winegrowers' Sustainable Trust is a voluntary group of winegrowers that have taken a pledge to produce grapes and wine using environmental, economic and social sustainability practices. Vinea has strict environmental standards and require high quality farming practices. The program has 27 vineyard members, representing 954 acres through the Walla Walla Valley, amounting to about 66% of the valley's total acreage. Vinea growers are dedicated to holistic, environmentally friendly viticulture practices that respect

the land, conserve natural resources, support biodiversity and provide for long-term vineyard viability. For more information, visit www.vineatrust.org. Their MISSION IS TO: develop and implement a sustainable vineyard management program, synonymous with the Walla Walla Valley (the Walla Wally Valley AVA is shared by both Oregon and Washington State), internationally recognized for its strict environmental standards and high quality farming practices. **Goals**: *1) Membership:* Attract Walla Walla Valley and other winegrowers dedicated to investing in sustainable viticulture and implementing these practices over the long term. *2) Stewardship:* Implement proven

Large Picture Right: *A vibrant Biodynamic compost heap at the Beaux Frères vineyard. The compost heap is inoculated with a biodynamic mixture. This innoculant stimulates biological activity and produces a more active and nutritious compost and healthier vine.*
Inserted Picture: *Shows a small hole, about 15 cm deep, that we dug. Initially steam poured out as the hole was exposed. Although the dissipating heat wasn't measured , I estimate that it must have been over 110°F.*

holistic, environmentally friendly viticultural practices that respect the land, conserve natural resources, support biodiversity and provide for long-term vineyard viability. Obtain international recognition through certification with the International Organization of Biological Controls I.O.B.C.

3) Quality: Produce world-class wines of distinction by further strengthening the partnership between growers, vintners and consumers. **4) Viability:** Enhance the image and prestige of Walla Walla Valley wine grapes, specifically those grown by members of Vinea, the Winegrowers Sustainable Trust. Establish Walla Walla as a leader in sustainable viticulture and generate awareness and regard for this position among Washington state vintners, growers, elected officials, the community at large, members of the trade, media and consumers. For more information, visit www.vineatrust.org.

Tilth Certified Organic.

Founded in 1974, Oregon Tilth is a nonprofit research and education membership organization

Large Picture Right: Healthy Pinot Noir Grapes farmed Biodynamic at the Beaux Frères vineyard. Inserted Picture: A well forming Pinot Noir berry from the same vineyard.

dedicated to biologically sound and socially equitable agriculture. It is an agricultural organization with a unique urban-rural viewpoint. Primarily an organization of organic farmers, gardeners and consumers. Tilth offers educational events throughout the state of Oregon, and provides organic certification services to organic growers, processors, and handlers internationally.

Demeter Certified Biodynamic ®.

Based on international standards since 1928, the Demeter Association certifies farms and products Biodynamic. The certification is offered for agricultural farms, processing industry and handlers coming in contact with certified products. In order for a farm to be certified it must demonstrate that it has undergone Biodynamic stewardship for a minimum of two years. This stewardship is defined by the certification guidelines. Processors and handlers must also demonstrate compliance to their respective standards but a two-year minimum is not required. In general, organic farming certification and the Demeter certification have many of the same practices. However, Biodynamic agriculture does have certain practices that are unique: 1) The whole farm has to be managed as a living organism. 2) The maintenance of a healthy, diverse ecosystem. This

embraces the expectation that the farmer supports a broad ecological perspective which includes not only the earth, but the rhythms of the earth and as well the cosmic influences. 3) Soil husbandry and nutrient self-sufficiency. The use of Biodynamic inoculants to build healthy soil through more active (naturally enriched) compost, thus stimulating plant health. 4) Integration of livestock with a requirement that at least 80% of livestock feed comes from the farm. This is not mandatory and some horticultural operations may be excused from this requirement. 5) The use of genetically engineered plant materials and organisms have been prohibited since 1992.

Biodynamic ® In-Conversion

Biodynamic status is given to farms that are operating according to Demeter Certified Biodynamic® standards but have yet to fulfill the two-year minimum stewardship requirement.

LEED ® The Leadership in Energy and Environmental Design

(LEED) Green Building Rating System™ is a nationally accepted benchmark in the United States for the design, construction, and operation of high performance "Green Buildings." LEED promotes a whole-building approach to sustainability. This performance is recognized in five key areas of environmental and human health. These are:

1) Sustainable site development
2) Water savings
3) Energy efficiency
4) Materials selection
5) Indoor environmental quality.

The LEED Rating System was created with consistent, credible standards for what constitutes a green building. The rating system is developed and continuously refined via an open, consensus-based process that has made LEED the green building standard of choice for Federal agencies and state and local governments nationwide. It has been proven that LEED-certified buildings have reduced operating costs, whilst at the same time providing healthier and more productive occupants, and conserving natural resources. Certification requirements and prerequisites are based on the "credits" or points achieved within each category. A building can achieve a total of 69 possible points, and certifications are based upon the total amount of points. The levels are:

Certified 26-32 pts., **Silver** 33-38 pts., **Gold** 39-51 pts. & **Platinum** 52-69 pts.

Sustainable Sites (14 Possible Points)
Prerequisite - Erosion & Sedimentation Control
Site Selection / Urban Redevelopment / Brownfield Redevelopment / Alternative Transportation / Reduced Site Disturbance / Storm water Management / Landscape & Exterior Design to Reduce Heat Islands / Light Pollution Reduction.

Water Efficiency (5 Possible Points)
Water Efficient Landscaping / Innovative Wastewater Technologies / Use Reduction.

Energy & Atmosphere (17 Possible Points)
Prerequisite - Fundamental Building Systems Commissioning. Prerequisite - Minimum Energy Performance Prerequisite - CFC Reduction in Equipment
Optimize Energy Performance / Renewable Energy / Additional Commissioning / Ozone Depletion / Measurement & Verification / Green Power.

Materials & Resources (13 Possible Points)
Prerequisite - Storage & Collection of Recyclables
Credit 1 Building Reuse / Construction Waste Management / Resource Reuse / Content / Regional Materials / Rapidly Renewable Materials / Certified Wood.

Indoor Environmental Quality (15 Possible Pts.)
Prerequisite - Minimum IAQ Performance
Environmental Tobacco Smoke (ETS) Control / Carbon Dioxide (CO_2) Monitoring / Increase Ventilation Effectiveness / Construction IAQ Management Plan / Low-Emitting Materials / Indoor Chemical & Pollutant Source Control / Controllability of Systems / Thermal Comfort / Daylight & Views.

Innovation & Design Process (5 Possible Pts.)
Innovation in Design / LEEDTM Accredited Professional

Gravity Flow or Free Flow.

An ideal gravity flow facility could have as many as seven levels: **1)** grape receiving, sorting and loading, fermentors and presses, **2)** fermentor unloading and pomace removal, **3)** settling, **4)** barrel storage, **5)** blending, **6)** bottling, and **7)** the dock for truck loading. The purpose of "Gravity Flow" is to reduce unnecessary pressure on the grapes and wine and naturally to reduce energy too.

Carbon Neutral®

Oregon Governor, Ted Kulongoski signed the Climate Change Integration Act (HB 3543), establishing state goals for reductions in greenhouse gas emissions, creating a Global Warming Advisory Commission for the state, and initiating the Climate Change Research Institute within the state's university system including the Carbon Neutral Initiative for Wineries.

There are three steps to this program. The first step for participating wineries is to conduct an energy audit. Reducing energy use is one of the keys to reduce carbon emissions. The Energy Trust of Oregon will provide free energy audits for any winery/vineyard that uses either PGE or Pacific Power for its current electricity use or Northwest Natural Gas or Cascade Natural Gas. Energy Trust will also work with interested participants to conduct a solar power assessment.

The second step entails measuring greenhouse gases (basically carbon/CO_2) and creating a footprint for the winery and/or vineyard operation. A group of consulting firms (Ecos Consulting, Maui Foster & Alongi, Inc. and Quantec) have agreed to coordinate development of a carbon assessment tool which will address issues specific to the Oregon wine industry.

The third and final step is the development of a "Carbon Reduction Plan." The plan needs to identify energy reduction strategies for the winery.

Seventeen wineries and vineyards have joined the Carbon Neutral Challenge Initiative, and many others are considering joining. The participants include: Abacela, A to Z/Rex Hill, Benton-Lane Winery, Bethel Heights Vineyard, Chehalem Winery, Cooper Mountain Vineyards, King Estate, Lange Winery, Lemelson Vineyards, Mahonia Vineyards, Resonance Vineyard, Seven Hills Winery, Sokol Blosser Winery, Soter Vineyards, Stoller Vineyards, Torii Mor Winery, and Willamette Valley Vineyards. For further information see The Oregon Environmental Council's web site at http://www.oeconline.org/.

Picture Right: *A healthy organic leaf at King Estate in Southern Oregon.*

The AVAs of Oregon

Oregon has 15 approved winegrowing regions with 734 vineyards including 303 vineyards/wineries, and produces 72 grape varieties. Impressively, almost 57% of the planted acreage is represented by the Pinot Noir grape. Oregon's major white grape is the Pinot Gris, which stands for 13% of the total planted acreage. Together these two grape varieties make up 70% or 9 859 acres (Fig. xxx) of the total 14 100 planted acres in Oregon.

Artisan wines are what Oregon winemak-ers like to produce. Their stewardship for environmental farming and high-quality wines are surpassed by very few even in Burgundy, France, the home of "Clas-sical" Pinot Noir. However, 10 year old Pinot Noirs from good Willamette Valley wineries will really knock your socks off!

From the landscape soaring above the Columbia River Gorge to the green, roll-ing hills of the Willamette Valley and the high mountain valleys of Southern Or-egon these picturesque, almost Norman Rockwell-like, settings together with the sublime artisan wines is Oregon in a bottle. If this doesn't whet your appetite then nothing will!

Most Oregon wineries are relatively small with just over 5 000 cases produced an-nually. So if you want to find these gems, this won't be through your local store; nonetheless, if you take a leisurely drive down one of Oregon's many country roads you'll find these wineries tucked into the foothills as one with the breathtaking landscape. Apart from the superior wines and breathtaking views you'll also be able to savor many delicious and wine-friendly dishes offered by a number of very good chef-owned restaurants in the region. For those of you wishing to stay for a couple of days, Oregon is littered with charming inns, bed & breakfasts and boutique hotels where you can rest your liver.

For those of you who can't make a trip into the wine regions of Oregon many of the wineries have an on-line wine club where you can purchase some of their wines.

Sustainable agriculture, or in this case sustainable winegrowing, is an environmentally friendly and responsible practice and increasingly recognized as vital to a terroir-based winegrowing philosophy in Oregon. Wine quality and agricultural sustainability go hand in hand. In 1997 Low Input Viticulture and Enology (L.I.V.E.) was incorporated to promote sustainable, low-impact wine farming in Western Oregon. L.I.V.E. gives vineyards the recognition for their agricultural practices, according to

	Planted Acreage 2005	Crush by Variety 2005	Winery Sales by Case (9 liter cases) 2005
Cabernet Franc	109	190	2 921
Cabernet Sauvignon	504	428	24 277
Chardonnay	842	1 532	136 211
Gewurztraminer	214	245	12 198
Merlot	550	629	43 777
Muller Thurgau	96	319	15 233
Pinot Blanc	190	390	1 757
Pinot Gris	1 885	4 312	267 772
Pinot Noir	7 974	12 075	782 836
Sauvignon Blanc	59	49	3 034
Syrah	402	503	13 457
Tempranillo	108	135	2 422
Viognier	118	147	4 343
White Riesling	524	988	77 902
Zinfandel	64	117	4 841
All others	461	794	134 143
TOTALS	14 100	22 853	1 527 124 9 liter cases

Graph Left: The total number of planted acres for each of the major varieties, their crush amounts in tons, and number of 12 x750ml bottle-cases produced. The given information originates from the 2005 Oregon Vineyard and Winery Report, National Agricultural Statistics Service, Oregon Field Office.

Rosé, White, Blush, Other Still & Sparkling Wines

the guidelines of The International Organization for Biological Control, based in Geneva, Switzerland. However, in this book we refer to all vineyards with L.I.V.E. and other associated environmental practices as "Sustainable Agriculture." Some of these ecological practices include:

1) the vineyards should minimize their environmental footprint;

2) only natural, organic, elemental-spray solutions can be used to combat vine diseases like mildew and botrytis (primarily sulfur);

3) natural and indigenous predatory insects and bacteria are allowed to control noxious pests;

4) compost derived from natural vine cuttings and verma compost are utilized instead of industrial fertilizers to feed soils and young plants;

5) foliar sprays and pulverized plant, and mineral elements are used to help maintain the health of our plants during the dry summer months;

6) biodiversity in the vineyard is practiced by promoting all plant and animal species

naturally indigenous to the vineyard - this diversity is also encouraged by planting wild flowers and varieties of cover crops as well as plant species throughout the property. This creates a balanced ecosystem with naturally occurring insects and fungi that compete biologically with vineyard pests.

There are certainly many other organic, biodynamic and sustainable practices in use but this is not the forum to discuss them.

	Number of Vineyards 2005	Planted Acreage 2005	Production 2005	Wineries 2005
Applegate Valley	33	428	486	12
Columbia River, Walla Walla, and at large	64	997	2458	25
North Willamette Valley	434	9307	15397	199
Rogue Valley	69	1413	2815	16
South Willamette Valley	83	1342	2654	33
Umpqua Valley	51	613	119	18
TOTALS	**734**	**14100**	**23929**	**303**

Graph Above: The graph shows the total number of vineyards, planted acres, production (tons) and wineries in Oregon. The information originates from the 2005 Oregon Vineyard and Winery Report, National Agricultural Statistics Service, Oregon Field Office. *Map Right:* There are 16 American Viticultural Areas (AVAs) in Oregon.

AMERICAN VITICULTURAL AREAS OF OREGON

Sub-AVAs of the Willamette Valley AVA

Areas Included in the Southern Oregon AVA

1	Willamette Valley	5	Dundee Hills	9	Red Hills Douglas County	13	Columbia Gorge
2	Chehalem Mountains	6	McMinnville	10	Rogue Valley	14	Columbia Valley
3	Yamhill-Carlton District	7	Eola-Amity Hills	11	Applegate Valley	15	Walla Walla Valley
4	Ribbon Ridge	8	Umpqua Valley	12	Southern Oregon	16	Snake River Valley

There are 16 American Viticultural Areas (AVAs) in Oregon. They are, in accordance with their registration dates:

Columbia Valley - 1984,
Umpqua Valley - 1984,
Walla Walla Valley - 1984,
Willamette Valley - 1984,
Rogue Valley - 1991,
Applegate Valley - 2001,
Columbia Gorge - 2004,
Dundee Hills - 2004,
Yamhill-Carlton District - 2004,
Southern Oregon - 2004,
McMinnville - 2005,
Ribbon Ridge - 2005,
Red Hill Douglas County - 2005,
Eola-Amity Hills - 2006,
Chehalem Mountains - 2006,
Snake River Valley - 2007.

Willamette Valley

Willamette Valley

The Willamette Valley was named after the Willamette River which flows through it. 150 miles long and at its widest up to 60 miles wide, it is Oregon's largest AVA. It also represents about 60% of the vineyards and 65% of the wineries in the entire State of Oregon. It extends from the Columbia River in Portland south through Salem and to the Calapooya Mountains near Eugene. The Willamette Valley also includes six sub-appellations:

Chehalem Mountains,
Dundee Hills,
Eola-Amity Hills,
McMinnville,
Ribbon Ridge, and
Yamhill-Carlton District.

Stats:
199 wineries and recently over 10,000 acres of wine grapes.

Wine History:
The first pioneers responsible for Willamette Valley's modern winemaking culture began in 1965 when three UC Davis graduates (David Lett, Charles Coury, and Dick Erath) left California for Oregon. They believed that Oregon was an ideal place to grow cool-climate varieties, though many experts at that time believed the contrary;

Picture Right: *Typical winter with low lying clouds in the Willamette Valley.*

-24-

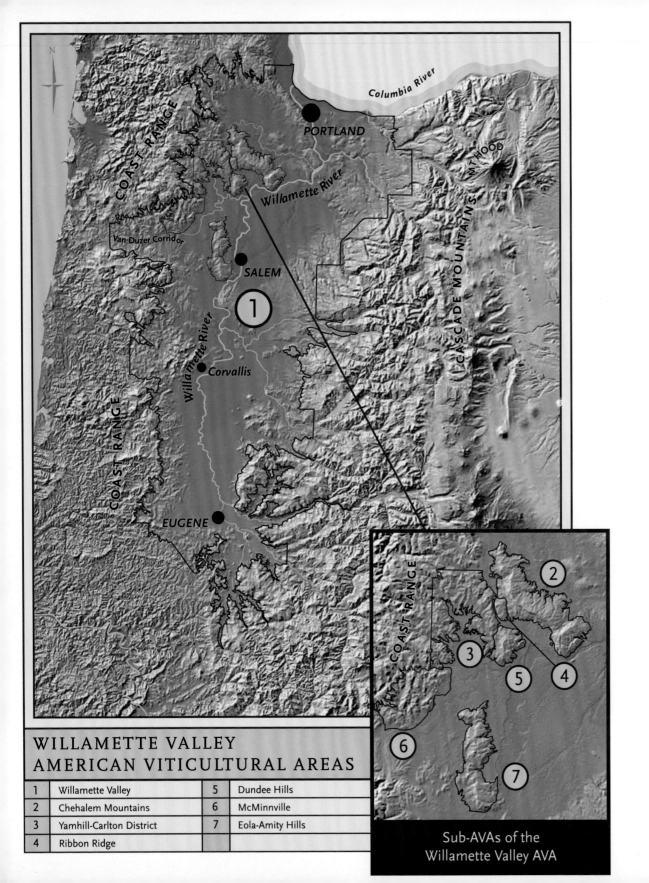

Sub-AVAs of the
Willamette Valley AVA

nevertheless, history has shown that Oregon can compete, join and in many cases produce better quality than many classical and modern elite winemaking regions in the world.

The trio was the first in Oregon to plant Pinot Noir, not to mention small amounts of related varieties, such as Pinot Gris, Chardonnay, and Riesling. These wine pioneers whole-heartedly believed that Oregon would one day become an important wine-growing region. Good on them! as the Australians would say.

Other believers were not far behind. Within the next decade the Willamette Valley grew further when David and Ginny Adelsheim,

Map Left: The map illlustrates the 7 sub-appellations (AVAs) in the Willamette Valley. Take note of the topography, a major influence in the weather patterns as the valley is protected from the west and east on both sides. However, an important aspect is shown just west of Salem, where the Van Duzer Corridor is found. This corridor admits cool Pacific air into the valley. This cool air turns to fog as it rolls over the fingers and hills surrounding the valley, an extremely important factor in quality grape growing. Cool in the morning and evening with warm daytime temperatures.

Ronald and Marjorie Vuylsteke, Richard and Nancy Ponzi, Joe and Pat Campbell, Susan and Bill Sokol Blosser and Myron Redford all planted vineyards. As in most traditional wine communities, these families worked closely with each other and in a collaborative spirit by sharing advice and encouragement as they all moved towards making superior wines.

In the 1979, three years after the "1976 Judgment in Paris", Steven Spurrier put Napa Valley on the map, which I assume inspired David Lett to introduce his wines into the Gault-Millau French Wine Olympiades, where he won top Pinot Noir honors against France's best labels.

A "new world" or "modern style" of winemaking hit the stage and a worldwide wine revolution began with California and Oregon in the forefront. In 1984, the Willamette Valley became an official AVA and today it is recognized as one of the premier wine-producing areas in the world.

If you ask a Burgundian what region can make "the second best Pinot Noir in the world" he will certainly say Willamette Valley. However, Willamette Valley is not only known for its magnificent Pinot Noir but also other cool-climate varieties as Pinot

Gris, the Dijon clone of Chardonnay and Pinot Blanc.

Climate:

Mild throughout the year, with dry, warm summers and cool wet winters. The Willamette Valley is known for its abundant moisture; however, it rains mostly during the winter months, and not in the growing season. The coastal marine influences along with the temperate climate provide excellent growing conditions within the Valley, which is ideal for cool climate grapes, especially Pinot Noir. In comparison with the rest of the state, the valley has more daylight hours during the growing season, yet another ingredient for quality. During the 100± day period from flowering to harvesting, the Willamette Valley enjoys warm days and cool nights, and the rolling hills offer good temperature swings that allow the wine grapes to develop their flavor and complexity while retaining their natural acidity.

Soils:

Around 10,000 to 15,000 years ago the Missoula Floods, which originated in Montana, deposited a bed of gravel, silt, rock and boulders over the original volcanic and sedimentary seabed. The most common type of soil in the Willamette Valley soil is

its original volcanic red Jory soil; however, it is only found 300+ feet above the valley floor as these were above the Missoula Floods. The higher ground therefore offers very high grade soils with the old volcanic red Jory, which also offers extremely good draining to boot preventing root rot and increase the quality of the grapes. Sedimentary-based soil can be found below the 300 feet.

Topography:
The coastal mountain range to the west, the Cascades to the east and the hills of the north protect the Willamette Valley from the harsh winter months. While most of the valley's vineyards are above 200 feet, located to the west of the Willamette River, and are on or near the leeward slopes of the Coastal Range, there are some which are much higher. In the Chehalem Mountains for instance, the tallest point, Bald Peak, rises 1,633 feet above sea level.

Predominant Varieties:
Pinot Noir, Pinot Gris, Chardonnay, White Riesling, Cabernet Sauvignon, Syrah, Merlot, Müller-Thurgau, Gewürztraminer, and Viognier.

Recommended Wineries to Visit:
Willamette Valley Vineyards offers spectacular views from its tasting room and tower. Excellent grape typical wines which go well with a variety of foods. Scott Paul and Ken Wright are excellent choices as they both offer some excellent examples of grape typical, food-friendly wines. Other recommended winers inclue: Van Duzer and Domaine Coteau.

Chehalem Mountains

Location:
Chehalem Mountains is a sub-appellation to the Willamette Valley region. The Chehalem Mountains AVA is approximately 20 miles in length and 5 miles wide. It lies some 19 miles southwest of the Portland and stretches to about 45 miles east of the Pacific Ocean in the west.

Stats:
100 vineyards, 31 wineries, 1,600 vineyard acres.

Wine History:
Chehalem Mountains became an approved American Viticultural Area in 2006 but its history began in 1968 when Dick Erath purchased 49 acres in Dopp Road in Yamhill County. Naturally, he called his new property Chehlam Mountain Vineyards. About five years later, in the mid 70s other pioneers such as the Adelsheim and Ponzi families. Today there are over 30 wineries and approaching more than 100.

Climate:
Annual precipitation ranges from 37" (94mm) to 60" (152mm). The variations are mainly due to the diversity in the elevation above sea level, 200' (61m) to 1,633' (498m). The 430 meter disparity not only accounts for a doubling in rain but also in the largest temperature variation in the Willamette Valley. The temperature difference naturally affects the ripening, and subsequently the same Pinot Noir grapes can be harvested as much as 20 days apart.

Soils:
Chehalem Mountains have an interesting soil combination of Columbia River basalt, ocean sediment, and wind-blown calcareous silt or clay (loess).

Topography:
With the highest mountains in the Willamette Valley, Chehalem Mountains consist of several hilltops, ridges and spurs and

Picture Right: *Bergström Vineyards in the fall.*

fingers that emerge from the Willamette Valley floor. The viticultural areas are 200 ft (61m) over sea level. Bald Peak is the tallest point.

Predominant Varieties:
Pinot Noir, Pinot Gris, Chardonnay, Pinot Blanc, Syrah, Gamay Noir, Riesling, and Auxerrois Blanc.

Recommended Wineries to Visit:
Adelsheim Vineyard grows and produces very good grape typical varieties which are excellent matches with food. Bergström Wines is another very good producer of quality grape typical wines. Lovely view of the Chehalem mountains are available from both properties.

Things to do:
Portland is Oregon's largest city and is just 30 minutes by car from the Chehalem Mountains AVA, which lies at the northwest end of the Willamette Valley. Portland offers a myriad of cultural activates such as art, outdoor entertainment, and some extremely interesting restaurants. There are also a number of smaller towns such as Forest Grove, Newberg, Dundee and Mc-Minnville that offer some charming inns and bed and breakfasts, including some intimate, chef-owned restaurants serving wine-friendly Pacific Northwest cuisine. For those wishing to grow wings, visitors can even take hot air balloon rides to get a bird's eye view of the rolling hills, rivers, tundra and grapes that you so love.

Dundee Hills

Location:
About 28 miles southwest of Portland you'll find Dundee Hills. Dundee Hills is a sub-appellation within the Willamette Valley. Rising above the Willamette and Chehalem Valley floor, Dundee Hills offers spectacular rolling hills with views of Mt. Hood and Mt. Jefferson's majestic snowy peaks.

Stats:
50 vineyards, 25 wineries, 1,700 vineyard acres

Wine History:
Dundee Hills was approved as an AVA in 2005. However, winemaker David Lett planted the first Pinot Noir in the Dundee Hills in 1965, naming it The Eyrie Vineyard. Dick Erath of Erath Vineyards and the Sokol Blosser family soon followed with other winemakers who settled on the south-facing slopes to plant many of Oregon's first vineyards. Another repsected local is Jim Marsh. Jim was originally a prune grower and when asked why he changed from prunes to grapes he answered, "I can drink a lot more wine than I can eat prunes." A remarkable man in many ways he practices organic growning and to the fullest without irrigation and using sod to retain moisture and increase vigor. His wine you'll find under the Arterberry label.

Contrary to popular belief, Jim has found another approach to controlling the patch of Phylloxera that he found in his vineyard. "By keeping the Phylloxera infected vine soils moist and covering them with a good portion of sod I have been able to prevent the soils from drying-out, this is how the Phylloxera crawl out, plus I am improving the vines nutrition with extra sod. This keeps the vine vigorous and the Phylloxera at bay. Today I cannot even find evidence of those infected vines".

These pioneers paved the way for some of America's finest wineries such as: Torii Mor, Archery Summit, Lange, and Argyle. If Oregon had classed growths such as Premier Grand Cru and Grand Cru as in Burgundy, Dundee Hills would without doubt be the Grand Cru and DRC of the modern world. Here you'll find some of America's most fascinating and grape typical wines as well as modern, eco-friendly vineyards and wineries that have set the stands for all others to attain.

Climate:

Dundee Hills area is effectively an island protected from great climatic variations by surrounding geographic features. The Coastal Range to the west lessens the effects of the Pacific Ocean's heavy rains and windstorms, and causes a rain shadow over the Dundee Hills area, resulting in just 30 to 45 inches of annual precipitation, most of which falls in the winter months outside of the growing season. Because of their slope and elevation, Dundee Hills vineyards benefit from warmer nights and less frost and fog than the adjacent valley floors.

Soils:

Dundee Hills is known for its rich, red volcanic Jory soils over sedimentary sandstone. This combination together with the volcanic basalt, clay, loam and silt deposits make up this unique quality. These rich soils usually reach a depth of between 4 to 6 feet not to mention providing excellent drainage for healthy vines and quality wine grapes.

Topography:

Part of the North Willamette Valley hill chain, as a result of intense volcanic activity and the collision of the Pacific and north American plates, the Dundee Hills area rises above the surrounding Willamette Valley and is defined by the 200 ft lineal contour surrounding the AVA. The highest peak of 1,067 feet (325m). The area of hills comprises a north-south spine with ridges and fingers, as well as small valleys on its east, south and west sides.

Predominant Varieties:

Pinot Noir, Pinot Gris, White Riesling, Chardonnay, Pinot Blanc, Pinot Meunier, Melon, Muscat Ottonel, Muller-Thurgau, Dolcetto.

Recommended Wineries to Visit:

An abundance of quality can be found in these hills! Torii Mor with their Japanese gardens and French style Burgundies along with Domaine Serene with their superb Tuscan Manor and elegant wines to Archery Summit with their amazing cave cellars and fruity wines. Sokol Blosser also provides an array of very good food-friendly wines. Other wineries of interest include: A to Z Wineworks, Maresh Red Barn, Bella Vida Vineyards, Duck Pond, Erath, Lange, Domaine Drouhin, Stoller and the Anderson Family.

Things to do:

The Dundee Hills is only 45 minutes from Portland; nevertheless, it offers you a memory of vineyards for a lifetime. Notwithstanding the ability to fulfill your appetite for premium wines, every Sunday from May through October, you can also visit the farmer's market where you'll be able to find fruits, produce, artisan cheeses, handcrafted items and much more. Naturally, the nearby vineyard-filled hills also offer a variety of charming inns and bed and breakfasts with a few restaurants serving wine-friendly cuisine.

Eola-Amity Hills

Location:

Totaling 37,900 acres (15,300ha) Eola-Amity Hills is a sub-appellation of the Willamette Valley AVA. It is located just west-northwest of Salem, Oregon's state capitol.

Stats:

30 wineries, and 1,460 vineyard acres.

Wine History:

The Salem area has an agricultural history dating back to the 1850s. However, it wasn't until the 1970s that a few pioneers decided to plant grapes. One of these pioneers was Don Byard of Hidden Springs. Today, Eola-Amity Hills produces world-class, handcrafted cool-climate varietals. Eola-Amitiy Hills became an official America Viticultural Area in 2006.

Climate:

The Eola-Amity Hills region has a temperate climate. It has warm summers and mild winters with most of the rain falling outside of the growing season. The annual average precipitation is around 40 inches (101mm). Temperatures range from high averages 62 degrees F (16°C) in April to 83 degrees F (28°C) in July. These conditions are conducive to cool-climate good quality grapes. The "Van Duzer Corridor" provides a break in the Coastal Range that allows the cool Pacific Ocean air to flow through providing Eola-Amity Hills with perfect conditions by dropping temperatures during the late summer afternoons, helping to keep grape acids firm and sugar levels stable.

Soils:

In principal, the soil content of the Eola-Amity Hills is chiefly volcanic basalt from ancient lava flows, marine sedimentary rocks and alluvial deposits at the lower elevations of the ridge. This produces a combination of rather shallow, rocky but well-drained soils, which typically produce small grapes with greater concentration of acids and skin tannins to sugar.

Topography:

Developed out of intensive volcanic activity in its past, and the collision of the Pacific and North American plates, Eola Hills is still part of the north Willamette Valley hill chain. The Eola Hills run mainly on a north-south ridge with numerous lateral fingers and ridges on both sides that run east-west. The majority of the region's vineyard sites exist at elevations between 250' (76m) to 700' (213m).

Predominant Varieties:

Pinot Noir, Pinot Gris, Chardonnay, Pinot Blanc, Viognier, Dolcetto, and Syrah.

Recommended Wineries to Visit:

Cristom is one of Oregon's top wineries. Do not miss a visit to this very talented team. They make exceptional, grape typical wines. Bethel Heights and Amity also offer many excellent choices.

Picture Right: A view of Archery Summit's vineyard, in the Dundee Hills, as you drive up the road.

Things to do:

The Eola-Amity Hills region is just northwest of Salem and in the North Willamette Valley. Close to the State Capital, great shopping, and fine-dining, the Eola-Amity Hills region also offers a lively arts community with top-notch theaters, museums, galleries and a variety of festivals. The incredible 80-acre "Oregon Garden" and its Frank Lloyd Wright-designed "Gordon House" is only 30 minutes by car. The scenic country roads of Eola-Amity Hills will take you by many wineries and tasting rooms, as well as other artisan culinary stops, including Willamette Valley Cheese Co.

McMinnville

Location:

McMinnville is a sub-AVA of Willamette Valley AVA and lies 40 miles southwest of Portland and extend another 20 miles south-southwest.

Stats:

600 vineyard acres, 14 wineries

Wine History:

The McMinnville AVA was established in 2005. However, agriculturally, McMinnville has long been a farming community that dates back to the 1850s when their main harvest was berries, tree fruits and livestock. David Lett changed that in 1970 when he purchased an old Turkey farm and redesigned it into a vineyard and winery. Naturally others followed and in 1987, McMinnville held the very first International Pinot Noir Conference. In recent years, an annual The Pinot Noir Festival takes. It is a very popular three-day event where winemakers and enthusiasts from all over the world congregate for Pinot Noir tastings, winery tours, and seminars.

Climate:

McMinnville is protected from the Coastal Range, and as a result, both the south- and east facing vineyards receive rather less rainfall than sites just 15 miles to the east. The "Van Duzer Corridor," a break in the Coastal Range, offers the vineyards situated on the more southerly facing sites, an advantage by providing them with the cooling Pacific Ocean winds. This helps to reduce the evening temperatures in the region whilst at the same time keeping the grape acids and sugars in balance. McMinnville is, on average, warmer and drier, than other Willamette Valley AVAs and has therefore less problems with frost.

Soils:

The alluvial deposits include: marine sediment, loams and silts. As compared to other appellations in the Willamette Valley, these soils dry (low moisture content) and are uniquely shallow.

Topography:

McMinnville's elevation plain ranges from 200' (61m) to 1,000' (300m). At its highest on the east and southeast slopes of the Coastal Range foothills McMinnville doesn't offer the awe-inspiring views of Dundee; however, geologically, it has a distinctive feature. The "Nestucca Formation," is a 2,000-foot thick bedrock formation that extends west of the city of McMinnville towards the slopes of the Coastal Range. What is unusual about this, though, is that the ground water is affected by the natural intrusions of marine basalts. This, according to local producers, affects the grapes and wines and imparts a unique flavor and development characteristics.

Predominant Varieties:

Pinot Noir, Chardonnay, Pinot Gris, Pinot Blanc, Riesling, Cabernet Sauvignon, Syrah, Zinfandel, Müller-Thurgau

Recommended Wineries to Visit:

Maysara Winery or Momtazi Vineyard offer

good, grape typical, certified, biodynamic wines that go well with food.

Things to do:

The annual trek to the Pinot Festival is recommended. In addition, the historic downtown (old town) McMinnville is home to urban wine-tasting rooms, top-notch restaurants serving the finest examples of Oregon wine. If you like planes, the town also offers the Evergreen Aviation Museum, which is home to Howard Hughes' world famous Spruce Goose, a gigantic WWII seaplane (also known as the Flying Boat) along with other types of planes (SR-71) and much more.

Ribbon Ridge

Location:

About 22 miles southwest of Portland and 4 miles northwest of Dundee you'll be able to find Ribbon Ridge. Ribon Ridge AVA is a sub-appellation of the Willamette Valley AVA and it is an enclave within the larger Chehalem Mountains AVA.

Stats:

20 vineyards, 5 wineries, 500 acres of wine grapes

Wine History:

Harry Peterson-Nedry planted the first wine grapes at his Ridgecrest Vineyards in 1980, followed by the first commercial vineyard with the planting of 54 acres of Pinot Noir and Chardonnay. Other vineyards were soon planted in this relatively small ridge, which, today, is home to five wineries. The appellation became official in 2005.

Climate:

The geographical features of the Chehalem Mountains to the north, south and west, protect Ribbon Ridge's grape-growing hillsides. This provides Ribon Ridge with a slightly warmer and drier mirco-climate when compared to the adjacent valley floors. As a consequence of this warmer climate, Ribbon Ridge's is well suited for early grape growth in the spring, producing consistent and even ripening over the summer and due to the topography (fingers and hill sides) a long, full maturing season in the fall.

Soils:

The Ribbon Ridge region consists of moderately deep, well-drained silty-clay loam

Picture Right: A bunch of Pinot Noir from the Torii Mor vineyard just before harvest.

soils are part of the Willakenzie soil series known for its low fertility and suitability for growing high-quality wine grapes. The sedimentary soils are primarily younger, finer and more uniform than the volcanic and alluvial sedimentary soils of neighboring regions.

Topography:

One of the smallest AVAs in Oregon, Ribbon Ridge is a mere 3.5 miles (5.6km) long by 1.75 miles (2.8km) wide. The ridge extends from the Chehalem Mountains and rises some 683 feet (208m) from the Chehalem Valley floor, giving it an enclave or island-like appearance.

Predominant Varieties:

Pinot Noir, Pinot Gris, Gamay Noir, Muscat, Sauvignon Blanc, Chardonnay, Riesling, and Gewürztraminer.

Recommended Wineries to Visit:

Beaux Frères, a partnership between Robert Paker and his brother in-law, make excellent grape typical Pinot Noir. Other recommened wineries to see are Brick House and Patricia Green who both make very good varietals.

Picture Right: Some Pinot Noir grapes just prior to harvest.

Things to do:

Ribbon Ridge is just 30 minutes southwest of Portland, Oregon's biggest city, where there's plenty of arts and culture, outdoor fun and culinary endeavors to experience. Naturally, North Willamette Valley's wine-producing AVAs, including Ribbon Ridge, are smaller towns such as Forest Grove, Newberg, Dundee and McMinnville that provide a fest of wine-tasting opportunities, charming inns and bed and breakfasts; not to mention, an impressive array small of chef-owned restaurants serving wine-friendly Pacific Northwest cuisine. Visitors can enjoy the scenic beauty from the variety of golf courses within driving distance or even take a hot air balloon ride.

Yamhill-Carlton District,

Location:

Yamhill-Carlton District AVA is a sub-appellation of the Willamette Valley AVA. It's located 35 miles (56km) southwest of Portland and 40 miles (64km) east of the Pacific Ocean.

Stats:

60 vineyards, 20 wineries, 1,200 acres of grapes.

Wine History:

Yamhill-Carlton District was officially established in 2004, but like most appellations, Yamhill-Carlton District had an agricultural history with orchards, nurseries, wheat, livestock and logging. Just when the North Willamette was beginning to plant its vineyards, Pat and Joe Campbell started Elk Cove Vineyards in 1974, and soon thereafter produced the first commercial wine in the Yamhill-Carlton area. Other pioneers quickly followed suit and today this AVA is recognized as one of the country's finest producers of cool-climate varietals.

Climate:

The Yamhill-Carlton District is protected in the north by the Chehalem Mountains, in the east by the Dundee Hills, and in the west by the Coastal Range. This protection results in less rain fall than the surrounding areas and moderate growing conditions perfectly suited for cool-climate grapes.

Soils:

Yamhill-Carlton has a sand and siltstone base covered with ancient marine sediment and a coarse-grained soil. Ideal for drainage and vine-stress viticulture practices. However, the grapes grown in such soil often result in wines with lower acid levels than those made from grapes grown in basaltic or wind-blown soils. Naturally, the warmer weather conditions also affect the acidity levels.

Topography:

Yamhill-Carlton vineyards are protected in the north by the Chehalem Mountains, in the east by the Dundee Hills and in the west by the Coastal Range. The Yamhill-Carlton AVA lies on an elevation of between 200' (61m) and 1,000' (305m). This helps to avoid the frost in the valley and high elevation areas. The temperatures are therefore suitable for effective and in some cases early ripening.

Predominant Varieties:

Pinot Noir (82%), Pinot Gris (7%), and Chardonnay (4%).

Recommended Wineries to Visit:

WillaKenzie is another fine producer with sustainable agriculture and fine grape typical wines that match well with food. Elk Cover offer lovely rolling hills and a good selection of food friendly wines. Anne Amie make some of the most gorgeous whites in the area and offer spectacular views from their terrace. Other wineries of interest include: Leemelson, Belle Pente, and Penner-Ash who all produce excellent wines.

Things to do:

The Yamhill-Carlton appellation is about an hour's drive from Portland and lies at the north end of the Willamette Valley. There are wonderful scenic views of vineyards, farms, green hills and forests such as the hamlets of Carlton and Yamhill. Forest Grove, Newberg, Dundee, and McMinnville offer a great variety of charming inns and bed and breakfasts, and a good selection of wine-friendly Pacific Northwest cuisine.

Southern Oregon

Southern Oregon

Location:

The Southern Oregon AVA is in the southwest portion of the state. It is approximately 125 miles (200km) in length and 60 miles (96km) at its widest. It stretches from just south of Eugene all the way down to the California border. It encompasses 4 sub-appellations (AVAs):

Umpqua Valley,
Rogue Valley,
Red Hill Douglas County, and
Applegate Valley.

Stats:

120 vineyards, 17 wineries, 3,000 acres of wine grapes

Wine History:

The Southern Oregon AVA became official in 2004. Traditionally though, Southern Oregon has the longest history when it comes to grape growing within Oregon. Peter Britt operated a winery in Jacksonville back in 1852. Another pioneer, from US Davis, Richard Sommers, founded Hillcrest Vineyards in the Umpqua Valley in 1961. In the 1970s a number of vineyards followed suit. Today vineyards are growing both cool- and warm-climate varieties.

Climate:

Even though the majority of Southern Oregon AVA has the warmest growing conditions in the whole of Oregon, there are a few cool microclimates within its varied hillsides and valleys that enable Southern Oregon to successfully produce some very good varietals. The region is drier, has a warmer climate, and receives more sun-

Picture Right: The fog moving through the Stoller vineyard in Dayton in the fall. Next Page: A summer/winter picture looking down the Del Rio Vineyard & Winery in southern Oregon.

days and less rain (±40%) than the Willamette Valley.

Soils:
Southern Oregon's soils consist of mainly sedimentary bedrock from the 200 million year old Klamath Mountains in the west.

Topography:
The Southern Oregon AVA appellations are typically situated in high mountain valleys at elevations between 1,000' (305m) to 2,000' (610m). The eastern and southern areas receive more precipitation than the northern and western areas as they are protected by coastal mountains.

Predominant Varieties:
Pinot Noir, Merlot, Cabernet Sauvignon, Pinot Gris, Syrah, Chardonnay, Cabernet Franc, White Riesling, Tempranillo, Gewürztraminer, Viognier

Things to do:
Winemaking and art and artisan cheeses go hand in hand. In Southern Oregon you'll be able to find all of these. There is a thriving arts community with museums, galleries, plus two well attended art and music

Picture Left: Late autumn. Looking up the road to Archery Summit in the Dundee Hills.

festivals: The Britt Festival in Jacksonville and The Oregon Shakespeare Festival in Ashland. The area is ripe with culinary activities, from artisan chocolate making, not to mention another festival, the Ashland Chocolate Festival. Southern Oregon is also home to Carter Lake, North America's deepest lake, and Oregon Caves National Monument with mountains for hiking and skiing, and an abundance of natural wilderness to explore and legendary rivers for rafting and fishing.

Applegate Valley

Location:
Applegate Valley is a sub-appellation of the larger Rogue Valley AVA also in Southern Oregon AVA. From the California border, it stretches 50 miles (80km) north to the Rogue River just west of Grants Pass.

Stats:
23 vineyards, six wineries and 235 vineyard acres.

Wine History:
The Applegate Valley AVA became official in 2001. Its history going back to the foundation of wineries in Oregon when it began in 1852 when a settler named Peter Britt planted the States first grapes. He opened Valley View Winery, Oregon's first official winery in 1873. Unfortunately Valley View closed in 1907 and it wasn't until the 1970s, after modern pioneers began discovering the neighborhood again. Not until a few families settled down and set their roots Applegate Valley experienced a resurgence of winemaking. Today, this area turns out a diversity of wines and is considered an important winegrowing region.

Climate:
With a moderate climate, Applegate Valley generally enjoys a warm, dry climate and about 25.22" (64mm) of rain annually. The days are hot with 3-4 weeks of over 90ºF (32ºC)temperatures during the growing season; however, the cool nights offer some reprieve for the vines and the fruit can mature in perfect warm-climate conditions.

Soils:
Applegate Valley's soils are well drained as they lie on alluvial fans for stream terraces with and typically of granite origin.

Topography:
The Siskiyou Mountains surround Applegate Valley and the Siskiyou National Forest

borders the Applegate Valley to the west, and the Rogue River National Forest to the east. Spectacular views are available. The vineyards are usually at 2000" (610m) or higher.

Predominant Varieties:
Merlot, Cabernet Sauvignon, Pinot Noir, Syrah, Chardonnay, Pinot Gris, Riesling, Cabernet Franc, Viognier, and Zinfandel.

Recommended Wineries to Visit:
Devitt Winery must be Oregon's smallest winery. A little eccentric but unique. They produce only 1500 cases per year; however, they are very good grape typical examples. Don't expect to find a castle but rather a garage, and you will not be disappointed. Small, down to earth but good.

Things to do:
The Britt Festival in historic Jacksonville and the Oregon Shakespeare Festival in Ashland are well known festivals in the region where both music and art are celebrated in style. Medford offers shopping, cafés, market-fresh restaurants, and charming inns and bed and breakfasts. The stunning mountain setting offers a wilderness full of hiking, skiing and white water rafting down the Rogue River. In Central Point you'll be able to find the famous Rogue Creamery, which produces one of the world's greatest blue cheeses.

Red Hill Douglas County

Location:
Red Hill Douglas County AVA is an enclave and sub-appellation of the Umpqua Valley AVA and encompasses 5,500 acres (2,220ha) and is a single vineyard AVA, one of just a few in the country. It lies about 30 miles north of Roseburg and parallels Interstate 5 and near Yoncalla.

Stats:
Single vineyard AVA (Red Hill Vineyard) with just 220 acres (89ha) planted.

Wine History:
Red Hill Douglas County appellation was approved in 2005. However, the Applegate and Scott families, pioneers of Southern Oregon, settled there in the mid-1800s. In 1876, Jesse Applegate planted Douglas County's first established vineyard in Yoncalla.

Climate:
Red Hill Douglas County has a relatively mild climate. Nevertheless, the influence of Pacific Ocean creates a rather wetter climate than the surrounding Umpqua Valley. On the other hand, the average daytime temperature is around 75ºF (23.8ºC) during growing season. Other regions in the Umpqua valley can see temperatures soar over 105ºF (40.5ºC). The area generally enjoys a frost-free growing season.

Soils:
The iron-rich, red volcanic Jory soils, formed by the volcanic basalt, and the clay, loam and silt form the basis of the soil composition. The top soil is well drained, with depths exceeding 15' (4.57m), in some cases. It is considered by some to be premium and excellent for vines and good grapes.

Topography:
Rolling hills formed by the Umpqua Formation and the volcanic rocks of the Pacific Ocean floor. Elevation slopes gently from around 800' (244m) to 1,200' (366m).

Predominant Varieties:
Pinot noir, Chardonnay, and Riesling.

Things to do:
The Applegate Trail is part of American history. It passed through this area in the mid 1840s and was a way for the pioneers to reach the western valleys of the Oregon Territory. There are beautifully kept cov-

ered bridges, historic homes, museums, pioneer cemeteries and bunches of antique shops mixed with charming cafés and restaurants throughout the region. Nature is legendary in the Umpqua region and fishing on its river banks can serve many well. There is a historic Steamboat Inn resting on the North Umpqua River in the Umpqua National Forest that is well worth a visit. Well-regarded by fly-fishing experts as a tradition that dates back to 1957. Crater Lake National Park with its outdoor recreation activities is just a two and a half hour drive from Umpqua Valley.

R*ogue Valley*

Location:
Three adjacent river valleys (Bear Creek, Applegate and Illinois Valley) which extend from the foothills of the Siskiyou Mountains make up The Rogue Valley AVA. It is the southernmost winegrowing region in Oregon and extends from the foothills of the Siskiyou Mountains along the California border north to the Rogue River. It is 60 miles (96km) long by 70 miles (112km) wide and encompasses the Applegate Valley sub-appellation.

Stats:
16 wineries, 130 vineyards, with more than 2,200 planted acres (888ha).

Wine History:
Rogue Valley became an official appellation in 2001. However, its history dates back to the 1840s when newly landed European immigrants began planting grapes. They were joined by Peter Britt in 1852, and in 1873 he opened Valley View Winery, Oregon's first official winery. Valley View closed in 1907; nevertheless, the Wisnovsky family began to use the name again in 1972. Other winemakers started to recognize that the valley had potential when an Oregon State University professor planted an experimental vineyard in 1968.

Soils:
The soil composition ranges from sandy loam to hard clay with metamorphic, sedimentary and volcanic derived soils in the Rogue Valley.

Topography:
Vineyards here are typically at elevations of 1,200' (365m) to 2,000' (610m). To assist in drainage exposure, they are planted on slopes and hillsides rather than the valley floor. The convergence of the Klamath Mountains, the Coastal Range and the Cas-

cades are responsible for the Rogue Valley's diverse landscape.

Predominant Varieties:
Merlot, Cabernet Sauvignon, Pinot Noir, Syrah, Chardonnay, Pinot Gris, Riesling, Cabernet Franc, Viognier, and Tempranillo.

Recommended Wineries to Visit:
Del Rio Vineyards is a must if you are in the region. They have spectacular vineyards streching along waving hills. Good grape typical wines that match well with food.

Things to do:
The Rogue Valley is named after the legendary river that flows through it. Ginger Rogers and Clark Gable, 1930s Hollywood, made the river famous by declaring it as their favorite fishing spot. This is Nature's playground with: hiking, rafting, scenic wilderness, fishing lodges, tranquil fishing holes and just plain fresh air. The Britt Festival in historic Jacksonville and the Oregon Shakespeare Festival in Ashland are both near. Market-fresh restaurants, charming inns and bed and breakfasts, cafés and boutique shopping, are all available.

Umpqua Valley

Location:

Umpqua Valley AVA sits with the Willamette Valley AVA to the north and between the Cascade Range to the east, the Coastal Range to the west and the Rogue Valley AVA to the south. The AVA stretches 65 miles (104km) from north to south, and is 25 miles (40km) from east to west.

Stats:

60 vineyards, 12 wineries, and 1,200 planted acres (484ha).

Wine History:

The Umpqua Valley received its classification in 1984. The Umpqua Valley's wine-growing history dates back to the 1880s. The first vineyard was planted soon thereafter by a number of German immigrants that had worked for the Beringer Bros., the oldest continuously operating vineyard in Napa Valley. In 1961 Richard Sommer established Hillcrest Vineyards near Roseburg and just eight years later, in 1969, Paul Bjelland of Bjelland Vineyards founded the Oregon Winegrowers Association in the Umpqua Valley. The 1970s brought new wineries including Henry Estate Winery, whose winemaker Scott Henry developed trellis system, used in many countries today, which increases grape yield, among other benefits.

Climate:

One of Oregon's more diverse climates with both conditions favorable to both cool and warm varieties. With 3 distinct climatic sub-zones:

1) The Northern area has a cool, maritime-influenced climate where Pinot Noir and other cool-climate varieties thrive. It has approximately 50" (127mm) of rainfall annually so irrigation is therefore unnecessary.

2) The Central area intermediate or moderate climate where both cool and warm varieties do quite well.

3) The area south warm, dry and in some cases even arid. Irrigation is necessary and warm climate varieties such as Tempranillo, Syrah and Merlot thrive here.

Soils:

As varied as the climate is in the Umpqua Valley, so are the soils. There are more than

Picture Right: A view of the organic landscpe in the King Estate. The various flowers from a good source of food for the natural insects within the vineyards. This way the insects do not eat the grapes but their preferred meal.

150 soil types here; nevertheless, metamorphic, sedimentary, and volcanic rock is still common throughout the region. The valley floor shows mostly deep alluvial or heavy clay materials, while the hillsides show mixed alluvial, silt or clay structures. Excellent diversity for winegrowing.

Topography:

The complex topography of the Umpqua Valley is a result the convergence of the Klamath Mountains, the Coastal Range and the Cascades are responsible for the Umpqua Valley's diverse landscape. If the valley was to be renamed a more appropriate name would be "The 100 Valleys of Umpqua."

Predominant Varieties:

Pinot Noir, Chardonnay, Pinot Gris, Cabernet Sauvignon, Riesling, Syrah, Merlot, Gewurztraminer, Tempranillo, and Grenache.

Recommended Wineries to Visit:

Henry Estate Winery offers grape typical wines in a variety of styles and varieties. Good food-friendly wines. Scott Henry's invented trellis system is used in canopy management internationally. Abacela Vineyards & Winery also offer a large varietal selection and should not be missed.

Things to do:

This is Nature's playground with hiking, rafting, scenic wilderness, fishing lodges, tranquil fishing holes and just plain fresh air. The Britt Festival in historic Jacksonville and the Oregon Shakespeare Festival in Ashland are both near. Market-fresh restaurants, charming inns and bed and breakfasts, cafés and boutique shopping, are all available. Diamond Lake is also very close.

Eastern Oregon

Columbia Gorge

Location:

In the heart of the Columbia Gorge, just about 60 miles (96km) east of Portland, you'll find the Columbia Gorge AVA astride the dramatic Columbia River. Located adjacent to the Columbia Valley AVA It is both a Washington and Oregon AVA. The appellation encompasses approximately 40 miles (64km).

Stats:

20 Oregon vineyards, 14 Washington vineyards, 6 Washington Wineries, 6 Oregon Wineries with 400+ vineyard acres (191ha).

Wine History:

The Columbia Gorge AVA received its official status in 2004. However, its history dates back to the 1880s, when the town of White Salmon, in Washington State, was founded by the Jewitt family. Soon thereafter, other pioneer families followed suit. The native American vines (Vitis Lambrusca & Vitas Riparia) were planted and some of these are still to be found today. However, serious wine-making did not begin until after the 1970s. The Columbia Gorge became famous when Lewis and Clark trekked through on their way to the Pacific Ocean in 1802.

Climate:

The climate in the Columbia Gorge AVA differs drastically. The high desert climate lies to the east and it receives a mere 10" (254mm) of annual rainfall and irrigation is required. On the other hand, the cooler, marine-influenced climate lies to the west and it receives 36" (910mm) annually with no irrigation.

Soils:

The soil in the Columbia Gorge wine region contains a more fine grain sand, silt, loam type mixture instead of the volcanic "Jory" based soils found commonly in the western part of the state.

Topography:

The sloping landscapes astride the narrow-winding Columbia River Gorge, flanked by the valley walls, which range from steep volcanic rock faces to more gentle-terraces provide a warm sheltered climate with excellent drainage for grape-growing. Mt. Adams and Mt. Hood, two very impressive geographical sites and both part of the central Cascade Mountain Range are found to the north and south of the Columbia Gorge.

Predominant Varieties:

Chardonnay, Pinot Noir, Syrah, Cabernet Sauvignon, Gewürztraminer, Riesling, Pinot Gris, Merlot, Sangiovese, and Zinfandel.

Recommended Wineries to Visit:

Cathedral Ridge Winery provide spectacular views of Mt. Hood and the Gorge. They offer good varietal examples that match well with food. Don't miss a stroll in their lovely gardens. Erin Glenn Vineyards with their tasting room and winery downtown offer good grape typical wines in an old US Mint which has been converted to a wine cellar and tasting room. other wineries to visit include: Pheasant Valley Winery, Phelps Creek Vineyard, The Pines and Mt. Hood Vineyards all offering an interesting selection of wines to taste.

Things to do:

A National Scenic Area, the Columbia River Gorge contains spectacular concentrations of nature at its best. High waterfalls, hiking and mountain trails, Mt. Hood (southwest is Oregon's tallest peak), picturesque landscapes and much more.

Entertainment in the form of skiing is also available. There are ski resorts which even have night-skiing. If you're a cherry buff, there are literally thousands of Bing and Rainier cherry trees, and the area is renowned for having the nation's most prolific winter pear crop). Visitors can experience the Columbia River's outdoors/spots activities with world-class windsurfing and kite boarding. In addition to the many charming stores, visitors and locals have many market-fresh, wine-friendly restaurants to choose from.

Columbia Valley

Location:

With 11 million acres (4.45 million ha) the Columbia Valley AVA is extremely large and diverse. The vast majority of the six sub-appellations are in Washington State and only a small part in Oregon stretching from The Dalles to Milton-Freewater. The Columbia Valley AVA is 185 miles (296 km) wide and 200 miles (320 km) long.

Stats:

50 wineries with 29,000 vineyard acres (11740ha).

Wine History:

The Columbia Valley AVA became official in 1984. However, the Columbia Valley wine history, on the Oregon side, dates back to the early 1900s, when the first pioneers or rather settlers planted their Zinfandel grapes (many feel that it was actually the Primitivo variety brought from southern Italy) in the town of The Dalles. Some of these Zinfandel vines, now more than 110 years old, still produce wine grapes in "The Pines 1852 Vineyard," whose proprietor rejuvenated the land in the early 1980s.

Climate:

The Continental High Desert Climate dominates the Columbia Valley AVA. The hot encourages good fruit sugars and vigorous vines, while the cool desert night breeze ensures that grapes retain their natural acidity. With a mere 6" to 8" (150 to 200mm) of annual rainfall. Irrigation is therefore a necessity throughout the region.

Soils:

After the ice-age (about 15,000 years ago) the melting of the ice packs caused incredible floods (the Missoula Floods) in the area. The region's soil composition includes the deposited silt and sand from the floods in addition to the wind-blown loess sediment. These are well drained soils that are good for vines growth.

Topography:

The majority of the Columbia Valley rests on the Columbia River Plateau and encompasses the numerous valleys formed by the Columbia River and its tributaries. This also includes the Snake, Walla Walla and Yakima rivers. The Columbia Valley region has mountains to the west and north, while the Columbia River acts roughly as its southern boundary, with the Snake River (near Idaho) as its eastern border.

Predominant Varieties:

Merlot, Cabernet Sauvignon, Chardonnay, Sauvignon Blanc, Riesling, Gewürztraminer, Semillon, Pinot Gris, Chenin Blanc, and Syrah.

Recommended Wineries to Visit:

Wheatridge in the Nook Winery offers some interesting varietal wines. For those of you who wish to venture on the fence—King Estate has a vineyard in the Columbia River Basi of Oregon and Washington State. The wine is actually made in Washington but grown in Oregon called 2005 NxNW Walla Walla Cabernet Sauvignon. Excellent grape typical characteristics and a realy fun label for those of you who like a little more information about the wine you're drinking.

Things to do:

The Columbia Valley AVA stretches across the Columbia River from the eastern part of the Gorge into Washington State. Excellent outdoor activities are available in the form of windsurfing and kite-boarding.

For fishing enthusiasts, there is good Walleye and Sturgeon fishing. The area is home to the Columbia Gorge Discovery Center and Wasco County Historical Museum. Visitors to these centers will gain excellent knowledge about the area's natural and Native American history, not to mention the trials and tribulations of Lewis and Clark and The Oregon Trail. The town of Hood River is a really charming western town with fantastic views of the majestic Mt. Hood. North America's longest ski season can be found here too. Spectacular views are to be had in the entire region.

Walla Walla Valley

Location:

The Walla Walla Valley AVA is a sub-appellation of the larger Columbia Valley AVA. As with the Columbia Valley, the Walla Walla AVA also shares its appellation with Washington State. The appellation stretches from foot of the Blue Mountains, across the Columbia River to the southeast corner of Washington and into the northeast corner of Oregon. Although all but one winery reside within the Washington state almost 50% of the AVA's planted acreage lies in Oregon.

Stats:

Oregon has 31 or approximately 60% of vineyards with a total of 572 acres (231ha) and one winery. The entire AVA (Oregon & Washington) has 70 wineries, 52 vineyards, 1,200 vineyard acres (485ha).

Wine History:

The appellation became official in 1984. However, its viticultural and vinification history dates back to the 1850s with some

*Picture Right: A small Botrytis infected bunch in the late fall. **Following Page**: Ell Cover Vineyards.*

Italian immigrants. Blue Mountain Vineyards was established by the Pesciallo family in 1950; though, they closed their doors within a decade. Recent history began in the 1970s with a number of pioneers. In Oregon winemaking is Zebra Cellars with its three estate vineyards, producing over 10 varietals.

Climate:

The Cascade Mountain Range, which lies to the west, shields the Walla Walla AVA from excess precipitation. It receives a mere 12.5" (317mm) of rainfall per annum so irrigation is required. The latitude affords long sunshine-filled days with cool night temperatures producing well balanced sugar/acid levels. These conditions support good grapes development, flavor and complexity while retaining the grape's natural characteristics.

Soils:

The Missoula floods (15,000 years ago) brought with it an abundance of cobbles and minerals. This in combination with the well-drained loam, silt, loess provides excellent soil for growing grapes.

Picture Left: *Looking over the vineyards of Elk Cove in the Yamhill-Carlton District in Willamette Valley.*

Topography:

The vineyards are at the foot of the Blue Mountains with elevations typically ranging from 650' (182m) to 1,500' (366m). The Cascade Mountain Range lies to the east.

Predominant Varieties:

Cabernet Sauvignon, Merlot, Syrah, Chardonnay, Cabernet Franc, Sangiovese, Viognier, Dolcetto, Grenache, Malbec, and Nebbiolo.

Recommended Wineries to Visit:

Zerba Cellars has a large collection of varietals that will suit many tasters.

Things to do:

The "Alps of Oregon" not only provide good outdoor activities such as snowboarding and skiing but the town of Milton-Freewater also offers Oregon's only Walla Walla AVA winery. Downtown Walla Walla provides a plethora of quaint places to overnight. There are a number of good market-fresh restaurants, and the historic architecture and rich arts community will not go unnoticed. In Joseph, you'll be able to visit a number of bronze foundries and art galleries, in addition to restaurants, cafés and bed and breakfasts.

S*nake River Valley*

Location:

The Snake River AVA was approved in April 2007. It includes 8,263-square miles in southwestern Idaho and southeastern Oregon. These designations allow vintners and consumers to attribute a given quality, reputation, or other characteristics of a wine made from grapes grown in an area to its geographical origin. The use of AVAs also allows vintners to describe more accurately the origin of their wines to consumers and helps consumers to identify wines.

The new Snake River Valley AVA includes Baker and Malheur Counties in southeastern Oregon; however, it also encompasses Ada, Adams, Boise, Canyon, Elmore, Gem, Gooding, Jerome, Owyhee, Payette, Twin Falls, and Washington Counties in southwestern Idaho.

Stats:

Presently the AVA has 15 wineries, 46 vineyards, and 1,107 acres of commercial vineyard production.

Picture Right: *A view of one of the four barrel cellar rooms at Adelsheim.*

Selected Wineries & Vineyards of Oregon

Treasures of Oregon

The Willamette Valley is the largest and most respected AVA in Oregon; nevertheless, some outstanding wines are produced in other Oregon AVAs too. Although I have left out a few treasures on the Oregon wine scene the purpose of my selection has been to highlight some eco-friendly innovators and to show the diversity within the Oregon wine industry.

The King Estate offers some of the most spectacular wines that I have tasted in a long time. The Willamette Valley Vineyards offers fantastic grape typical varietals at excellent prices. "Domaine Serene topped Domaine de la Romanée Conti in a blind tasting of 3 wines from each producer in vintages 1998, 1999, and 2000. Domaine Serene wines placed first, second and third in 1998 and 1999 and first and second in 2000." Cristom has continually set the mark for others to achieve. Their wines are outstanding and if you ask any winemaker in Oregon which winemaker they respect most, the vast majority will say Steve at Cristom. Adelsheim produce some wonderful varietals showing elegance and finesse. Sokol Blosser, the leaders in eco-friendly winemaking in Oregon for decades also make some tremendous wines. Beaux Frères with their biodynamic and organic approach make some very interesting wines. Torri Mor, committed to "Green

Building" and organic wines, produce some brilliant wines. The list can go on: Hawks View Vineyards, Archery Summit, Bergström, Domaine Drouhin, Lange Estate Winery & Vineyrds, Amity Vineyards, Wil-laKenzie, Penner-Ash Wine Cellars, Erath, Elk Cove, St Innocent Winery, Shafer Vineyard Cellars, Ponzi Vineyards, Argyle, Lemleson, Anne Amie, Bethel Heights, Rex Hill, Duck Pond Cellars... There are literally 100 vineyards that deserve special recognition for their outstanding eco-friendly programs and tremendous wines.

Most producers in Oregon practice organic farming with a sustainable, eco-friendly program proving that environmentally conscious producers can make some of the world's best wines. I have included a key at the beginning of the selected winery. This key should help to provide you with a quick eco-friendly reference guide pertaining to each vineyard. This book does not require vineyards to complete the required probationary period (which in some cases are 3 years); however, I do require that they follow the guidelines established by the various certifications.

Torii Mor Vineyard & Winery

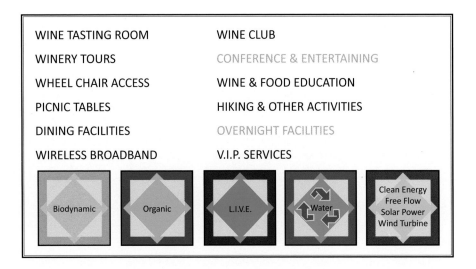

WINE TASTING ROOM	WINE CLUB
WINERY TOURS	CONFERENCE & ENTERTAINING
WHEEL CHAIR ACCESS	WINE & FOOD EDUCATION
PICNIC TABLES	HIKING & OTHER ACTIVITIES
DINING FACILITIES	OVERNIGHT FACILITIES
WIRELESS BROADBAND	V.I.P. SERVICES

Biodynamic · Organic · L.I.V.E. · Water · Clean Energy Free Flow Solar Power Wind Turbine

History: Originally planted in 1972, its vineyard terroir is one of the oldest in the Dundee Hills. Twenty-one years later, in 1993, Torii Mor was founded by the renowned neurological surgeon Dr. Donald Olson and his wife Margie. Don and Margie initially purchased the vineyard and winery to showcase its uniqueness. This has proven to be a good thing as Torii Mor has developed from a mere 1,000 cases per annum to more than 15,000 cases in 2007.

This "Grand Cru" in the Dundee Hills focuses on the natural quality of Pinot Noir, maintaining terroir and individual lot uniqueness. I had the privilege of tasting through their barrels for the last two consecutive years and I was extremely impressed with their dedication to maintain the terroir characteristics in their wines. Their artisan, handcrafted approach has produced wines that rival the best in the world.

Wishing to portray this unique soil that the vines thrive on, Dr. Olson created the TORII MOR name. After a great deal of reflection "Torii," which refers to the ornate gates most often seen at the entrances to Japanese gardens and "Mor", an ancient Scandinavian word for earth, were combined. The romantic image of the "Gate to the Earth Space" or passageway to beautiful things emerged. It could be argued that

Large Photo: *A view from the terrace overlooking the Olson vineyard at Torii Mor.* ***Inserted Picture:*** *Torii Mor's Aquafir, which is more than 5,000' below the surface, produces excellent pure natural water free from modern day pollutants.*

Pinot Noir, more than any other varietal, best shows terroir and could then be seen as the gateway to the earth.

Eco-orientation:
As the saying goes, "It's all in the name," well, that is the case with Torii Mor's anyway. It means "Gate to the Earth" and reflects their commitment to organic and sustainable farming. Torii Mor has its own water recycling plant, solar energy panels providing over 90,000 kwh of electricity, a water cooling wall, and their winery building has gone green. By green I mean LEED (Leadership in Energy and Environmental Design) certified, which means that the building is designed using the latest environmentally friendly techniques. A gravity flow winemaking process has also been installed – from the tanks into the sub-terrain barrel cellar. Recently, Torii Mor also committed to going "carbon neutral."

Acreage & Grapes:
Olson Estate (20 acres/8 ha) Pinot Noir, Pinot Blanc & Pinot

Pictures from Top Left (1): A view of the Japanese Haiku House Tasting Room, providng an intimate and social setting. (2): A wine tasting group in the Japanese garden at Torii Mor. (3): The Peace (Heiwa) Bell is a symbol for pease and harmony and stands adjacent to the Japanese gardens. (4): A view of Torri Mor Winery. It is "LEED" and Carbon-neutral" certified.

Gris); Hawks View (cc.acres / ha Pinot Blanc, Pinot Noir etc.).

Production:
Total production of around 15,000 nine bottle cases. 10,000 cases of Pinot Noir, 2,000 cases of Pinot Gris, 2,000 cases of Pinot Blanc, and others.

Wine Types & Styles:
I recently tasted Torii Mor's 1994 Olson Estate, Pinot Noir, and it was fantastic! After more than 12 years, it showed excellent fruit, good acids and fine tannins. Well balanced and offering a complex finish usually only found in Burgundy''s best wines. If Torii Mor should boast about something it should be their Pinot Noir. Pinot is their forté, followed closely by an astonishing Pinot Blanc.

Torii Mor make excellent classical style wines that show grape typicity. They produce a range of estate Pinot Noir wines, furthermore, a Pinot Blanc, Pinot Gris, a semi-sweet Late Harvest Gewürztraminer and a popular Port wine. Oak Usage: French oak 96%, Hungarian oak 4%. 88% new oak, 6% - 1 year old & 6% - 2 year old oak.

Recommended Wines:
1) Torii Mor, Olson Estate Pinot Noir, 2006. (90 pts) A classical wine style. The nose

shows good grape typicity with excellent fruit displaying both dark and light cherries, violets, boysenberries followed by a spicy touch and a hint of French oak. The palate has fine, round tannins, good fruit and firm acidity. It is in balance with its alcohol. Long aftertaste. Storage potential (12-15 years).

2) Torii Mor, Hawks View Pinot Noir, 2006. (90 pts). Classic in style. Good grape typicity. The nose explodes with a mix of red cherries, cranberries, strawberries, pepper and a touch of French oak characters. The palate is well balanced with good fruit and fine tannins supported by good acidity levels. Long length. Stoeage potential (12-15-years).

3) Torii Mor, Olson Estate, Pinot Blanc, 2006 (89pts). Classical in style. Good aromatics with fruity, floral and tropical fruits characters. The palate shows good fruit supported by good acidity levels. Alcohol is balanced and well integrated. Lingering length. Storage potential (3-5 years).

Owner/s: Dr. Don & Margie Olson.

Winemaker/s: Jacques Tardy is a native of Nuits Saint Georges, Burgundy, France. Jacques grew up in a family that has been heavily involved in the French wine industry for five generations, both in wine-making and vineyard management. Jacques was educated at the Lycée Agricole et Viticole of Beaune, earning a degree in 1974 in Viticulture and Enology. After he completed a year of mandatory military service, he returned home, leased vineyards and made his first wine under his own Jacques Tardy label in 1976.

After several years of making wine in France, Jacques moved to California in 1982 to work at the J. Lohr Winery in San Jose, California. Jacques started first in the cellar and was soon promoted to Cellar Master, a position he held for more than five years.

With the desire to make quality Pinot Noir, Jacques and his family moved to Oregon in 1990 to explore job opportunities. Jacques started as co-winemaker at Montinore Vineyards, in Forest Grove, Oregon, and was promoted to winemaker in 1992. In 1998 Jacques added to his wine-making duties the management of the 240 acre

Pictures Right: Torii Mor's Jory soils are more than 3 meters (9+ feet) in depth. They are rich, red volcanic over sedimentary sandstone. This combination together with the volcanic basalt, clay, loam and silt deposits makes the soil extremely viable and unique for growing Pinot Noir.

vineyard after the vineyard manager left the company, a position he held until fall 2004 when he took over as winemaker at Torii Mor winery in Dundee. The quality red and white wines that Jacques has produced since 1990 have earned several gold medals and other awards of distinction. While at Torii Mor, Jacques has crafted his signature "Deux Verres" Burgundian style wine, as well as furthered new world Oregon style "terroir" high quality wines.

Other items of Interest: There's a renewal taking place at Torii Mor these days. Their newly built winery will be LEED certified, they have joined the "carbon-neutral" train to a better healthier atmosphere, their sustainable and organic farming practices have become part of their name and philosophy "Gate to the Earth." Not only are they focusing on protecting their unique "terroir" but they are also designing a number of educational programs to support their staff the public.

To mark this emergence and to honor his lost son Leif, who died in 1985, for his forward thinking ability, Don has established a new "Peace Bell" in the Japanese Gardens. In Japan, Peace Bells signify "Balance and Harmony," as with Torii Mor's revival.

General Information:
Torii More Vineyard & Winery
www.toriimorwinery.com

Winery Address (Open to Public):
18325 NE Fairview Dr.
Dundee, OR 97115
(503) 554-0105

Tasting Room:
Tasting Fee: $5.00
Hours: daily 11-5

Varieties/Wine Styles:
Chardonnay, Pinot Blanc, Pinot Gris, Pinot Noir, Port and Late Harvest Gewürztraminer.

Winery Features:
Tasting Room, Picnic Area, Wheelchair Accessible and Retail Sales.

Wine Club:
Yes. 10% discount and free tastings with membership.

Large Picture Right: A view of the Olson Vineyard at Torii Mor. Inserted Picture: Don and Margie Olson with Corky.

Willamette Valley Vineyards

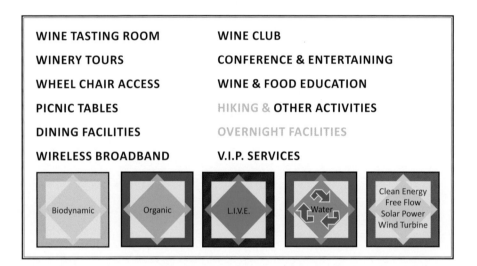

WINE TASTING ROOM   WINE CLUB

WINERY TOURS   CONFERENCE & ENTERTAINING

WHEEL CHAIR ACCESS   WINE & FOOD EDUCATION

PICNIC TABLES   HIKING & OTHER ACTIVITIES

DINING FACILITIES   OVERNIGHT FACILITIES

WIRELESS BROADBAND   V.I.P. SERVICES

Biodynamic Organic L.I.V.E. Water Clean Energy Free Flow Solar Power Wind Turbine

History: Jim Bernau, a native Oregonian, founded Willamette Valley Vineyards in 1983. Seeking to make elegant and classical style Pinot Noir he pioneered his way into the promising new winegrowing region – the Willamette Valley Appellation. At the time, many wine experts of the day thought that it was a questionable risk in planting vines in such a cold climate. History has proved all these skeptics wrong.

However skeptical the others were, Jim was determined, and in 1983 the Estate site was established in an overgrown prune orchard sitting on top of an ancient volcanic basalt flow. This unique site proved to be an asset to Jim. The Jory red soils along with the fractured rock sub-terrain proved to be an excellent terroir offering perfect nutrition, drainage and microclimate conditions. Jim's heart raced when he realized this. Instantly, he knew that this is where he would grow small cluster, intensely flavored, aromatic Pinot Noir grapes.

By day, Jim was a small business lobbyist for the Oregon wine industry; however, with the help of a small tractor, he spent his evenings clearing the first 50 acres, planted Pinot Noir, and hand-watered his vines with hundreds of feet of garden hose. Still without a winery, he spent the next six years improving the quality of his grapes by nurturing the vines. In 1989 he was able to build his own winery. Desiring to share his dream with others, he conducted the first self-underwritten public stock offering in

*Large Photo: Entry to the conference room, restaurant, tasting room and lookout tower. **Insert:** A picture of the Willamette Valley Estate Pinot Noir.*

the U.S. and collectively united hundreds of Oregon wine enthusiasts with his vision. Since that time the winery has consistently produced highly rated Pinot Noir, earning the Wine Enthusiast Magazine's designation as one of "America's Great Pinot Noir Producers." "Our wines have been served at the White House, the James Beard House and are recommended by many wine critics."

Increasing their Pinot Noir plantings in 1997 with the purchase of Tualatin Estate Vineyards, one of the oldest vineyards in Oregon, Willamette Valley Vineyards continue to narrow their focus on sustainably farmed estate fruit and in 2007 contracted the highly acclaimed Elton Vineyards in the Eola-Amity AVA. "We are now one of the leading producers of Pinot Noir in Oregon."

Their approach is to grow by hand, through eco-friendly means, the highest quality fruit. By adopting careful canopy manage-

Pictures from Top Left (1): Post harvest pruning in the Willamette Valley Vineyards. (2): A fall picture looking up the vineyards towards the tasting room. (3): The views from the lookout tower above the main building. (4): The terrace overlooking the estate vineyards.

ment and sustainable agricultural methods they achieve wines that express purity of fruit and distinction of place. In order to preserve the terroir and microclimate of each lot, the lots are fermented and barreled separately, thus retaining their unique Willamette Valley Appellation.

Eco-orientation: Serving as stewards of the land is paramount for everyone at Willamette Valley Vineyards where all their vineyards are certified sustainable through LIVE (Low Input Viticulture and Enology) and Salmon Safe. Additionally, they use biodiesel in all their tractors and delivery vehicles, employees receive 50 gallons free each month, and they offer a ten cent refund on all wine bottles returned to their tasting room. In 2007 they were certified by the Rainforest Alliance to use FSC certified corks in their wine bottles. In addition to a "Social Pledge" to keep the land free from all pollutants, Jim has agreed, with other wineries in Oregon, to go "carbon-neutral."

Acreage & Grapes: 48 acres at the Estate Site. 190 planted (220 total) at Tualatin Estate Site. 60 acres at Elton. All vineyards are planted primarily with Pinot Noir clones: Pommard, Wadenswil, 667 and 777. Additionally small plantings of 113, 114, and 115 along with the Dijon clone Chardonnay, Pinot Gris, and Riesling.

Production: Willamette Valley Vineyards produces between 75,000 to 85,000 cases annually. This is usually determined by harvest, quality and weather conditions. More than 50% of the production is in Pinot Noir.

Wine Types & Styles: Willamette Valley Vineyards primarily produce a classic style of Oregon Pinot Noir. Their "Willamette" brand is most commonly seen in the retail stores; nevertheless, they also produce several single vineyards and a winemaker's cuvee (called the signature cuvee). All Single Vineyard brands come from vineyards where they've managed the farming and that can produce certified sustainable wines. Like their name their focus is on "terroir", which presents the microclimates and soils of the Willamette Valley. Willamette Valley Vineyards also produce an acclaimed Pinot Gris. *Oak Usage*: Mainly French Oak barrels.

Recommended Wines:
1) Signature Cuvee 2005. Classical in style with good Pinot Noir typicity. The nose shows a complex aroma with black cherry, raspberry and spices. The palate is well balanced with fine round tannins, good fruit and acidity levels and well integrated with alcohol. Long finish and aftertaste. Storage potential (10-15+ years).
2) Estate Pinot Noir 2005. Classical style. Good Pinot Noir characters. The nose shows some darker berries, cherry, leather, smoky and spice characters. The palate is balanced with firm but fine tannin structure integrated well with the fruit, acid and alcohol. Long finish. Storage potential (10-12 years).
3) Willamette Valley Pinot Noir 2005. Grape typical. The nose shows ripe fruit, black cherries, and floral spicy characters. The palate displays a balanced wine with fine tannins, good fruit and acid levels and good integration of alcohol. Medium to long finish. Storage potential (6-9 years).

Owner/s: A small publically traded winery. Jim Bernau is founder, principle owner, and oversees all operations. Many of the employees share in ownership of the winery.

Pictures Right Top: Harvest at Willamette Valley Vineyards. (2): A spectacular view looking up the estate vineyard towards the winery and tasting room.

Winemaker/s: Forrest Klaffke is their senior winemaker and Don Crank III (promoted from assistant winemaker in 2006) serves beside him as a winemaker.

Forrest is a traditional hands-on winemaker and has been in the cellar for 30 plus years. He began winemaking at Sebastiani in CA and migrated to Oregon in the early 90s to make small batch Oregon wines. His wealth of knowledge from years of observation and experience in the cellar has been critical to our success. Although he was promoted to winemaker in 2002, he was assistant winemaker for 14 years.

Don Crank III moved to Oregon from the east coast – interested in becoming a winemaker. He has a B.S. degree in biochemistry with an emphasis in fermentation science from Perdue University. In 2002 he joined Willamette Valley as a cellar worker, but was quickly promoted. Don't ask Don a question unless you want a highly technical answer. Together he and Forrest make a great team each bringing their own unique set of skills to the table – a combination of hands-on and scientific experience.

Other items of Interest: All of their wines under the Willamette Valley Vineyards label are 100% Willamette Valley Appellation fruit. They do not source from outside our appellation for these wines.

General Information:

Willamette Valley Vineyards
www.willamettevalleyvineyards.com
Winery Address (Open to Public):
8800 Enchanted Way SE
Turner, OR 97392   Tel:(503) 588-9463
Tasting Room:
Tasting Fee: Complimentary Tasting; however the reserve tasting costs $6. Reserve includes free Riedel wine glass. Hours: 11am-6pm year round, 7 days a week, except major holidays.
Additional Tasting Room:
Tualatin Estates, 10850 NW Seavey Road
Forest Grove, OR 97392
Tours Available: By Appointment Only
Varieties/Wine Styles:
Chardonnay, Pinot Gris, Pinot Noir, and Riesling.
Winery Features:
Tasting Room, Second Tasting Room, Wedding Facilities, Reception Facilities, Picnic Area, Bus/RV Parking, Wheelchair Accessible and Retail Sales.

Large Picture Right: The tasting room with its spectacular views over the valley. ***Inserted Picture:*** *Jim Bernau, the founder of Willamette Valley Vineyards, helping with the harvest.*

Adelsheim Vineyard

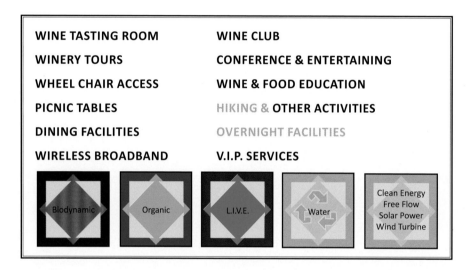

WINE TASTING ROOM	WINE CLUB
WINERY TOURS	CONFERENCE & ENTERTAINING
WHEEL CHAIR ACCESS	WINE & FOOD EDUCATION
PICNIC TABLES	HIKING & OTHER ACTIVITIES
DINING FACILITIES	OVERNIGHT FACILITIES
WIRELESS BROADBAND	V.I.P. SERVICES

Biodynamic   Organic   L.I.V.E.   Water   Clean Energy Free Flow Solar Power Wind Turbine

History: After a trip to Europe where Ginny and David Adelsheim became inspired by the artisan hand-made approach to wine and food they dreamed of planting their own vineyard. This became reality in 1971 when they found, nestled in the Chehalem Mountains, a gentle, sloping field rich with clay-loam soil and a southern exposure. Less than a year later, in 1972, the Adelsheims began planting their original 15-acre vineyard at Quarter Mile Lane with Pinot Noir, Chardonnay, Pinot Gris, and Riesling.

Relying on family and friends for assistance, they battled the elements, weeds, mildew, birds and deer. However, the years paid off and after working in a cramped winery basement, with a simple crusher and press, and 20 Burgundy barrels, David Adelsheim made their first 1,300 cases of wine in 1978.

Producing small quantities of Pinot Noir, Chardonnay and Riesling from the estate vineyard they also purchase some Sémillon and Merlot grapes from other vineyards.

As the Quarter Mile Lane vineyard matured to full yield, their production grew by 50% annually. In 1982, a fully equipped 6,000 square-foot winery was built adjacent to the Adelsheim's home.

In 1989 the first vineyard expansion occurred when Adelsheim leased a 19-acre

Picture Right: *Ginny Adelsheim co-founded Adelsheim Vineyard in 1971. She is the artist responsible for the Adelsheim Vineyard's acclaimed series of label drawings.*

ADELSHEIM
VINEYARD

YAMHILL COUNTY
WHITE RIESLING

site across the road from the original estate vineyard at Quarter Mile Lane. Today, Bryan Creek Vineyard is an important source of our Pinot Noir, Pinot Gris, and Pinot Blanc. They also purchased a 52-acre site in the Chehalem Valley. Planted with Pinot Gris and Burgundian clones of Pinot Noir and Chardonnay, the Calkins Lane Vineyard is also home to the new Adelsheim vineyard winery. Another 120 acres were planted at the Ribbon Springs Vineyard in 1995.

Eco-orientation: The Adelsheim estate is farmed with a focus on low-impact, sustainable viticulture: synthetic herbicide sprays are never utilized, and water-efficient drip irrigation optimizes the potential of soils with lesser moisture retention. Cover crops, soil amendments and canopy management are fine-tuned in order to focus vine energy, while high-density plantings, Burgundian clones and green harvesting encourage low yields, averaging two tons per acre.

Pictures from Top Left (1): Entry to the tasting room and conference center. (2): One of four underground barrels caves in the cellar. (3): Entrance doors leading towards the tasting room. (4): Adelsheim's two level gravity flow sorting and fermentation room. Note the small fermentation tanks that are helpful in keeping individual vineyard lots separate.

Acreage & Grapes: The Adelsheim estate vineyards now comprise nine exceptional sites totaling 170 acres. They are The Estate Vineyards: Quarter Mile Lane Vineyard, Bryan Creek Vineyard, Calkins Lane Vineyard, Ribbon Springs Vineyard, and the Ellis Vineyard. Auxerrois, Chardonnay, Late Harvest/Dessert/Ice Wine, Pinot Blanc, Pinot Gris, Pinot Noir, Syrah and Tocai Friulano grape varieties are planted.

Production: 27,000 cases in the following categories:
- *Willamette Series*; Willamette Valley Pinot Noir and Willamette Valley Pinot Gris.
- *Reserve Series*; Elizabeth's Reserve Pinot Noir and Caitlin's Reserve Chardonnay.
- *Wacky Whites* (and Pinks); CH (Stainless Steel Chardonnay), Pinot Blanc, Auxerrois, Tocai Friulano, and Deglacé which is a dessert Pinot Noir.

Adelsheim Vineyard was one of Oregon's earliest producers of single vineyard Pinot Noirs with a first release in 1986. Single vineyard wines are very limited in production and available first to members of their wine club.

Wine Types & Styles: I had the fortune to taste their 1994 Olson Estate, Pinot Noir, last years and after 11 years in the bottle is showed excellent fruit, good acids and fine tannins. Well balanced and offering a complex finish only found in Burgundy's best wines. It is their forté followed closely by an astonishing Pinot Blanc. Oak Usage: French oak 100%.

Recommended Wines:
1) Adelsheim, Elizabeth's Reserve, Willamette Valley Pinot Noir 2005, (2,495 cases produced). The wine shows good grape typical aromas with dark-cherry, sage, lavender, clove and a touch of other spices followed by a rustic hit of smoke from the oak ageing. The taste is well-balanced with soft round tannins and good fruit. The alcohol level is in balance. Good storage potential.
2) Adelsheim, 2005 Willamette Valley Pinot Noir (10,213 cases produced). This wine displays grape typical characteristics with good red-berry fruit, dark cherry aromas and a touch of spiciness. Good balance of fruit, tannins, acidity and alcohol with a long aftertaste. Good storage ability 5-6 years.
3) Adelsheim, 2006 Willamette Valley Pinot Gris (15,380 cases produced). Good grape typical characteristics with a soft citrus aroma mixed with pears, peaches, apples, and a touch of spiciness. Good fruit and acidity balance and a long length. Storage potential 2-3 years.

Owner/s: David & Ginny and Adelsheim, Jack & Lynn Loacker.

Winemaker/s: Dave Paige joined Adelsheim Vineyard as winemaker in September, 2001, after working with Pinot noir at three different California wineries for 12 years. He continues to provide fresh vision regarding winemaking techniques and equipment, while maintaining stylistic continuity with our past.

Erik Kramer joined Adelsheim Vineyard as assistant winemaker in 2005 after working for several wineries in Washington, Oregon and New Zealand. Erik's position entails coordinating proper execution of wine-making activities, monitoring wine quality, and conducting lab work and bench trials.

Chad Vargas became Adelsheim Vineyard's vineyard manager in the fall of 2006 after working as a viticulturist for two years at

Pictures Right: The spiral stair case leading down to the winery, barrel cellar, and tour tasting room.

Kendall-Jackson. He holds BS and MS degrees in Crop Science and Plant Pathology and has a wealth of experience in vine nutrition and pest and disease management. Chad is responsible for quality control and sustainability programs, financial planning and training related to our expanding vineyard operations.

Other items of Interest: Adelsheim grow a very unsual variety called Auxerrois — not the Malbec from Cahors in south-west france but a crossing between the Pinot Noir and Gouais Blanc. It is quite rare and only about 500 acres are found worldwide. It presents a refreshing wine with quince, pear and honey characters and good acidity levels.

General Information:
Adelsheim Vineyard
www.adelshiem.com

Winery Address:
16800 NE Calkins Lane
Newberg, OR 97132
(503) 538-3652
Open to Public

Tasting Room:
Tasting Fee: $10.00
Hours: Wed-Sun 11-4

Tours Available:
By Appointment Only

Varieties/Wine Styles:
Auxerrois, Chardonnay, Late Harvest/Dessert/Ice Wine, Pinot Blanc, Pinot Gris, Pinot Noir, Syrah and Tocai Friulano.

Winery Features:
Tasting Room, Wheelchair Accessible and Retail Sales, Wine Club, Broadband, Entertaining.

Large Picture Right: The terrace overlooking the rolling vineyard. Inserted Picture: The winemaker, Dave Paige, busy selecting the barrel lots.

Domaine Serene

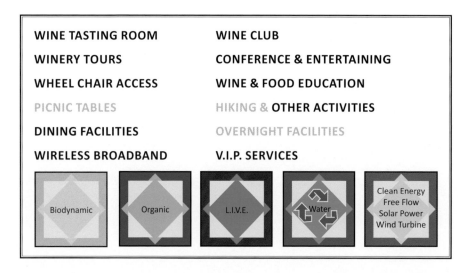

WINE TASTING ROOM	**WINE CLUB**
WINERY TOURS	**CONFERENCE & ENTERTAINING**
WHEEL CHAIR ACCESS	**WINE & FOOD EDUCATION**
PICNIC TABLES	HIKING & **OTHER ACTIVITIES**
DINING FACILITIES	OVERNIGHT FACILITIES
WIRELESS BROADBAND	**V.I.P. SERVICES**

Biodynamic Organic L.I.V.E. Water Clean Energy Free Flow Solar Power Wind Turbine

History: A passion for Pinot Noir led Ken & Grace Evenstad to Oregon in 1989. The intense purity of fruit that comes from this area of Oregon was the driving factor for the establishment of Domaine Serene in the Northern Willamette Valley.

In 1989, The Evenstads purchase 42 acres atop the renowned Red Hills of Dundee, Yamhill County, Willamette Valley, Oregon. The quality of the newly purchased site establishes the winery as a major player in the market. In the next few years, the Estate vineyards Mark Bradford, Fleur de Lis and Etoile will be planted on the West facing slope.

1990. Domaine Serene (named after their daughter Serene Evenstad Warren) produces their first wine from contracted fruit. " Joel Myers becomes Vineyard Manager, bringing many years of Yamhill County vineyard experience to the job.

In 1995, Domaine Serene purchases 41 adjoining acres with east facing slopes, which in the next two years will become Grace, Clos du Soleil and Gold Eagle Vineyards, and in 1997, they purchase another adjoining south-facing slope of 59 acres. The vineyard is re-named Côte Sud Vineyard.

The Evenstad Estate Vineyard property now totals 142 acres and consists of east-west and south-facing slopes.

Large Photo: A post-harvest, late fall, view of the weather coating Domaine Serene's Estate Vineyard.
Insert: *Domaine Serene's wine-tasting room with spectular views of the Willamette Valley.*

In 1998, an additional 80-acre hilltop property is purchased in the Red Hills as the new winery site.

Inspired by gravity-flow Ken and Grace designed the first model of the now spectacular multi-level winery. Ernest R. Munch was chosen as architect, Walsh Construction for general contractor, and Jordon Design Group for design.

In 1999, Domaine Serene purchases a 90-acre gentle east-facing slope on the Jerusalem Hill in the Eola Hills of Yamhill County.

2000. Construction begins on the new five-level winemaking facility atop the red Jory hills of Dundee, Oregon.

2001. In September, Domaine Serene moves into their new winery.

Eco-orientation: The winery's Sustainable Farming Practices program emphasizes environmentally friendly farming methods in wine grape production to promote

Pictures from Top Left (1): The view as you enter the front gates of the spectacular Tuscan estate atop the Dundee Hills. (2): The entrance way. (3): Ken & Grace Evenstad. (4): Another view of Domaine Serene which is built on five levels to enable gravity-flow.

responsible stewardship of the land and natural resources. Domaine Serene adheres to the following farming principles:

100% dry-farmed.

More than half of Domaine Serene's total acreage at each of the three Estates (Evenstad, Jerusalem Hill and Winery Hill) is set aside for natural habitats of wildlife and flora.

Vineyard layout and the use of natural grasses provide effective erosion control. In order to preserve natural resources and to encourage deep root development for the health of the vine, Domaine Serene does not use irrigation.

Cultural practices such as hedging, leaf pulling and dis-budding in combination with natural products control disease in fruit production. A commitment to maintaining low vigor vines and ultra low crop levels.

Acreage & Grapes: Evenstad Estate, in the Dundee Hills, ranges in elevation from 520-800 feet. Their seven vineyards face east, south and west, with views of the Cascade Mountains, the Coastal Range, and the Willamette Valley. Clones, rootstocks, microclimates, slope and elevation allow for the creation of distinct and complex wines. There are seven producing vineyards on the Evenstad Estate: Mark Bradford, Fleur de Lis, Etoile, Gold Eagle, Clos du Soleil, Grace and Côte Sud. Planted with Pommard, Wadenswil and Dijon clones.

Production: 15,500 cases.

Wine Types & Styles: Domaine Serene Vineyards and Winery produce really good estate-grown Pinot Noir and Chardonnay. Domaine Serene is without doubt one of the top five wineries in Oregon. They produce grape typical wines with finesse and length. I am therefore not surprised that "Domaine Serene topped Domaine de la Romanée Conti in blind-tasting of 3 wines from each producer in vintages 1998, 1999, and 2000. Domaine Serene wines placed first, second and third in 1998 and 1999 and first and second in 2000." **Oak Usage:** French oak 100%

Recommended Wines:
1) Domaine Serene, Evenstad Reserve 2005, Pinot Noir Willamette Valley shows elegant Pinot Noir typicity with aromas of dark cherry, raspberries and touch of pomegranate followed by some spicy tobacco characteristics. The palate is well balanced with good round tannins, acids, and fruit. Alcohol and oak is well integrated.
2) Domaine Serene, Etoile Vineyard, Chardonnay 2005 shows the subtle elegance of Chardonay. Grape typical with good citrus characteristics of pear, lemon, apple followed by a slight herbacious and sur-lie character (which I love) and some vanilla from the integrated oak. Excellent length and with good fruit, acidity and alcohol balance.
3) Domaine Serene, Rockblock, Seven Hills Vineyard (Walla Walla Valley), Syrah 2004. Pack with red and dark berries followed by a spicy tobacco character. Good balance with soft round, fine tannins, good acid, fruit, oak and alcohol balance.

Owner/s: Ken & Grace Evenstad

Winemaker/s: In 1998 Winemaker, Tony Rynders joins Domaine Serene and produces the award-winning 1998 Pinot Noir and Chardonnay. A Wisconsin native, Tony made his way out west in 1986 and never looked back, moving between California, Washington and Oregon. A three

Pictures Right Top: A view from the side of the estate where you can also notice the various levels. (2): Some stainless steel fermentation tanks in the large, space-friendly winery.

month tour of Europe unleashed a fascination for wine and motivated him to seek out a career in the wine industry. After his inaugural winery experience in California in 1989, Tony enrolled in the Viticulture and Enology program at U.C. Davis and received his Master's Degree in Enology in 1993. Tony has a wide diversity of winemaking experiences spanning well over a decade. Since 1998 he has been Winemaker for Domaine Serene. He previously served as Red Winemaker at a major Washington State producer and also worked in wineries in Oregon, Italy, Australia and California.

Other items of Interest: Domaine Serene's farming practices are designed to produce low crop levels to insure a concentration in flavor. On average, for the last fourteen years, they have harvested approximately 1.7 tons per acre. Naturally a rigorous summer harvest (green harvest) takes place, and fruit is sometimes dropped two or three times prior to picking. Like most of the Willamette Valley, all of Domaine Serene's grapes are handpicked and hand-sorted on a conveyer belt to remove all imperfect fruit. The various small lots from each vineyard are kept separate in small open-top fermentors and in small French cooperage selectively sourced from several French forests. There is minimal intervention and only gentle gravity flow movement of wine from beginning to end. Pinot Noir is in barrel about 14-18 months, not fined or filtered, and is racked only at bottling. The Estate-grown Dijon clone Chardonnay is fermented in small, French cooperage and aged sur lies for 10-15 months. Bottled wines are aged about one year before release, often longer for single vineyard Pinot Noir.

General Information:
Domaine Serene
www.domaineserene.com
Winery Address:
6555 NE Hilltop Lane
Dayton, OR 97114 * Tel:(503) 864-4600
Open to Public
Tasting Room:
Tasting Fee: $15.00 (Refundable with purchase)
Hours: Thursday to Sunday, 11am-4pm
Tours Available:
By Appointment Only
Varieties/Wine Styles:
Chardonnay, Pinot Noir and Syrah.
Winery Features:
Tasting Room, Wheelchair Accessible and Retail Sales.

Picture Right: Lovely cellars which rival the finest in Europe. Inserted Picture: Copper doors leading into the cellars.

Cristom

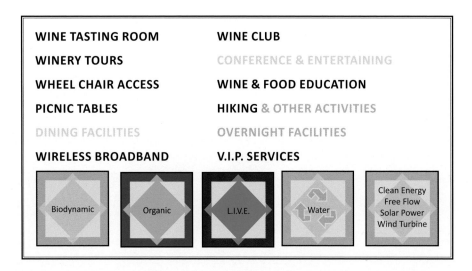

WINE TASTING ROOM	**WINE CLUB**
WINERY TOURS	CONFERENCE & ENTERTAINING
WHEEL CHAIR ACCESS	**WINE & FOOD EDUCATION**
PICNIC TABLES	**HIKING** & OTHER ACTIVITIES
DINING FACILITIES	OVERNIGHT FACILITIES
WIRELESS BROADBAND	**V.I.P. SERVICES**

Biodynamic · Organic · L.I.V.E. · Water · Clean Energy Free Flow Solar Power Wind Turbine

History: Cristom's founder and owner, Paul Gerrie, used his skills as an engineer and avid researcher to pursue his passion for wine. On his travels to France, he was introduced to the traditional growing practices of the Burgundy region. He learned that soil, microclimate (terroir) and site were critical elements in developing good fruit with complexity and finesse.

After a visit to the International Pinot Celebration in 1991, Paul decided the time was right to leave the East Coast and bring his family and his passion for great Pinot Noir to Oregon's burgeoning wine country. A couple of months later, with the help of Michael Etzel, the co-owner and winemaker of Beaux Frères, they looked at potential vineyard sites. In 1992, the current property was purchased and the first vintage arrived in September the same year.

"When I found our property, I knew it was the right place." Believing in Oregon, and the potential for its terroir, Paul, his wife Eileen, and the children Christine and Tom moved and called Oregon their new home. It was then that Paul built the winery from ground up, naming it after his children. Subsequently, "the proof is in the pudding" as the old saying goes and his proof is in the wines that they produce today.

Large Photo: The winery and tasting room with the large barrel cellar in the basement. *Insert:* A view of the barrels in the cellar.

But their journey wasn't complete without a winemaker who shared Paul's vision of "letting the land make the wines, so Steve Doerner who, after a quarter century of experience, still believes the winemaker's job is to "optimize what nature — the vineyard — provides" joined the team. Like most trained scientists, Paul and Steve are keen observers. While they are still advocates of tradition, they continually experiment both in the vineyards and in the cellar. A recent example is the introduction of Viognier to the Willamette Valley. Cristom was one of the first to plant it, even though conventional wisdom assumed the climate was too wet. "We planted it on our sunniest acre and got nice vintages right away," explained Steve.

Eco-orientation: Cristom is fully Organic in their Eileen Vineyard. They also practice L.I.V.E. (Low Input Viticulture & Enology) and are engaged in the certifica-tion process. Their sustainable approach is to minimize off-farm inputs such as agricultural chemicals and fertilizers, and to maximize biodiversity.

Acreage & Grapes: 65 Acres. All Cristom Pinot Noir vineyards are named in honor of family matriarchs:

Marjorie. Grape: Pinot Noir. Clones: Pommard, Wadensvil, 114, 115, and 777. Size: 8.5 Acres. Planted: 1982. Named for Paul Gerrie's mother, is our oldest vineyard. Originally planted on its own roots in 1982, it now consists of five different clones on their own roots.

Louise. Grape: Pinot Noir. Clones: Pommard, 113, 114, 115, and 777. Size: 9 Acres. Planted: 1993. Named for Paul's maternal grandmother, was the first vineyard established by Cristom, and was planted using new rootstocks and clones. Our first release from this vineyard was 1996.

Jessie. Grape: Pinot Noir. Clones: Pommard, Dijon, 113, 114, 115, and 777. Size: 11.5 Acres. Planted: 1994. Named for Paul's paternal grandmother, is Cristom's steepest vineyard. The first release was the 1998 vintage.

Pictures from Top Left (1): Entrance to the Cristom Vineyards. (2): Canopy management in practice. Cutting away unnecessary leaves in the vineyard. (3): One of the barrel rooms in the basement. (4): Looking out of the tasting room through the magnificent doors, made in the early 1850s, onto the Emilia vineyard lot.

Eileen. *Grape:* Pinot Noir. *Clones:* Pommard, Wadensvil, 114, 115, and 777. *Size:* 8.5 Acres. *Planted:* 1982. Named for Paul's wife, is planted at Cristom's highest elevation. The first release from this vineyard was the 2000 vintage.

Emilia. *Grape:* Pinot Gris. *Clones:* Dijon, 146 and 152. *Size:* 5 Acres. *Planted:* 1993-1996. Named for Paul's mother-in-law, is Cristom's lowest vineyard.

Germaine. *Grape:* Chardonnay. *Clones:* Dijon, 75 and 95. *Size:* 4.5 Acres. *Planted:* 1993. Named for Steve Doerner's maternal grandmother, it is a densely planted Chardonnay vineyard with earlier ripening Dijon clones.

Other vineyards include:

Viognier. Clones: 01. Size: 1 Acre. Year Planted: 1993. This vineyard was one of the first dedicated to this varietal in the Willamette Valley. It is planted on Cristom's warmest site to ensure the Northern Rhone Valley varietal will ripen to maturity. Its first release was in 1996.

Syrah. *Clones:* 174, 383, 470, and 877. *Size:* 2.5 Acres. Encouraged by the success of our Viognier vineyard, we recently cultivated another Northern Rhône varietal. Our first released 2005.

Production: 10,000 cases.

Wine Types & Styles: Unquestionably, one of the top five wineries in Oregon. Steve makes excellent grape typical wines with very good storage potential. **Oak Usage:** French oak 100%.

Recommended Wines:

1) Cristom Estate, Syrah, 2004. Classic in style with excellent grape typicity. The aromas have generous but elegant fruit, white & black pepper, spice, dark plums, leather and with a hint of tobacco along with a generous amount of fruit. The palate is well balanced and fully integrated with firm but round tannins, good acidity and perfect fruit to alcohol balance with a long finish. Good storage potentional. If you can get a few bottles of this you will not go wrong!

2) Cristom, Eileen Vineyard, Pinot Noir, 2004. Classic in style. Wonderful grape typical aromas bound by floral characters and hints of sweet-dark-cherry

Pictures Right: Entry to the tasting room and conference center. Notice the beautiful work and detail on the old doors that were manufactured some time around the 1850s.

with a touch of spice, some smokiness, tobacco leaf, and cedar wood. Youthful firm but round fine tannins integrated with the fruit, acidity and alcohol balance. Good length. Excellent storage potential.

3) Cristom Estate, Pinot Gris, 2005. Classic Steve touch with excellent grape typical characteristics. The nose shows good citrus characters of lime blossoms, minerals, and a touch of spiciness. Nice malo-lactic fermentation (MLF) creaminess on the palate withwell balanced acid and fruit. Good Sur-Lie characteristics. Long finish.

O*wner/s:* Paul Gerrie.

W*inemaker/s:* Steve Doerner went to Oregon with a Biochemistry degree from UC Davis, and fourteen years of winemaking experience from a well known Pinot Noir producer in California. With no winemaking background Steve started his career with an open approach to winemaking. Steve soon learnt not to inoculate his wines, to use "Old World" winemaking techniques and native yeasts which all influence the way he makes wine today. If you ask most winemakers in Oregon whom they respect, they will most likely reply Steve at Cristom!

G*eneral Information:*
Cristom Yineyards
www.cristomwines.com

Winery Address:
6905 Spring Valley Road NW
Salem, OR 97304 * Tel:(503) 375-3068
Open to Public

Tasting Room:
Tasting Fee: $15.00 (Refundable with purchase)
Hours: Thursday to Sunday, 11am-4pm

Tours Available:
By Appointment Only

Varieties/Wine Styles:
Chardonnay, Pinot Gris, Pinot Noir, Syrah, and Viognier.

Winery Features:
Tasting Room, Wheelchair Accessible, Retail Sales, and Wine Club.

*Large Picture Right: Entry to the tasting room and conference center with the large brown double doors leading into the cellar. **Inserted Picture:** A picture of Steve Doerner, winemaker at Cristom.*

Hawks View Vineyard

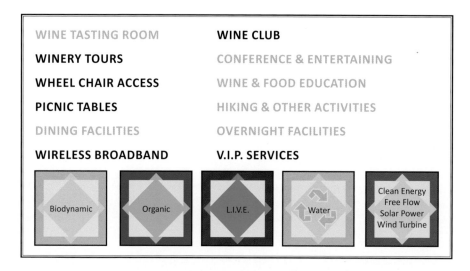

WINE TASTING ROOM   WINE CLUB

WINERY TOURS   CONFERENCE & ENTERTAINING

WHEEL CHAIR ACCESS   WINE & FOOD EDUCATION

PICNIC TABLES   HIKING & OTHER ACTIVITIES

DINING FACILITIES   OVERNIGHT FACILITIES

WIRELESS BROADBAND   **V.I.P. SERVICES**

Biodynamic | Organic | L.I.V.E. | Water | Clean Energy Free Flow Solar Power Wind Turbine

History: The property was purchased from the Benziger family from California in early 2002, and over the last five years the Kemps have invested heavily into the vineyard with both resources and time. This investment has proven to be worthwhile as Hawks View is now one of Oregon's leading vineyards with exceptional grape typical quality fruit and eco-friendly sustainable farming. Their reputation for providing wineries with the best Pinot Noir available is now acknowledged by many as one of the elite top ten vineyards in Oregon. If we were to "delimit or grade" the land using the Quinta system from Portugal or the Appellation Controlée from the Champagne region of France then Hawks View would score very high and receive a "Grand Cru" status based on its micro-climate (aspect, soil types and mineral content, annual precipitation and sunshine, drainage) and its dedication to vineyard management.

Hawks View was named for the abundance of hawks (8 of them) that live on the property and despite the close proximity to urban/suburban areas, the vineyard is home to many species of wildlife, including deer, heron, birds, coyotes, fox, and the occasional cougar who all take their annual share of Pinot grapes too.

Topography: Facing east astride the rolling hills of the Chehalem mountains and situated between the elevations of 250 feet and 450 feet, Hawks View Vineyard offers

Large Picture Right: A picturesque view from the terrace of the manor house. Wonderful views of the 5 peaks of the Cascades can be seen from here. **Inserted Picture:** *From the left, Jack and A.J. Kemp.*

picturesque views of the 5 major peaks in the Cascade Range (from North to South)
- Mt. Rainier
- Mt. St. Helens
- Mt. Adams
- Mt. Hood
- Mt. Jefferson

Eco-friendly Wines and Vineyard: Hawks View employs L.I.V.E. practices (though not certified) it is a major focus of which they are proud. Their mantra is "to allow the fruit to express the nuances of the site by employing sustainable and low impact farming practices." This is done through diligence, quality handwork, and giving each one of their 56,000 grape plants individual attention from pruning to harvest.

Hawks View is home to a strong insect population fostering a lively ecosystem that affords an insecticide free vineyard. The native grasses along with the natural flora are maintained between the rows of vines. This serves two purposes within their ecosystem.

Pictures from Top Left (1): The water falls and pond as you enter the driveway at the manor house. (2): A view from the estate's manor shows the gently flowing landscape with spectacular views of the Cascades. (3): The ecosystem includes an abundance of insects. (4): Natural flora between the vines.

Firstly, A.J. Kemp explains "It provides a natural habitat with natural food sources for the insect population; otherwise, they would dine on our preferred food, the Pinot Noir grapes. Because we provide the insects with their natural and preferred foods in the flora of their choice, they leave us alone and we have no need for pesticides."

Secondly, the natural flora also helps to keep the already well drained soils drier. This forces the vines to grow down to seek water. Longer deeper roots are also vital to the vines' ability to benefit from the mineral rich soils at Hawks View which gives it its unique "Terroir."

The Laurelwood soils allow for powerful canopy development that generally ripens the fruit very evenly and around a week before the rest of the Willamette Valley.

Other items of Interest: The Southern end of the property is home to the oldest and largest known Chestnut Tree west of the Mississippi River. It was even featured in the February 1990 issue of National Geographic Magazine in an article entitled Back from the Brink – Chestnuts. The tree is described as "mightiest of the survivors at 69 feet tall and 16 feet around, the Chestnut was planted in about 1885."

Vineyard Terroir: Vineyard reflects good planning, execution, good solar exposure, and correct slopes for proper air circulation and water drainage. The soil is Laurelwood silt loam, which is a proven soil for Pinot Noir. The soil runs deep and is well drained; nevertheless it can retain water in time of low precipitation. It exhibits good nutrient balance and exceptional fertility with low clay content and providing the vines with a platform for vigor. The vineyard is located in the newly approved Chehalem Mountains AVA and the site contains two distinct plantings totalling 46.22 acres:

Lot one was planted in 1991 on own-rooted Pinot Noir (29.74 acres)
- Hanzell
- Dijon 115
- Wadenswil
- Pommard
- Dijon 777

Own-rooted Pinot Gris (2.67 acres)
- Davis Clone

Lot two was planted in 1997 and grafted rootstock Pinot Noir (13.81 acres)
- Dijon 777 – Riparia Gloire
- Dijon 667 – Riparia Gloire
- Dijon 114 – 101/14
- Dijon 115 – 101/14

- Coury – S04
- Wadensvil – 3309

Production: Hawks View, in an average vintage, produces approximately 90 tons of fruit, or 2 tons of fruit per acre. The site has shown it can handle well over 100 tons in good vintages.

Eight (8) wineries purchase fruit from the Hawks View sites. Each site clearly managed with a distinctive goal of vineyard designation so that wine from any one particular site has its own distinct grape typicity and flavor profile.

Although the entire vineyard provides consistent and excellent fruit, A.J. Kemp's favorite block is the Muirfield Block which has received consistent vineyard designation since 1995. It faces southeast on gentle slopes and has 4.75 acres. Planted in 1991 on its own-roots, it is mixed with both the Dijon and Wadenswil clones. Asked why he likes this particular block consistently, A.J. replied, "it has consistently produced the highest scoring wines."

Pictures Right: Shows the aspect of the vineyard with gentle slopes. The vineyard lies at an elevation of between 250 to 450 feet above sea level. Evidence of the red Jory soils can also be seen in the higher elevations.

Wine Types & Styles: Pinot Noir from the Hawks View Vineyards show a feminine, floral bouquet, with hints of cranberry, strawberry, and other luscious red fruits followed by a spicy touch. The palate shows excellent acids and together with the fruit and tannins it provides a very balanced wine with good length in the aftertaste. The wine usually benefits from extended barrel and bottle aging.

What's Next: While the initial investment was focused upon growing premium Pinot Noir destined for vineyard designation, the Kemp's, at the urging of winemakers from around the region, have begun building an Estate winery focused upon expressing the nuance and complexity that is Hawks View Vineyard.

Hawks View's philosophy will be to utilize only a portion of the vineyard's fruit for their own production. They are proud to be associated with many reputable wineries, so they will continue to provide viticultural services and Pinot Noir fruit to their quality vineyard designated wineries.

General Information:
Hawks View Vineyards
www.hawksviesvinyard.com

Vineyard Address:
20175 SW Edy Road
Sherwood, OR 97140
Tel:(503) 710-1408
By Appointment Only

Tasting Room:
Tasting Fee: $15.00 (Refundable with purchase)
Hours: By appointment only!

Tours Available:
By Appointment Only

Varieties/Wine Styles:
Pinot Noir and Pinot Gris.

New Winery Features:
Tasting Room, Conference Center, Wheelchair Accessible, Retail Sales, Weddings, and Wine Club.

Large Picture Right: To the untrained eye this might look like an untrained or unmaintained vineyard; however, this is what environmentally friendly vineyards and sustainable agriculture are about. Good healthy ecosystems. Inserted Picture: A picture of the estate manor jutting over the rolling slopes of the Hawks View Vineyards.

Archery Summit

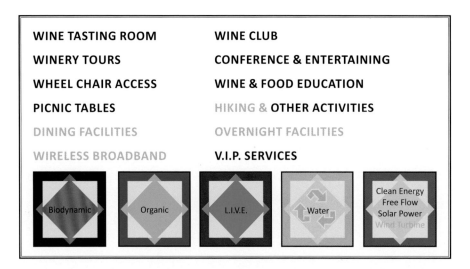

WINE TASTING ROOM   WINE CLUB

WINERY TOURS   CONFERENCE & ENTERTAINING

WHEEL CHAIR ACCESS   WINE & FOOD EDUCATION

PICNIC TABLES   HIKING & OTHER ACTIVITIES

DINING FACILITIES   OVERNIGHT FACILITIES

WIRELESS BROADBAND   V.I.P. SERVICES

Biodynamic   Organic   L.I.V.E.   Water   Clean Energy Free Flow Solar Power Wind Turbine

History: While traveling with the US Ski team, Gary Andrus discovered his passion for wine in the 1960s. After studying wine in France he and his family founded a winery in California in 1978. Gary moved north to Oregon and established Archery Summit. Subsequently, the winery was designed to integrate classical architecture with a 100% gravity-flow winery.

Built into the hillside of the estate vineyard, the winery has five floors, two above ground and three below. An innovative part of the 100 percent gravity-flow process is an elevator system on the lowest floor, 60 feet below the vineyard, which lifts the tanks of blended wine to barrel or bottling level. The first crush was in 1995.

Eco-orientation: Biodynamic and organic certified. The gravity-flow winery is designed to minimize energy use and maximize fruit care. This is achieved through careful handling of the grapes. The grapes are received in small capacity bins, hand-sorted, and de-stemmed on the top floor travel downward one floor at a time to our fermentation hall, aging caves, and bottling area, all without character-damaging pumps.

Archery Summit believes in a hands-on cultivation and natural pest-control, going so far as to find beneficial insects on leaves

*Large Picture Right: A view of Archery Summit Winery and tasting room entrance. **Inserted Picture:** Notice the slope of the Archery Summit estate vineyard. There is probably at least a 30 degree incline with excellent drainage.*

in the cranberry fields and bringing them back to their vineyards. With many of their vines are planted in narrow rows on very steep slopes. These steep slopes require special care and even hand-mowing. This personal style continues in the winery.

The vines are densely planted and vertically trellised vines are forced to compete, producing smaller berries with fewer, more concentrated clusters. Leaves are hand-thinned to ensure maximum sunlight reaches the grapes. Clusters are sacrificed to further reduce yields. And, unlike most vineyards, where fruit grows chest-high for ease of harvest, we train ours closer to the rootstock, warmth of the earth.

Acreage & Grapes: A total of 115 acres of acres, including the vineyards in Dundee Hills. The estate vineyards are planted with the Dijon clones (113, 114, 115, 667 and 777), site-selected and blended with existing mature rootstock.

Pommard and Wadenswil clones are also found on some of their other sites.

Pictures from Top Left (1): Another view of the steep vineyard slopes at Archery Summit. (2): A vineyard worker trimming the leaves and spraying for mildew. (3): The magnificent gravity flow winery with towering ceilings. (4): The caves at one of the lower levels of the winery.

Production: 18,000 cases.

Wine Types & Styles: Archery Summit makes good grape typical Pinot Noir. The styles represent a mix of both classical (oxidative wine-making with open fermenters) and modern wine-making (anaerobic, fruit driven) styles.

Oak Usage: 100% french oak.

Recommended Wines:
1) Archery Summit Estate, Pinot Noir, 2004. Ruby-red color. The nose is aromatic, fruity with a spicy, smoked meat and vanilla character followed by dark cherries and blackcurrants. The palate is well balanced with fine but firm tannins and tons of good fruit, balanced with the acids and alcohol levels. Long fruity finish. Storage potential (10-15 years).

2) Archery Summit, Red Hills Estate, Pinot Noir, 2004. Dark blue-red color. An aromatic nose filled with spices, ripe blackberry, blue berry and a touch of oak flowed by some good floral characters. The palate presents a good fruit, fine round tannins balanced with alcohol and acids. Some vanilla is also evident in the long aftertaste. Storage potential (10-12 years).

3) Archery Summit, Arcus Estate, Pinot Noir, 2004. Deep red color. A smoky, cherry, and blackberry aroma followed by a touch of vanilla, oak and floral characters on the nose. The palate has good acidity levels balanced with the fruit and fine tannins. Good alcohol integration. Long finish. Storage potential (12+ years).

Owner/s: Pine Ridge Winery, California.

Winemaker/s: Anna Matzinger knows that good winemaking is part science and part intuition, but in most part, its intuition that drives her. "I know that chemistry is part of the winemaking process," said Anna. "But you can't rely on test results to make good wine!"

Anna began her winemaking career as a lab technician for Beringer Vineyards in Napa Valley. However, it was her time working harvest and helping make wine in New Zealand, Australia and California that helped develop her own artisan balance of wine-science and winemaking.

Anna joined the winemaking team at Archery Summit in 1999, and became winemaker after Sam Tannahill. Her deft touch and intuition is only confirmed by the good reviews of her wines.

"Being in the vineyard, crawling inside the tanks, punching down the caps, and making judgments on barrel selection and length, that's where the wine is made. You have to see and feel the fruit coming in to know what you'll be dealing with a year from now," commented Anna.

The vineyard manager, Leigh Bartholomew's experience stems from Washington State, Chile, New Zealand, Burgundy and California. She has a Master's degree from the University of California at Davis. "The vineyard sites are exceptional as we have the kind of sites which permit us to expand our thinking, to constantly challenge and change how we grow grapes from vine spacing to pruning and clone selection," Leigh said with an energetic smile in her eyes.

Other items of Interest: THE CAVES. Carved out of the hillside beneath the winery, Archery Summit has a few underground aging caves which were modeled on the subterranean cellars of the Côte

*Pictures Right: A view from the winery looking down over the vineyard and the Willamette Valley. Notice the classical rose bush at the end of the row. This is used to identify any potential viiruses or diseases that might plague the row. **Inserted picture top:** A view of Archery Summit from Sokol Blosser Winery.*

d'Or. These caves are insulated with the surrounding volcanic rock, and the temperature in the caves remains between 55-59° F throughout the year, with humidity below 75 percent.

A spectacular sense of "Old Europe" is felt as you pass between these barrels and domed caves. The narrow passageways are lined with 550 French oak barrels.

Special visits and V.I.P. dinners and tastings are also provided in these spectacular settings.

The vines of Archery Summit Estate, which surround the winery at the south end of the Dundee Hills, consistently produce a Pinot Noir achieving high scores. Planted at the same that the winery was built, the vineyard is comprised of a select mix of rootstocks and clones.

Estate lot size:
16 acres
Planted 1994, 1995
Clones: 113, 114, 115, 667, Pommard Clones and Wadenswil Clones
Appellation: Dundee Hills
Exposure: South

General Information:
Archery Summit
www. archerysummit.com

Winery Address:
18599 NE Archery Summit Rd
Dayton, OR 97114
(503) 864-4300
Open to Public

Tasting Room:
Tasting Fee: $15.00

Tours Available:
By Appointment Only

Varieties/Wine Styles:
Pinot Noir

Winery Features:
Tasting Room and Retail Sales.

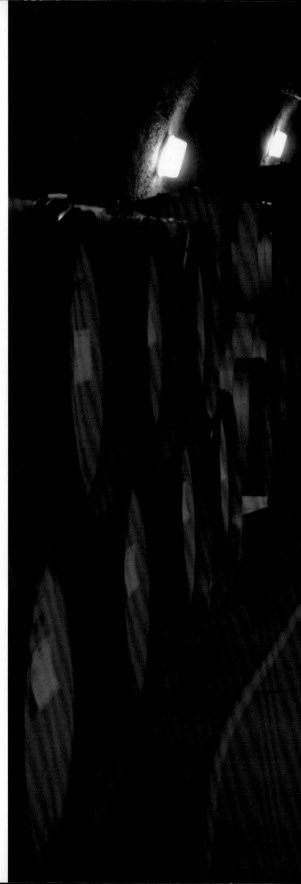

Large Picture Right: *The caves with maturing wines. The horizontal barrel, at the bottom of the picture, shows a barrel washing stand. The barrels are placed onto the metal stand and hot water is shot up into the barrel to clean it. A lot smarter and easier to operate than most other systems, like a simple garden variety hose.*

Sokol Blosser Winery

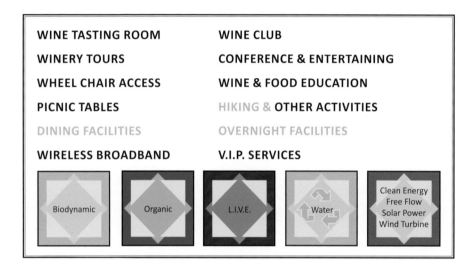

WINE TASTING ROOM	**WINE CLUB**
WINERY TOURS	**CONFERENCE & ENTERTAINING**
WHEEL CHAIR ACCESS	**WINE & FOOD EDUCATION**
PICNIC TABLES	HIKING & **OTHER ACTIVITIES**
DINING FACILITIES	OVERNIGHT FACILITIES
WIRELESS BROADBAND	**V.I.P. SERVICES**

Biodynamic | Organic | L.I.V.E. | Water | Clean Energy Free Flow Solar Power Wind Turbine

History: Recognized as pioneers in Oregon wine, Bill and Susan Blosser, with a lot of youthful self-confidence, energy and determination, planted their first vines in 1971. At that time there was no wine industry in the valley so their entrepreneurial spirits and willingness to trial and error was abounded.

Six years later, in 1977, they built their first winery in the beautiful Dundee Hills of Willamette Valley. At the time, their winery was considered by many to be state-of-the-art; however, as technology improved and grape processing techniques advanced, in 2002, they realized that they had to embark on a large remodeling and construction project to keep their facility in the forefront.

In 1991, Susan Sokol Blosser took over from Bill as winery president. Her "Green or Eco-friendly" hand has seen many innovative changes to the Sokol Blosser Winery and landscape. In 1997 they were the first vineyard to be certified as "Salmon Safe." One year later, Russ Rosner joined as winemaker. Another eco-friendly step forward was in 2000 when Sokol Blosser, after the 3 year probationary period, achieves sustainable "LIVE" certification. Not stopping there, in 2002 after completing the new underground cellar and remodeling the crush pit area they became "LEED certified, Silver." Also that same year they began farming organic and three years later (2005) the vineyard received a USDA organic certifica-

Large Picture Right: The terrace outside of the tasting room overlooking the vineyards. Inserted Picure: The tasting room nestled amongst the trees. Offers spectacular views over the vineyard.

tion from Oregon Tilth. Understanding the importance of clean energy, a 25kW photovoltaic solar panel system was installed in 2006, furnishing 33% of the business's total energy needs.

Although the Oregon wine industry has grown to over 300 wineries and more than 13,000 acres of vineyards, Sokol Blosser has survived, grown and prospered as a family-owned and run operation, and feels proud to have been part of developing and shaping Oregon's now prominent wine industry.

Their goal, as in 1971, remains the same today – "to strive to create wines of world class quality that are produced sustainably, mindful of the environment and your health, and that express the distinctive flavors of our hillside vineyards. Sokol Blosser wines reflect who we are - our values and our sense of place."

Pictures from Top Left (1): The entry to the Sokol Blosser Winery (2): Another picture of the shaded wine tasting room. (3): The 25kW photovoltaic solar panel system which was installed in 2006. It furnishes 33% of the winery's total energy needs. (4): A walk-through vineyard with many of the varieties grown on the Sokol Estate. Here visitors can roam freely with being concerned about contaminating the rest of the vineyard.

Eco-orientation: Dedicated eco-friendly, world class quality wine. Following the principles of "The Natural Step," and pursue environmentally friendly practices by farming their estate vineyards organically. The estate vineyards have been certified "green" by LIVE. They use 50% biodiesel in our farm tractors. Their underground barrel cellar was built to US Green Building Council standards and they became the first winery in the country to earn the prestigious LEED (Leadership in Energy and Environmental Design) certification. They use unbleached paper products for labels, wine boxes and gift bags whenever possible, and they recycle everything from office paper to pallet shrink wrap.

Acreage & Grapes: 87 acres surrounding winery in Dundee, Oregon.

Production: 55,000 cases.

Wine Types & Styles: Sokol Blosser uses 2.5 ton open-top fermenters to ferment their Pinot Noir. The Pinot is given two days of pre-fermentation maceration, then punched down gently three times per day during a seven day fermentation. Finally, the wine is given a very long (twenty-two day) post-fermentation maceration. As

the newly fermented wine rests in contact with the skins it extracts color, complexity and tannins.

After the barrel cellar was completed, they remodeled their old winery facility to provide ample room for tanks and a large open space to store fermenters during harvest and case goods during bottling. Their newly refurbished crush pit area allows for hand sorting of all grapes before processing with the intent to simulate gravity-flow during de-stemming and crushing so as to handle the grapes as gently as possible.

The Sokol Blosser wine style is typical Oregonian. It combines "old world" winemaking practices with a modern touch. Good fruit and tannins levels with controlled alcohol levels and firm acids.

Recommended Wines:

1) Sokol Blosser, Dundee Hills Pinot Noir, 2004. Deep, dark blue-red color. Aromatic nose with good black cherry and raspberry, followed with hints of spice, vanilla and oak. The palate reveals good balance of fruit, acid, and round/octagon tannins with a long finish and good alcohol integration. Storage potential (8-12 years).

2) Sokol Blosser, Dundee Hills Cuvée Pinot Gris, 2004. Good grape typical aromas. The nose shows some spices with citrus characters of apple and pear followed with hints of mineral, earthy, smoky and lees. Very good acid levels with good fruit and length. Good alcohol integration. Storage potential 6-9 years).

3) Sokol Blosser, Estate Müller-Thurgau, 2006. An aromatic wine shows tropical fruit and floral characters. These are represented by orange blossom, mango, honeysuckle, golden delicious apples and jasmine. The palate has some refreshing effervescence that along with the good acidity levels balances the semi-sweet residual sugar levels. Good alcohol integration. Storage potential (4-5years).

Owner/s: The Sokol Blosser family: Susan, Bill, Nik, Alex and Alison.

Winemaker/s: Winemaker Russ Rosner joined Sokol Blosser in 1998 with more than ten years experience at Robert Mondavi. Russ conceptualized our Pinot Noir Single Block program when he noted the distinctiveness of the barrels from different blocks of estate Pinot Noir.

Picture Right Top: Sokol Blosser's famous underground wine cellar which is LEED certified and houses over 900 barrels. Picture Right Bottom: Some wine maturing in the cellar.

"We hand sort through every grape before it goes into a fermenter or is pressed. For Pinot Noir, the grapes are de-stemmed without crushing, to preserve as many whole berries as possible. For white varietals, the grapes are whole-cluster pressed," said Russ eagerly.

Other items of Interest: Cellar Club members and guests are usually invited to kick-off harvest at our exclusive annual "Cellar Club Harvest Party." The event includes a Vineyard Walk with Susan & Alex Sokol Blosser to taste grapes and learn about our organic farming practices. After a good healthy walk, members visit their underground barrel cellar with winemaker Russ Rosner and taste the latest current releases. No charge, but reservations are required.

After the walk and the current vintage cellar tasting things move downstairs to the Winery for their Harvest Dinner prepared by legendary Ciao Vito. Naturally, the Sokol Blosser family and staff are present for the fresh, local and sustainable dinner which is paired with Sokol Blosser wines. The cost for this memorable evening runs at $85 per guest.

General Information:
Sokol Blosser Winery
www.sokolblosser.com

Winery Address:
5000 NE Sokol Blosser Ln
Dayton, OR 97114
(503) 864-2282

Open to Public

Tasting Room:
Tasting Fee: $5-15
Hours: 10-4pm

Tours Available:
By Appointment Only

Varieties/Wine Styles:
Late Harvest/Dessert/Ice Wine, Muller-Thurgau, Pinot Gris, Pinot Noir and Late Harvest Riesling.

*Large Picture Right: Entry to the tasting room and conference center. **Inserted Picture:** Barrels waiting for quality lot selection in the blending area of the cellar.*

Bergström Wines

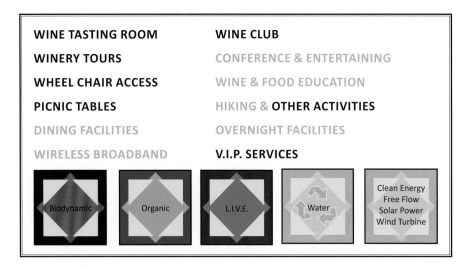

WINE TASTING ROOM	**WINE CLUB**
WINERY TOURS	CONFERENCE & ENTERTAINING
WHEEL CHAIR ACCESS	WINE & FOOD EDUCATION
PICNIC TABLES	HIKING & **OTHER ACTIVITIES**
DINING FACILITIES	OVERNIGHT FACILITIES
WIRELESS BROADBAND	**V.I.P. SERVICES**

Biodynamic   Organic   L.I.V.E.   Water   Clean Energy Free Flow Solar Power Wind Turbine

H*istory:* The Bergström Winery was founded in 1999 by John and Karen Bergström and their son Josh Bergström. After Josh's return from Burgundy where he studied viticulture and Enology at the CFPPA in Beaune as a postgraduate student, the family made 10 barrels of Pinot Noir from purchased fruit in the Dundee Hills. In 2001 Josh's sister Kendall and her husband Paul de Lancellotti joined the family business, and the winery was constructed at its current location on the Calkins Lane bench of the Chehalem Mountains AVA. Now at 10,000 cases of production per year of Pinot Noir, Chardonnay and Riesling, the Bergström Winery is owned by John and Karen Bergström and all five of the Bergström children and their families. Josh Bergström is still winemaker, vineyard manager and general manager of the business.

E*co-orientation:* All 35 acres of estate vineyards at Bergström Winery are farmed Demeter certified Biodynamic (about 50% of its total production). They have always held strong beliefs that wine should not be farmed using pesticides, herbicides, insecticides or systemic fungicides. Currently the Bergström Family is in negotiations to create long term growing projects with clients so that Bergström Winery can be 100% Biodynamic by the year 2010.

Large Picture Right: A view in late summer / early fall of the Bergström vineyards.

Acreage & Grapes: There are three major vineyard sites consisting of 35 acres.

The Bergström Vineyard is 15 acres of Pinot Noir planted in 1999 in the Dundee Hills at an elevation of 375 feet. It is south/southeast facing and is planted to Dijon Clones 114,115,667,777, Pommard, Wadenswil, 828 and selections from mother vines in Burgundy.

The de Lancellotti Vineyard is 15 acres of Pinot Noir and Chardonnay (4 acres of Chardonnay and 11 acres of Pinot Noir) planted in 2001, 2006 and 2007 at an elevation of 400 feet. It is south- and west-facing and planted to Dijon Clones 115,777, Pommard, Wadenswil, 667 and a wide variety of Chardonnay clones.

The Bergström Winery estate is a 5 acre vineyard located just below the winery at 385 feet of elevation planted to 2.5 acres of Pinot Noir and 2.5 acres of Chardonnay at a Burgundian spacing of 3'x3' and is farmed by hand.

Production: The Bergström Winery produces 10,000 cases of wine per year. 1,500 cases of white wine (Chardonnay and Riesling) and 8,500 cases of Pinot Noir. Bergström bottles two different chardonnays per year (Sigrid and Cumberland Reserve) one Riesling (Dr. Bergström Riesling) and several different Pinot Noirs based on their vineyard locations such as: Bergström Vineyard, de Lancellotti Vineyard, Winery Estate Pinot Noir, Shea Vineyard Pinot Noir, Nysa Vineyard Pinot Noir, The Whole Cluster Selection and others.

Wine Types & Styles: Food-friendly wines with very good varietal typicities and excellent balance between classic old world and new world styles. **Oak Usage:** 100% French oak.

Recommended Wines:
1) Bergström Winery. Bergström Vineyard, Pinot Noir, 2004. Shows an intense dark scarlet color. The aromatics

Pictures from Top Left (1): Entry to the Bergström Estate. (2): The tasting room. (3): Barrels being cleaned. (4): A view of the Bergstöm vineyards. Notice the fog moving through the valley. The weather is important to cool morning and evening temperatures.

explode in a concentrated mix of ripe red cherries, wild forest strawberries and intoxicating oak spice with a solid core of minerals and stone. This palate has fine, silky tannins with excellent acids which are in balance with the fruit and alcohol levels. Long balanced finish. Very good storage potential. 600 cases produced.

2) Bergström Winery. The de Lancellotti Vineyard, Pinot Noir, 2005. Deep / dark color with a blue/red hue. The nose is complex with an intense aromatic grape typicity. It shows good spicy characters with a combination of dark and red berries, cherry fruits, anise, cassis and marionberry. Reminds me of a Fixin in northern Burgundy. The palate has firm acids balanced with fruit and well developed tannins. Very long aftertaste. Good storage potential. 455 Cases produced.

3) Bergström Winery. Sigrid Chardonnay, 2006. Good light golden straw color. Grape typical characteristics with a rich aroma filled with pineapple, apples, lemon zest followed by well integrated oak and hints of vanilla. The palate has good acids and fruit balance with a slight astringency. Lovely balanced finish. Good storage potential.

A very good example of a food-friendly Chardonnay.

Owner/s: The Bergström family.

Winemaker/s: Josh Bergström is a native to Oregon where he earned his undergraduate degree in the Humanities and French at the University of Oregon in 1998. As a college student he interned for Rex Hill Winery and Ponzi Winery before travelling to Burgundy France to earn a postgraduate degree in Enology and Viticulture from the CFPPA in Beaune. Josh has been Bergström Winery's winemaker and vineyard manager since 1999 and general manager since 2006.

Other items of Interest: Bergström Winery has 40 acres of estate vineyard land that are Demeter certified Biodynamic farmed since 2004 and organically farmed since their plantings in 1999 (Bergström Vineyard) and 2001 (de Lancellotti Vineyard and the Winery Estate Block) Josh believes that

Pictures Right: Bergström's barrel cellar provides Josh with a lot of exercise.

Biodynamic farming is the truest form of "natural/holistic" farming which will bring out and preserve the uniqueness of each vineyard and farm while building better soil structure and balance for generations to come; "Wine is a maceration product which means that the only ingredient must be pure fruit from a unique source if it is to be a great wine for now and for the ages. If chemicals are used in vineyards such as pesticides or herbicides or insecticides, they will not only cloud the purity of the wine and vineyard site but destroy the uniqueness and potential of that piece of land."

Josh and the Bergström team also make wine from purchased fruit coming from 30 different and unique vineyard sites in the Willamette Valley including Shea Vineyard, Nysa Vineyard, Temperance Hill Vineyard, Eyrie Vineyard, Anderson Vineyard, Palmer Creek Vineyard, Carabella Vineyard and many others.

General Information:
Bergström Winery
www.bergstromwines.com

Winery Address:
18215 NE Calkins Lane
Newberg, Oregon 97132
(503) 544-0468
Open to Public

Tasting Room:
Tasting Fee: $25
Hours: Tastings will be offered 4 times daily at: 10:00, 11:30, 2:00 and 3:30.
RESERVATIONS ARE REQUIRED.
Wine club members receive complimentary tastings for up to four people.
Tours Available: Frequently

Varieties/Wine Styles:
Chardonnay, Riesling, Pinot Noir, and Pinot Gris.

Certificates:
Certified Biodynamic & Organic

Winery Features:
Tasting Room, Picnic Area, Bus/RV Parking, Wheelchair Accessible and Retail Sales.

Large Picture Right: *A view of the tasting room and winery at Bergström, a couple of guests and Corky the dog.* **Inserted Picture:** *Josh Bergström hard at work in the winery.*

Beaux Frères

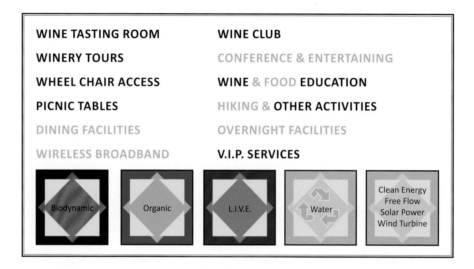

WINE TASTING ROOM	**WINE CLUB**
WINERY TOURS	CONFERENCE & ENTERTAINING
WHEEL CHAIR ACCESS	**WINE** & FOOD **EDUCATION**
PICNIC TABLES	HIKING & **OTHER ACTIVITIES**
DINING FACILITIES	OVERNIGHT FACILITIES
WIRELESS BROADBAND	**V.I.P. SERVICES**

Biodynamic Organic L.I.V.E. Water Clean Energy Free Flow Solar Power Wind Turbine

History: In 1986 while on vacation, Michael Etzel discovered an 88-acre farm for sale located in the Northern Willamette Valley on Ribbon Ridge in Yamhill County, Oregon. After some deliberation, Michael purchased the farm with his brother-in-law, Robert Parker, Jr. – and Michael started to transform the old pig and dairy farm into a Pinot Noir vineyard to reckon with started in 1988. At the same time that he was planting his own vineyard, Michael also worked four harvests at the Ponzi Winery.

The first harvest and crop was sold to Ken Wright and Dick Ponzi in 1990; however, he kept just enough grapes to make one barrel of wine.

In 1991, Robert Roy joined as the third partner. Subsequently, the barns on the property were renovated which also led to the creation of Beaux Frères Winery.

"Robert Parker, Jr. is one of three owners in Beaux Frères vineyard and winery. His interest in the property was spurred by his brother-in-law, Michael Etzel, who discovered the property in 1986. Robert lives in Maryland with his wife Pat, Michael's older sister, their daughter Maia, and various basset hounds and bulldogs. For twenty-four years he has written and published the independent wine journal The Wine Advocate and authored twelve best-selling books on wine. Robert never reviews Beaux Frères for his publications, but you will find his imprint in the winery's tasting

Large Picture Right: The Beaux Frères Winery showing the fermentation tanks in the foreground. **Inserted Picture:** *Michael Etzel taking a break from his duties.*

Beaux Frères

notes, and more importantly, in the philosophy that governs Beaux Frères and its pursuit of excellence."

E*co-orientation:* They practice biodynamic, organic and Low Input Viticulture & Enology (LIVE); however they are not yet certified.

A*creage & Grapes:* 33 acres under vine. Pinot Noir represents approximately 99.9%. 10 newly planted acres of Pinot Noir on the Upper Terrace of the Beaux Frères Vineyard, which has an average yield of 2 tons per acre. The vineyard manager is Michael G. Etzel and the assistant vineyard manager is Rogelio Rosales.

The vines are spaced one-meter apart in rows six-feet apart (at a density of about 2200 plants to the acre) and are trained in the single-Guyot method, with one fruiting cane per vine tied horizontally along the fruiting wire at about 24 inches above the ground.

Pictures from Top Left (1): *A drawing of the vineyard which is used on a number of labels.* ***(2):*** *Their compost heap which has an inside tempereature that could cook an egg.* ***(3):*** *Their humble tasting room.* ***(4):*** *The technical side of winemaking. Although a classical approach to winemaking is taken, one also needs to measure the wine's health and makeup.*

The Upper Terrace is planted with Pinot Noir Dijon clones 113, 114, 115, 667, and 777 on two different root stocks. The Terrace is a south-facing slope.

The Estate Vineyard is planted with the Pinot Noir Pommard and Wadenswil on their own roots. The vineyard is grown organic and biodynamic.

P*roduction:* The average total production is 3000 to 6000 cases. This varies on an annual basis as they are striving for the highest quality possible. The winery capacity is around 8000 cases. Beaux Frères makes only 3 Pinot Noir wines.

W*ine Types & Styles:* Beaux Frères Vineyard and Winery's position is to grow very ripe, healthy and intense fruit. This is done by maintaining low yields through a summer harvest (by passing through the vineyard on a number of occasions and dropping fruit). Additionally, the vineyards are not irrigated so that fermentation can capture the true reflection of the Beaux Frères Vineyard.

"Since our first vintage in 1991, the Beaux Frères philosophy remains the same: to produce a world-class Pinot Noir from tiny yields and ripe fruit that represents the essence of our vineyard. In pursuit of these goals, the Beaux Frères Vineyard was planted with tightly spaced vines, and yields are kept to some of the lowest in both the New and Old World," Michael said.

The grapes are harvested when they are physiologically (rather than analytically) ripe. Our winemaking philosophy is one of minimal intervention with clean fermentation utilizing indigenous yeast. The wines are stored in French oak for 12 to 14 months with changing percentage of new oak to match the strength of the wines. Beaux Frères is never racked until removed from barrel for bottling, which occurs without fining or filtration.

These non-manipulative, uncompromising methods guarantee a wine that is the most natural and authentic vineyard expression possible. Previous vintages demonstrate that these methods also allow our Beaux Frères to develop significant perfume, weight, and texture in the bottle.

Oak Usage: 100% French oak.

Recommended Wines:
1) Beaux Frères, The Vineyard Pinot Noir 2005. Good grape typical wine. The wine is classical in style reminiscent of northern Côte de Nuits (Fixin – just south of Dijon) in Burgundy. The color is dark blue-red with some purplish tones. The nose offers very good Pinot Noir characteristics with some spiciness, dark berry, cherry and raspberry tones accented by wonderful herbaceous, earthy and oak characters. The palate is well balanced with good fruit and acid levels. The tannins are round/octagon and the alcohol is well integrated. Storage potential (10-15 years).

2) Beaux Frères, The Upper Terrace Pinot Noir, 2005. Good grape typicity. The wine has many classical characteristics with a touch of Oregon. The color is deep and dark red. The nose is aromatic and displays very good floral, red berry, and cherry fruit with good earthy and oak tones. The palate is well balanced with good acidity levels, firm round tannins which is integrated with the fruit and alcohol. Long complex finish. Storage potential (15+ years).

3) Beaux Frères, Willamette Valley Pinot Noir, 2005 (formerly known as the Belles Soeurs). The wine is classical Oregon in style and shows good varietal typicity. It has a deep ruby red color. The nose displays both red and dark berries with cher-

Pictures Right: A fire truck from the 1950s is used to water the vineyard. (2): Beaux frères wines. (3): Michael and their biodynamic advisor mixing an inoculant for the compost heap. (4): The biodynamic box of goodies.

ries, raspberries and some blue berries. Good spicy characters and oak integration. The palate shows good fruit with firm acid levels with fine tannins followed by good alcohol and oak integration. Good length. Storage potential (8-10 years).

Owner/s: Michael Etzel, Robert Parker, Jr. and Robert Roy.

Winemaker/s: Michael G. Etzel is the Winemaker and Stephen Goff he Assistant Winemaker.

Other items of Interest: Beaux Frères means brother in-law in French.

General Information:
Beaux Frères Winery
www.beauxfreres.com

Winery Address:
15155 NE North Valley Rd.
Newberg, Oregon 97132
Tel: 503.537.1137
Call for an Appointment.

Tasting Room:
Visiting hours: Thanksgiving and Memorial Day weekends.

Tours Available: By appointment for mailing list customers, only.

Varieties/Wine Styles:
Pinot Noir

Certificates:
Certified Biodynamic & Organic

Winery Features:
Tasting Room, Picnic Area, Bus/RV Parking, and Wheelchair Accessible.

Large Picture Right: *Harvest time at the Beaux Frères vineyard.*

King Estate

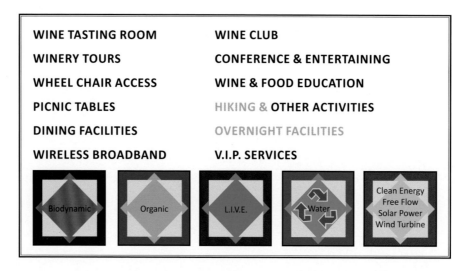

WINE TASTING ROOM	**WINE CLUB**
WINERY TOURS	**CONFERENCE & ENTERTAINING**
WHEEL CHAIR ACCESS	**WINE & FOOD EDUCATION**
PICNIC TABLES	HIKING & **OTHER ACTIVITIES**
DINING FACILITIES	OVERNIGHT FACILITIES
WIRELESS BROADBAND	**V.I.P. SERVICES**

Biodynamic · Organic · L.I.V.E. · Water · Clean Energy Free Flow Solar Power Wind Turbine

History: King Estate was started in 1991. The King family had been interested in the nascent Oregon wine industry dating back to Ed King III's move to Oregon in 1979 to enter the University of Oregon's MBA program. By the early 1990s Ed III had acquired two small vineyards through local timberland and farm land acquisitions. Meanwhile, Ed III's father, Ed, Jr., who had sold his aviation electronics firm, King Radio Corporation, in 1985, was also becoming more interested in wine due to his travels in Europe. Ed, Jr. retired with the sale of his company and spent much of his time sailing and at his homes in Arizona and Nevada. Ed, Jr. has always been the principle financer of the winery, though many other family members now own interests in the company. Ed Jr. visited Oregon regularly over the first decade of the winery and in 2001 began to spend his summers in Oregon. Ed III has continued to live in Oregon since the inception of the winery.

The launching pad for King Estate was the purchase of a 600 acre parcel near Lorane, Oregon in 1991. The property was first viewed by Ed III when he visited the Lorane Valley to see it was for sale on a cattle ranch. The ranch had once been entirely planted with fruit trees and the slopes reminded Ed III of the two small vineyards he already owned. He felt the ranch could be the location for the major winery project that he had discussed with his father. It turned out that the ranch was also for sale, and not just the hay. Time would prove that it was a

Large Picture Right: Fall at the King Estate. **Insert:** *The diverse flora is typical for organic wineries. Here the insect population and ecosystem can support good organic growth without pesticides.*

very good place to grow grapes as well. The location is somewhat unique in terms of its position in the state, a stone's throw south of the Willamette Valley, and close enough to the Oregon coast to be influenced by maritime weather. While the location might qualify for its own appellation, King Estate has focused on creating a national interest in Oregon wines in general, rather than any specific location in Oregon.

The years have brought the company two major land acquisitions in the neighborhood, the Spring Hill Ranch and the Doughty Ranch. These contiguous properties, extended the Estate to the north and east, and brought the total acreage to over 1000 acres.

King Estate has developed relationships with distributors around the US, Canada, and overseas. Many of these relationships have developed into true partnerships, based on mutual goals and joint planning. King Estate is very well distributed in the US, and will be found in the best retail shops and restaurants.

King Estate has focused on the long view

Pictures from Top Left (1): Outside of the King Estate organic market. (2): The King Estate organic marketplace. (3):The terrace leading to the King Estate. (4): Healthy looking bunch of organic Pinot Noir grapes from the King Estate.

of the industry and King Estate's role in it. Their success has not been due to only one person's efforts or vision: rather, many people have contributed much over the years.

Eco-orientation: In 2002, King Estate vineyards, nursery, and all surrounding gardens and landscape received organic certification by the Oregon Tilth Certified Organic association.

Acreage & Grapes: The beautiful 1,033-acre organic estate includes 465 acres of organic vineyards with 143 acres of Pinot Noir, 314 acres of Pinot Gris – 314 Acres, and 8 acres of Chardonnay, Muscat, Gamay Noir, and Gewurztraminer.

Production: The majestic winery, which reflects the architectural tradition of a French chateau, encompasses approximately 110,000 square feet. Total production capacity is 400,000 gallons.

The winery is equipped with contemporary technological advantages including computer-controlled refrigeration, along with traditional old world amenities such as underground barrel aging cellars. King Estate is a winemaker's winery designed to facilitate the painstaking production methods necessary to craft the finest wines.

Wine Types & Styles: Pinot Gris – King Estate has made a long term, multi-level commitment to this exciting varietal with over 315 acres planted on the estate. Pinot Gris from this estate vineyard is distinctly known for subtle hints of lime, honeysuckle, and mineral notes on the nose, complemented by flavors of pear and stone-fruit.

Pinot Noir – King Estate has planted perhaps the most clonally-diverse Pinot Noir vineyard in the country. Currently 16 clones of Pinot Noir are planted on a variety of rootstock and trellising systems, including a broad range of highly regarded Dijon clones. Clonal diversity imparts and amplifies flavor and textural complexity. The Pinot Noir vineyards are noted for featuring raspberry, blackberry, and rose petal on the nose complemented by flavors of black cherry and a silky mouth feel.

Recommended Wines:
1) King Estate, Domaine Pinot Gris, 2006. Shows fantastic grape typical aromas with some spices, honeysuckle, orange peel, pear, honey and touches of tropical fruit. The palate has excellent acids and fruit balance with an impressive length and finish.
2) King Estate, Domaine Pinot Noir 2005. Exhibits excellent grape typicity with a touch of spices and lovely floral characters combined with red berries, cherries and raspberries. The palate is well balanced with firm acidity and fruit with soft, fine round tannins and a long finish.
3) King Estate, Signature Pinot Noir 2005. Good aromatics with typical variety characters of raspberry, strawberry, cherry and a floral vanilla combination. Very good tannin-acid-fruit balance and a long finish.

Owner/s: Ed King, Jr. & Ed King

Winemaker/s: John Albin, Director of Winemaking and Grower Relations. A U.C. Davis graduate in fermentation Science, John began making wine in Washington at Associated Vintners (Columbia Winery) and planted his own 'Laurel Vineyard' in 1981. John's relationship with King Estate Winery began during the planning stages of the winery. His vineyard was chosen as one of the first private vineyards to provide fruit to King Estate Winery and he has enjoyed an enriching partnership with King Estate

Pictures Right: *Entry to the King Estate* **(2):** *An impressive view of the King Estate as you drive up to the winery.* **(3):** *A private room for V.I.P tasting and conferences.* **(4):** *The terrace and outside seating area where you can savor the food created by their world class chef.*

-121-

ever since. In 1999, John began working at King Estate as a crush supervisor and continued with that position for six years. He coordinates the critical scheduling of harvest for King Estate's vineyards in addition to the seven outside vineyards we contract with.

Bill Kremer, Winemaker. Bill earned a Master of Science in Microbiology from the University of Washington and a Master of Science from U.C. Davis in Food Science-Enology. Bill joined King Estate in 1995. Bill directs the entire winemaking process and production staff, supervises bottling, coordinates packaging materials, and organizes the organic certification program for the winery. Before joining King Estate Bill worked as an Enologist for both Chateau Potelle in Napa and R.H. Phillips Vineyard in Esparto.

Lindsay Kampff, Winemaker. Lindsay Kampff joined the winemaking team at King Estate during the 2004 vintage. Lindsay earned a Chemistry degree from the University of California at Santa Barbara in 2001 and completed the UC Davis Winemaking Certificate Program in the Summer of 2006. She is native to California and started in the Sonoma County wine industry working for J. Vineyards and Winery and Jordan Winery. As the Winemaker at King Estate, Lindsay is responsible for quality assurance

of our wines from harvest to bottling.

Al Ehlow, Assistant Winemaker. Al Ehlow holds a degree in Viticulture and Enology from UC Davis, and brings eight years of experience in the Sonoma and Napa Valleys with Whitehall Lane, Alderbrook, and Merryvale wineries.

General Information:
King Estate
www.kingestate.com

Winery Address:
80854 Territorial Rd
Eugene, OR 97405 * Tel:(541) 942-9874

Tasting Room: Open to Public
Tasting Fee: $Varies (Refundable with purchase)
Hours: Sunday - Thursday 11am - 7pm, Friday & Saturday 11am - 8pm
Tours Available: Frequently

Varieties/Wine Styles:
Chardonnay, Late Harvest/Dessert/Ice Wine , Pinot Gris and Pinot Noir.

Certificates: Certified Organic

Winery Features: Restaurant, Conferene Services, Tasting Room, Picnic Area, Bus/ RV Parking, Wheelchair Accessible and Retail.

Large Picture Right: *A magnificent fall picture of King Estate.* **Inserted Picture:** *John Albin, Head Winemaker at King Estate.*

-122-

Henry Estate Winery

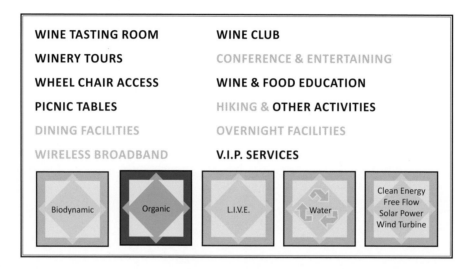

WINE TASTING ROOM   WINE CLUB

WINERY TOURS   CONFERENCE & ENTERTAINING

WHEEL CHAIR ACCESS   WINE & FOOD EDUCATION

PICNIC TABLES   HIKING & OTHER ACTIVITIES

DINING FACILITIES   OVERNIGHT FACILITIES

WIRELESS BROADBAND   V.I.P. SERVICES

Biodynamic   Organic   L.I.V.E.   Water   Clean Energy / Free Flow / Solar Power / Wind Turbine

History: Scott Henry, owner and founder of Henry Estate Winery, decided to begin growing grapes after a 13-year stint as an aeronautical engineer in California. Knowing well that the climate of the Umpqua Valley is similar to that of Burgundy, he and his friend, Gino Zepponi, scouted our family homestead for the best locations to grow grapes.

A small, family (Scott, Scotty & Syndi) owned and operated winery. "Our entire Henry clan pitched into plant the first 12 of what are today 40 acres of varietal grapes," said Scott proudly.

The newly constructed winery was opened just in time for the 1978 crush. Henry hired his friend Zepponi as a winemaking consultant. An engineer by trade, Henry began to ask questions, naturally this led to a learning curve which would see innovation after innovation. As demand grew, so did the winery, and, in 2000, production was expanded from 6,000 to 18,000 cases.

The Henry Estate is one of Oregon's oldest and most prestigious producers. The pioneering spirit of the Henry family has been an inspiration to many newcomers in the Oregon wine business. That inspiration and spirit is a foundation for the entire Oregon wine industry, and will continue to build the legacy and character of Scott Henry III.

Eco-orientation: They practice biodynamic, organic and Low Input Viticulture & Enology (LIVE); however they are not yet certified.

Large Picture Right: *Entrance to the Henry Estate.*
Inserted Picture: *Scott Henry III.*

A_creage & Grapes:_ 60 acres. The estate planted with Pinot Noir, Chardonnay, Pinot Gris, Gewürztraminer, Merlot, Müller-Thurgau, and White Riesling.

P_roduction_: 16,000 cases.

The Henry Estate is fortunate to have very rich soil and favorable climatic conditions. His vines produced a dense canopy with an abundance of fruit that had to be managed in order to sustain high-quality grapes for wine. "What was more challenging was the fact that as the vines grew older they also grew more vigorous," Scott mentioned.

"I tried many different methods to improve the degrading fruit quality and nothing was working to my satisfaction," he said. One of his ongoing vineyard trials revealed that vine vigor could be discouraged by increasing the number of canes from two to four per plant – this is contrary to what most viticulturists have been taught. Thus, he increased crop level to offset vigor and loosened bunch crowding to discourage

Pictures from Top Left (1): The hand-made colored glass adorning the tasting room's fron doors. (2): Scott Henry and his daughter Syndi Henry. (3): Vineyards in fall. (4): A number of the medals won by the Henry Estate wines.

bunch rot. However, this method simultaneously delayed ripening as the vine was required to work harder to ripen the fruit. "More leaf area and less leaf density after setting were therefore required," Scott said. Always striving for perfection, Henry developed a unique trellising system that optimizes the maturity of grapes.

Scott continues, "Four (versus the customary two) canes provide the fruit for each vine and four replacement spurs are selected for renewal growth. Shoot growth from the top canes is trained upward, while shoot growth from the bottom canes is trained downward to maximize canopy surface area and to control vigor. Shoot density is also halved, because only shoots from the top canes are trained upwards, and the remainder is forced to grow toward the ground. Because of their (unnatural) downward position the vigor is reduced in about half of the shoots. Growth between the two levels of fruit is separated shortly before bloom with the use of two catch wires, which originally rest midway between the two fruiting zones."

The engineer turned winemaker Scott explains, "The advantages of this system include increased yield, increased Brix and decreased Titratable Acidity. Experimentation does not show any differences between the fruit of the two tiers. While benefits are several, disadvantages of the system are primarily canopy management: the training process itself is a sensitive issue, upkeep is more demanding and consequently, cost is slightly higher than traditional methods."

" The wines produced from vines trellised in the Scott Henry System, however, are the decisive factor. They consistently show better color, fruit character on the nose and on the palate, and a better palate structure compared to what we could produce before," Scott said.

Today, there are over 10,000 acres planted in Australia, New Zealand, South America and the USA. "The Scott Henry Vertical Trellis System is used exclusively in our vineyards too," Scott says with a proud smile on his face.

Wine Types & Styles: A mixture between classical and modern wine styles. Their wines show a fruitier style commonly seen in Oregon's southern appellations.

Oak Usage: French and America oak.

Recommended Wines:
1) Henry Estate, Pinot Noir, 2005. Good varietal characteristics. The nose shows cherry, pepper, spicy tones with hints of vanilla, oak, and strawberry. The Palate displays good fruit and soft round tannins, moderate acidity levels, and well integrated oak and alcohol. Medium to long finish. Storage potential (4-7 years).

2) Henry Estate, Pinot Gris, 2006. Good varietal typicity. Aromatic nose with tropical hits of pear, peach, honeysuckle, and perfume followed with a hint of spice. The palate shows good fruit and acid. Long finish. Storage Potential (3-5 years).

3) Henry Estate, Müller-Thurgau, 2006. Grape typical. Aromatic nose showing tropical characters of peach, melon, citrus and apple blossom. The palate is medium bodied with good acidity levels and lots of fruit. Well integrated. Long finish. Storage Potential (3-7 years).

Owner/s: Scott Henry III

Winemaker/s: Scott Henry IV.

Other items of Interest: The whole Henry family is on hand to welcome you

Picture Right: The winery adorned with hundreds of French & American wine barrels.

to their annual celebration, Henry Goes Wine. Henry Goes Wine happens on the third Saturday in August each year. Families are invited to spend a beautiful summer day in the Umpqua Valley. Some of the entertainment includes live bands, carriage rides through the vineyard, winery tours and the popular potato salad contest. Kids are entertained with kites to fly, pony rides, and "Wizard of Ed" who makes fun balloon hats.

There is also great food for everyone to savor. Mo's seafood from the coast is a perennial favorite, offering everything from their award-winning clam chowder to blackberry cobbler. The Roseburg Jaycee's host the country barbecue from 4 p.m. – 6 p.m., which includes lamb kabobs and pork ribs, beans, salad, and fresh corn on the cob. A variety of drinks and Umpqua Dairy ice cream is offered as well.

General Information:
Henry Estate Winery
www.henryestate.com

Winery Address:
687 Hubbard Creekroad
Umpqua, OR 97486
(541) 459-5120
Open to Public

Tasting Room:
Hours: Daily 11:00am - 5:00pm
Tours Available:
Frequently

Varieties/Wine Styles:
Chardonnay, Gewürztraminer , Merlot, Muller-Thurgau , Pinot Gris, Pinot Noir, Riesling, Sparkling, Syrah and Viognier.

Winery Features:
Tasting Room, Wedding Facilities, Reception Facilities, Picnic Area, Bus/RV Parking, Wheelchair Accessible and Retail Sales.

Large Picture Right: *Entry to the tasting room and front end of the winery.* **Inserted Picture:** *The Scott Henry Trellis System which is used in many countries today. There are over 10,000 acres planted using his trellising technique.*

Hedged Shoot Tips

Del Rio Vineyards

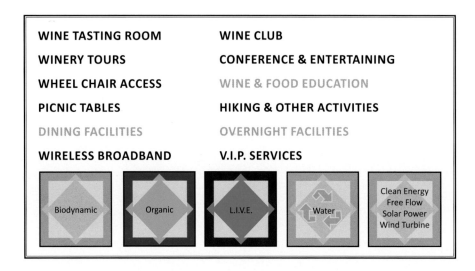

WINE TASTING ROOM	**WINE CLUB**
WINERY TOURS	**CONFERENCE & ENTERTAINING**
WHEEL CHAIR ACCESS	WINE & FOOD EDUCATION
PICNIC TABLES	**HIKING & OTHER ACTIVITIES**
DINING FACILITIES	OVERNIGHT FACILITIES
WIRELESS BROADBAND	**V.I.P. SERVICES**

Biodynamic | Organic | L.I.V.E. | Water | Clean Energy / Free Flow / Solar Power / Wind Turbine

History: Del Rio began its existence as the small community of Rock Point, founded by J.B. White in the early 1850s. John fought in the Rogue Indian Wars from 1855-1856, serving under Captain William A. Wilkinson. In exchange for his services, he received land. He was appointed as a judge in the Dardanelles precinct in 1857 and two years later established the post office in Rock Point.

In 1864 construction began on the Rock Point Hotel. On February 8, 1865, the hotel opened to the public with a grand ball.

At the same time one of the first telegraph stations was established in the area. Soon thereafter the small community of Rock Point began to flourish. Joining the hotel, and the post office, were homes, Abram Schuly's blacksmith shop, Hoymond and White's store, a saloon and a school. The record books from the Stage Company verify the regular use of the Rock Point Hotel as a stage stop.

In 1907, a new period began when F.K. Duel and others purchased the hotel and surrounding land. The property grew from a one-acre family orchard to an eight hundred acre valley orchard yielding leading varieties of pears, apples, cherries, peaches, apricots, walnuts and filberts.

The Del Rio Orchards were planted after 1907, during a rapid period of growth in the Rogue Valley known as the "pear boom".

Large Picture Right: Shows the "Rock Point Hotel" an old stage coach stop in the 1860s. Inserted Picture: A view looking across the railway tracks towards the Del Rio vineyards climbing up the slopes of the surrounding mountains.

The Orchard and hotel remained in the Duel family until 1997, when Lee and Margaret Traynham of California purchased the land. Realizing the historical significance of the structures, the Traynhamn's began full restoration. This included the Rock Point Hotel, which is one of the oldest structures in Southern Oregon.

They also began the transformation of a third generation pear orchard into one of Southern Oregon's premium wine grape vineyards. Naturally, this is a new start for the Rock Point Hotel as it now is open to the public and serves Del Rio Vineyard's own produced wines in the tasting room.

Eco-orientation: Organic and sustainable farming.

Acreage & Grapes: The rocky south-

Pictures from Top Left (1): Entry sign to the Del Rio Vinyards. (2): The lovely "country home" style tasting room. (3): The newly constructed cellars. When the author arrived, Rob Wallace, surprisingly enough, was found on his knees welding a new gangway, which was connected to a series of fermentation tanks in the adjacent fermentation room. What's more incredible is the fact that he built the entire winery too. (4): Here's a picture of Rob and Jolee Wallace. Down to earth and inspirational!

facing slopes of the vineyard drain well and provide excellent terrain for producing premium wine grapes. Del Rio Vineyards has 1000 acres of which 200,000 vines are planted on 215 acres. As a prime source of grapes to over 35 premium wineries in Northern Oregon, Del Rio produce a diverse selection of grape varieties such as: Sangiovese (Rodino clone), Merlot (181 clone), Grenache (03 clone), Pinot Noir (667 & 777 clones), Malbec (04 clone), Cabernet Sauvignon (04, 15 & 337 clones), Syrah (Noir clone), Cabernet Franc (332 clone), Pinot Gris (146 & 152 clones), Chardonnay 76 & 95 clones) and Viognier (01 clone).

Production: 4000 cases of Del Rio Vineyard's own wines.

Wine Types & Styles: As diverse as the varietals on the property.

Del Rio Vineyards has a climate that could be envied by most wine-growers. It has cool morning and evening breezes with 3,000 degree days (heating units) as compared to the 1,700 degree days in the Willamette Valley. This gives Del Rio the ability to grow and make a variety of styles from port to dry white. *Oak Usage:* French and American.

Recommended Wines:

1) Del Rio Vineyards & Winery, Claret, 2004. A Bordeaux blend comprised of 36% Cabernet Sauvignon, 27% Merlot, 27% Malbec, and 10% Cabernet Franc. The color is deep with a slight blue-red hue. The nose is aromatic and shows good fruit with a fruit cake, blackcurrant, cherry and spicy nose followed by well integrated oak and vanilla. The palate presents good fruit, soft round tannins and good acidity levels with alcohol and oak in balance. Medium to long length. Storage potential (7-10 years).

2) Del Rio Vineyards & Winery, Cabernet Franc, 2004. Deep, dark, ruby-red color. Grape typical. The nose shows a lovely herbaceous, spicy, tobacco, raspberry, and blueberry character. The palate is balanced with fruit, acid and fine tannins supported by good oak and alcohol integration. Long finish. Storage potential (5-8 years).

3) Del Rio Vineyards & Winery, Viognier, 2005. The wine shows good grape typicity. Pale-straw hue with a medium color. Aromatic wine with a lovely floral, tropical and citrus fruit character showing orange blossom, peach, apricot, mango and lemon grass with a touch of almond. The palate is full-bodied with good fruit and acidity. No bitterness in the aftertaste. Good alcohol integration. Long finish. Storage potential (3-5 years).

Owner/s: Rob and Jolee Wallace and Lee Traynham.

Winemaker/s: Winemaker Jeff Kandarian, a native of Central California, grew up in the San Joaquin Valley. Jeff graduated with a B.S. degree in Enology and a Minor in Chemistry from California State University in Fresno.

Completing his eighth crush in 2007, Jeff has worked with large, medium and small wineries. With his hands-on approach, Jeff remains active in all phases of the winemaking, whether supervising over 100 people or even consulting for a "Mom & Pop" winery.

His passion is Bordeaux and Rhone Red wines. His winemaking style is a "hands-off," minimalist approach to winemaking. This allows each wine from vintage to vintage to speak for itself. He believes that "truly great wines are a product of their environment," and that "if you work hard enough anything is possible." When Jeff is not making, drinking, or reading about wine, he spends his time with his family, friends, and cats.

Picture Right: *A bottle of the Del Rio Vineyards 2005 Viognier.*

He is a very proud husband and father. His other interests include traveling, the outdoors, sports (more viewing then participating these days), salt water aquariums, and cooking.

Other items of Interest: "Located at the entrance to Del Rio Vineyards, is the historic Rock Point Stage Hotel built in 1864. This building has been partially renovated to serve as Del Rio's wine tasting room. Much of the building has been restored to its original state, and the tasting room has the charm and warmth of days gone past.

Being one of the largest suppliers of premium wine grapes to over 20 Oregon vintners, Del Rio's tasting room offers the unique opportunity to not only feature their own Del Rio label, but a fantastic variety of fine wines produced throughout our local area. Surrounding the building is a comfortable picnic area, perfect for relaxing and enjoying a special vintage while taking in the spectacular view of Southern Oregon's largest vineyard."

General Information:
Del Rio Vineyards
www.delriovineyards.com

Winery Address:
52 N. River Road
Gold Hill, OR 97525
(541) 855-1212
Open to Public

Tasting Room:
Tasting Fee: $5.00
Hours: Sept - May: 11 to 5 p.m.
Jun - Aug: 11 to 6p.m.

Tours Available:
By Appointment Only

Varieties/Wine Styles:
Cabernet Franc, Cabernet Sauvignon, Chardonnay, Claret, Merlot, Muscat, Pinot Gris, Syrah and Viognier.

Winery Features:
Tasting Room, Wedding Facilities, Reception Facilities, Picnic Area, Bus/RV Parking, Wheelchair Accessible and Retail Sales.

Large Picture Right: *A view from the edge of the vineyard looking down towards the winery and tasting room.* **Inserted Picture:** *Winemaker Jeff Kandarian sitting aloft his wine barrels.*

Devitt Winery

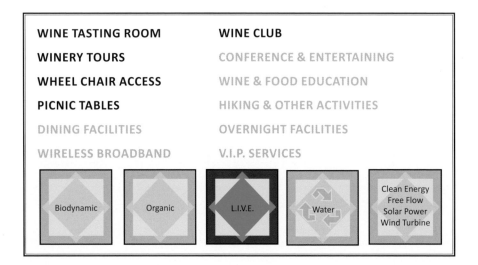

WINE TASTING ROOM	**WINE CLUB**
WINERY TOURS	CONFERENCE & ENTERTAINING
WHEEL CHAIR ACCESS	WINE & FOOD EDUCATION
PICNIC TABLES	HIKING & OTHER ACTIVITIES
DINING FACILITIES	OVERNIGHT FACILITIES
WIRELESS BROADBAND	V.I.P. SERVICES

Biodynamic · Organic · L.I.V.E. · Water · Clean Energy Free Flow Solar Power Wind Turbine

History: The Devitt's purchased the Oregon property in 1997 with the intention of establishing a vineyard for supplemental income by selling their grapes on to local wineries. They planted their first vines in 2001, on 5 acres that they trellised themselves.

Originally shipping the grapes to the northern part of the state, they started to question whether or not it was a good idea to go back into the wine business and to make wine again. "We had a full basement under our house that would suffice for wine storage, so the rest would not be too much of a stretch," said Jim.

In early 2003 they were approached by the owners of Old Stage Vineyard to farm, harvest and make wines from their grapes; however, Jim stated, "The thought of utilizing our basement for storage was now out of the question and we proceeded to build a winery, purchased the necessary equipment, barrels, tanks and sought the necessary permits." The first harvest and vintage in their new winery was in fall 2003.

Their grandson joined Devitt Winery last year and is working in the vineyard and winery. He is taking "distance learner" classes from UC Davis for a certificate in winemaking, and then will be taking classes in viticulture. Long-term plans call for planting an additional 12 acres at the Devitt Estate vineyard.

The philosophy of Devitt will continue to focus on winemaking based on good fruit from the vineyard. This will be acheived

Large Picture Right: *James Devitt checking the various wines and lots prior to blending.*

through proper pruning and canopy management with as little intervention as possible.

Eco-orientation: "Our philosophy is sustainable agriculture and L.I.V.E. (Low Input Viticulture & Enology) and always keeping in mind that wine is made in the vineyard– what you put on the grapes during the growing season is (to some extent) there at harvest time." Furthermore, Jim states, "We spray for mildew on a regular schedule, and nothing else. Fertilization and soil amendments are added during winter and before flowering."

Acreage & Grapes: A total of 14 acres with:
1) *9 acres* at Old Stage Vineyard consisting of Zinfandel, Merlot, Cabernet Franc and Cabernet Sauvignon, all mature vines. They harvest an average of 26 tons from this vineyard, making about 1500 cases of wine per vintage.
2) 5 acres at the Winery property planted with Pinot Noir, Syrah, Sangiovese, Tempranillo and Viognier producing about 9 tons of fruit annually.

Pictures from Top Left (1): The humble entry way into the Devitt winery. (2): Jim dropping fruit. (3): Raspberries (the Oregon winegrowers weed) galore on the Devitt property.

However, they plan to increase their estate planting by another 12 acres in the near future increasing the Devitt Estate winery property to 17 acres.
3) In addition, they crush about 10 tons of fruit from 2 local Applegate vineyards for an additional 500 cases of white and rosé wine.

Production: 1500 cases annualy with plans for 5000 cases in the next few years.

Wine Types & Styles: Kept in separate lots their wines are vinified in the following manner:

White wines: Whole cluster press and fermentation in 60gal (French oak with a mixture of 1/3 new and 2/3 neutral barrels) barrels. The barrels are racked and topped up after fermentation. The wine is left on its lees and stirred every 2-3 weeks for the next 8-9 months at which time it is blended together and bottled with minimal handling, producing complex wines.

Red wines: The grapes are de-stemmed into fermenters and allowed to cold soak for a few days, then inoculated with yeast and allowed to ferment until dry with punch down of the cap daily for color and tannin extraction. Upon completion of fermentation, the free run juice is racked into 60gal barrels. The cap is pressed and the juice is pumped into separate barrels. All wines are left in barrels until they undergo malo-lactic fermentation, then they are racked into a mix of French and American oak, new and neutral, and left for 12-18 months, topped up and stirred every couple of weeks. Prior to bottling, the barrels are combined, the wine lightly finned with egg whites, then bottled with minimal handling. After bottling and labeling, the wines are allowed to rest for a period of time before release.

All their wines are bottled 100% varietal and vineyard specific with the exception of the "Precipice" label which is a blend of 50% Merlot and Zinfandel. Oak Usage: All wines undergo oak cellaring after fermentation and before bottling in both French and American barrels, from various coopers.

Recommended Wines:

1) Cabernet Sauvignon, Estate Bottled, Rogue Valley, Old Stage Vineyard, 2003. Vivid, dark blue-red hues. Grape typical characteristics with blackcurrant, blue berry, and a touch of dark cherry integrated well with oak. The palate shows good firm tannins balanced with acidity and fruit. Long balanced finish with good storage po-

tential.
2) Cabernet Franc, Estate Bottled, Rogue Valley, Old Stage Vineyard, 2004. Excellent grape typicity. The nose is complex showing cherries, red berries, with some wonderful herbaceous characters and spicy oak. The palate is supported by fine to octagon tannins with good alcohol, acid and fruit balance. Very long finish. Good storage potential (10 to 15 years).
3) Chardonnay, Applegate Valley, Layne Vineyard, 2006. Good Chardonnay typical aromas with a touch of apples, pears, pineapple and well integrated lees and oak. The palate is balanced with good acid levels and round fruit with touches of lees and oak in the lingering finish. 5-8 years storage potential.

Owner/s: James and Susan Devitt

Winemaker/s: James Devitt was born on September 21, 1933, in Los Angeles, California. His parents were James and Rosie Devitt. He was educated in the Los Angeles city school system, attended general engineering school at UCLA from 1951 thru 1955 without graduating. Worked at

Pictures Right: Jim and Susan Devitt in the tasting room.

various electronic companies as an engineer until 1965, then started his own company manufacturing printed circuit boards for the electronics industry.

Desiring a change in lifestyle in 1971 he purchased 188 acres in Pope Valley, Napa County with the express desire to establish a winery. The Pope Valley property had a defunct winery building built in 1906 by Sam Haus, Swiss immigrants, and 17 acres of Semillon, Sauvignon Verte and Zinfandel grapes planted around 1900, also 6 acres of walnuts and 4 acres of mission olives. The plan was to plant an additional 15 acres of Zinfandel and make wine.

The first wine was made in 1972 from Zinfandel, Semillon/Sauvignon Verte and Riesling, released in 1973. Subsequent vintages were made with production increasing from 600 cases to 10,000 cases in 1985 with distribution in 33 states. In 1986 the winery was sold.

Other items of Interest: In the past 4 years the Applegate Valley has garnered its own American Viticulture Area, planted approximately 500 new acres, added 9 new wineries with at least 4 more coming next year which will bring to a total of 18 stand alone wineries with tasting rooms in this valley.

General Information:
Devitt Winery
www.devittwinery.com

Winery Address:
11412 Hwy 238
Jacksonville, OR 97530
(541) 899-7511
Open to Public

Tasting Room:
Hours: 11:00 - 5:00 7days
Tours Available:
Frequently

Varieties/Wine Styles:
Cabernet Franc, Cabernet Sauvignon, Chardonnay, Merlot, Pinot Noir, Sangiovese, Syrah, Tempranillo, Viognier and Zinfandel.

Certificates:
Certified Sustainable

Winery Features:
Tasting Room, Picnic Area, Bus/RV Parking, Wheelchair Accessible and Retail Sales.

Large Picture Right: A beautiful late fall picture from the vineyard. Inserted Picture: Devitt label.

Cathedral Ridge Winery

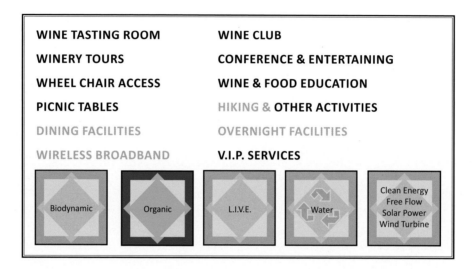

WINE TASTING ROOM	**WINE CLUB**
WINERY TOURS	**CONFERENCE & ENTERTAINING**
WHEEL CHAIR ACCESS	**WINE & FOOD EDUCATION**
PICNIC TABLES	HIKING & **OTHER ACTIVITIES**
DINING FACILITIES	OVERNIGHT FACILITIES
WIRELESS BROADBAND	**V.I.P. SERVICES**

Biodynamic — Organic — L.I.V.E. — Water — Clean Energy Free Flow Solar Power Wind Turbine

History: Founded in 1985 by Don Flerchinger, Flerchinger Vineyards became the second winery in Hood River, OR. The original winery building was opened in 1990 and some substantial additions have been made since them.

Don and his son Joe the Winemaker made fine Alsatian whites and reds until 2003 when the winery was purchased by Robb Bell.

Robb brought in Michael Sebastiani as winemaker and retained Lonnie Wright, of The Pines Vineyard and Winery, as the winery's grape specialist. This combination and a lot of hard work propelled the winery to an "Oregon Winery of the Year" from Wine Press NorthWest 2007.

Eco-orientation: Cathedral Ridge Winery is not organic certified; however, many of their purchased grapes are. The winery and its vineyards take a minimalist approach with an occasional mild chemical intervention only when required to protect the crop. Cathedral Ridge Winery only uses organic approved sprays and fertilizers, including kelp, elemental sulfur, whey, and a wide array of trace minerals. The approved chemicals are confined to occasional application of mild mildewcide.

Their winemaking philosophy believes in hands-off approach with absolute minimal levels of sulfite additions. They have a rigorous biweekly barrel checking and topping-up program, which inhibits potential problems with barrel and tank exposure.

*Large Picture Right: A picture of the entry from the estate gardens. **Inserted Picture:** Winemaker Michael Sebastiani is a fourth generation winemaker.*

A_creage & Grapes:_ The Estate Vineyard comprises 3.5 acres of Riesling and 1.5 acres of Pinot Gris. The winery also purchases only the best fruit from other regional and state growers who practice the same philosophy of sustainable organic agriculture. Cathedral Ridge Winery utilizes approximately 90-100 tons of fruit this year for a wide variety of wines and styles that best portray the Columbia Gorge and the Columbia Valley AVAs.

P_roduction_: Cathedral Ridge Winery produced approximately 7,200 cases in 2007. About 60% of the production consists of a number of red wines and the rest whites and rosés.

W_ine Types & Styles:_ "While it is cliché that Americans tend to overreach their bounds and make too many wines from varietals ill suited to their growing conditions we are the exception to the rule. In general terms, our approach is to simply get great fruit into the bottle. At Cathedral Ridge we have an amazing advantage, over most

**Pictures from Top Left (1):** The estate vineyards in the Columbia Gorge. **(2):** A view of the tasting room and lovely gardens overlooking the mountains in the background. **(3):** The entrance to the winery and cellar. **(4):** A vine in the estate property.

other wineries that purchase fruit, as the majority of the grape varieties that we use are within a 25 mile radius of the winery. Furthermore, the climate conditions are perfect for fruit development and ripening. Our climatic conditions are extreme and vary from rainforest to desert in as little as 30 miles. These conditions are traditionally favored by westerly breezes (up the Columbia River) during the growing season and cooling moisture laden mountain winds in the evening. The close adjacency of our grapes lets us pick at precisely the right time and we typically have our grapes yeasted and in the barrel, tank or bin w/ in 8 hours or less of being picked," an enthusiastic Robb, owner of Cathedral Ridge Winery, stated.

Continuing with a confident smile, Robb said, "Our style is to create early drinking wines which can be enjoyed soon after release. We demand grape typical wines that show strong varietals characteristics and wines with a beginning, a middle and an end. We believe in oak as a mellowing variable, not a tool to mask the grape and taste. Our wines have generally modest alcohol content and very low sulfites." **Oak Usage:** The 2007 vintage is 100% French Oak. Cathedral Ridge Winery believes that wines should not have a dominating oak character and this belief has led them to commit to using only the best (2nd year barrels) from

Opus One's top grade Cabernet Sauvignon. Robb continues, "In order to enhance the Cabernet Sauvignon complexities, we age the wine for 22 months in French oak and then blend in a touch of Syrah (less than 10%) to actually allow more of the Cabernet Sauvignon flavors to be exposed (at times, we can blend in another wine to release additional varietal flavors).

In the case of our Syrah, we were able to tone down some of its own highlights in order to allow its true richness to shine.

With Pinot Gris vineyards surrounding us in Hood River, Pinot Gris is becoming one of our mainstay wines. Due to its true varietal characters of pear and apple acidity, plus a traditional nuttiness quality with crisp fruit textures, Pinot Gris finds a natural home in the Hood River and Columbia Gorge region. We have found that our region is perfectly matched for growing and producing exquisite blends of Pinot Gris. We can use many of our grape growing and winemaking resources to create soft and fragrant Pinot Gris wines that continue to express its wonderful fruit and acidity. We include partial barrel fermentation, malolactic fermentation, sur lies stirring and extended barrel aging. These practices are blended with traditionally vinified Pinot Gris to enhance its delicate almond characters."

Recommended Wines:

1) Cathedral Ridge Winery, Cabernet Sauvignon, Bangsund Vineyards, 2005. Produced 173 cases. Good grape typical characteristics with hints of blackcurrant, blackberry, cherry and dark chocolate. The palate shows round soft tannins, good fruit and acid balance with integrated alcohol and oak characters. Medium to long finish. (Storage potential 10+ years).

2) Cathedral Ridge, Syrah, 2005. Bangsund, Baily, and Kortge grapes. 230 cases produced. Grape typical. Dark, deep in color. The aroma shows black and white pepper, dark berries, black berry and a touch of oak. The palate exhibits good fruit with medium octagon tannins, good acid levels with well integrated alcohol and a medium to long finish. Storage potential 10+ years).

3) Cathedral Ridge Winery, Pinot Gris, 2006. Estate (Hood River, OR) & Ziegler Vineyards (Underwood, WA) grapes. A medium, greenish-tint, light straw color. The nose has a touch of spices, lemon peel, orange blossom and pears with hints of honey. The palate is dry with firm acid levels and is in balance with the fruit and alcohol with a

Picture Right: *A bottle of Cathedral Ridge Cabernet Sauvignon 2005.*

-145-

touch of oaky lees in the aftertaste. Good finish. Storage potential (3-5 years).

Owner/s: Robb Bell.

Winemaker/s: Michael Sebastiani, a fourth generation winemaker. Michael Sebastiani was born and raised in the heart of the Sonoma Valley wine country. His first experiences in the industry started when I was 10, spending his summer vacations working in the vineyards. Michael grew up through the vineyards, from hand-labor, to tractor-work and then indoors learning winery mechanics and cellar-work.

In 1993, Michael Graduated from US Davis with a degree in Enology, in just three years, while he spent most of his time at the new family winery, Viansa. After graduation he started to work full time at the family winery. Since Viansa had its own destiny, he decided to leave the family winery in 2002 and pursue some of his ideas that wouldn't have worked with the Viansa model. He founded Generations of Sonoma Winery in 2003 and launched three new wine brands under the winery's umbrella. In addition to his venture in California he works with Robb Bell at Cathedral Ridge Winery where they are developing wines to represent the vast diversity of microclimates within the area.

Other items of Interest: The Columbia Gorge and Columbia Valley are home to Hood River and Mt Hood, which offer unique recreational opportunities for old and young alike. From golf to top rank rock climbing, from picturesque train rides to mountain biking, river excursions to jet boats up the Deschutes River.

General Information:
Cathedral Ridge Winery
www.cathedralridgewinery.com

Winery Address:
4200 Post Canyon Drive
Hood River, OR 97031 * Tel(541) 386-2882
Open to Public
Tasting Room:
Hours: 11-5PM Daily
Free tasting, no fee.
Tours Available:
Frequently
Varieties/Wine Styles:
Cabernet Sauvignon, Chardonnay, Merlot, Pinot Gris, Pinot Noir, Riesling, Syrah, Blush, Dry Riesling and Cabernet/Merlot
Winery Features:
Tasting Room, Wedding Facilities, Reception Facilities, Picnic Area, Bus/RV Parking, Wheelchair Accessible and Retail Sales, and Weddings.

Large Picture Right: *A view of Cathedral Ridge Winery and gardens.*

Erin Glenn Winery

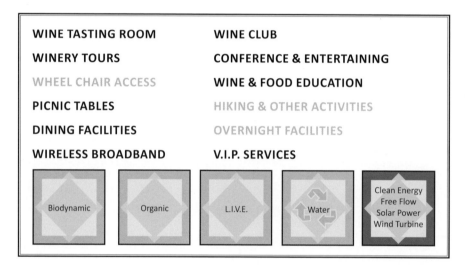

WINE TASTING ROOM	**WINE CLUB**
WINERY TOURS	**CONFERENCE & ENTERTAINING**
WHEEL CHAIR ACCESS	**WINE & FOOD EDUCATION**
PICNIC TABLES	HIKING & OTHER ACTIVITIES
DINING FACILITIES	OVERNIGHT FACILITIES
WIRELESS BROADBAND	**V.I.P. SERVICES**

Biodynamic · Organic · L.I.V.E. · Water · Clean Energy Free Flow Solar Power Wind Turbine

H*istory:* Erin Glenn, the winery, came into being in 2001. Over a bottle of local Zinfandel and roast venison, Tim and Erin Schechtel conceived their intent to become wine producers in an as yet undiscovered wine region. Joining a small group of growers, winemakers and entrepreneurs, they established their Estate vineyards on their home site between Cherry Heights and Chenowith Table at The Dalles, Oregon. At an elevation of 840 feet the vineyard site was below the level of the ice age floods and certainly inundated. However, being located on a side canyon of The Columbia Gorge, not all soils were lost. The site has been farmed over the last 100 years and most recently supported a dry land plum farm.

The Schechtel family wanted to honor their Irish heritage and hatched the name Erin Glenn – from the Celtic/Gaelic language (Erin meaning Ireland and Glenn meaning hidden valley). It has been written that the Celts actually invented the wine barrel during the Iron Age after much frustration with the fragile clay amphorae in which the Greeks and Romans stored their wine.

Finding their beginnings in The Columbia Gorge, home to Native American peoples for more than 10,000 years, was simply serendipity. Like their Celtic ancestors, the family at Erin Glenn wishes to instill in every vintage the love of the life and the land that supports us all by weaving a sense of place into every glass. Slainte!

Large Photo: Barrels ageing in the cellar. The wine in the two glass jugs on the right are used for topping up the barrels.

Eco-orientation: While Erin Glenn's estate vineyards are managed by low input sustainable standards, they are not yet certified. A lot of their fruit is also purchased from organic growers.

Water conservation is achieved with modern drip systems, cover crops and mulching. A state of the art soil moisture content system allows precise application of water to the vines.

Pest management is achieved by maintaining beneficial insects and vine health is fostered through foliar applications. Compared to cooler growing areas, the arid and windy climate (average rain fall 10") makes the vineyard less susceptible to many pests and mildew problems.

In addition to efforts at low input, low impact viticulture, Erin Glenn's single most eco-friendly practice is recycling. Erin Glenn's vineyard site has been reclaimed from pine forests which seeded in over an old plum orchard. A rain water reclama-

Pictures from Top Left (1): The brick walls and the candelabra add to the atmosphere as you enter the bacement cellar help to (2): A relaxing wine tasting bar. Spacious, comfortable setting with vaulted ceilings. (3): The staircase leading down into the magnificent wine cellar.

tion system has been installed that will supply additional water for irrigation and fire protection. The winery facility is a restored Civil War Era building, which has been retrofitted with a night-air cooling system to help maintain temperatures by storing cold in ancient masonry.

Recycled lumber, timber and barrels have been fashioned into tasting room counters, flooring, trim work and furniture. The winery observation platform is covered with decking manufactured with reclaimed plastics and ornamental iron work fashioned from recycled steel plates.

Acreage & Grapes: Estate vineyards are comprised of 3.5 acres of Syrah and 1.5 acres of Gewürztraminer. Contract vineyards for additional grapes come from nearby farms and range in size from 1 to 5 acres.

Production: 4,000 cases.

Wine Types & Styles: Wine varieties include Syrah, Cabernet Sauvignon, Merlot, Pinot Noir, Malbec, Tempranillo, Barbera, Dolcetto, Chardonnay, Gewürztraminer, Viognier, Rosé of Barbera, Sauvignon Blanc and Proprietary Blends.

Oak Usage: French, American, Hungarian.

Recommended Wines:

1) Erin Glenn Winery, Velvet Ass Rosé, Rosé of Barbera, 2006. Good Barbera characteristics. The nose is aromatic and fruity displaying red berry, cherry, raspberry and earthy tones. The palate is well balanced with smooth tannins, good acidity and fruit with a slight touch of residual sugar. The Alcohol is well integrated. Long fruity finish. Storage Potential (3-5 years).

2) Erin Glenn Winery, Chateau LeBeau Viognier, 2006. Grape Typical. Excellent and complex nose with bails of peaches and apricots and hints of other tropical fruits. The palate shows good firm acidity and clean fruit. It is well integrated and has a long finish. Storage Potential (3-5 years).

3) Erin Glenn Winery, Threemile, 2005. Blend of Cabernet Sauvignon, Merlot and Cabernet Franc. The nose is still rather closed but it does exhibit a complex wine with fruit dark berry characters of blueberries, blackberries, and plums. The palate shows octagon tannins with good acidity, fruit and oak. The alcohol is well integrated. Long finish. Storage potential: 6-10 years.

Owner/s: Tim & Erin Schechtel

Winemaker/s: Tim Schechtel is also the winemaker. With roots in German, Italian, French and Irish family traditions, Tim learned the basics of winemaking as well as curing and preserving fruits, meats and fish. Wine- and beermaking was just part of regular seasonal activities.

During the 1980s Tim planted some of the first test blocks of Pinot Noir in the Hood River Valley and partnered with a local grower who was committed to making his mark on local viticulture.

While largely self-taught, Tim has attended many industry programs and classes and does not hesitate to experiment. His single and simplest philosophy regarding wine business is "to restore a sense of place to wine. It's all about where you're from, not your scores."

Pictures Right: Erin Glenn Winery, Velvet Ass Rosé, Rosé of Barbera, 2006. Good Barbera characteristics.

O_ther items of Interest:_ Erin Glenn's cellar is a beautiful architectural relic of an age gone by. Encompassing more than 8000 square feet, the winery building was originally constructed to be the United States Mint at The Dalles city, 1864. President Abraham Lincoln authorized construction during the American Civil War.

The massive stone columns and brick arches are crafted in the style of classic roman masonry and provide excellent thermal mass for maintaining cellar temperatures and solitude for the maturing wines while providing an old world ambience.

G_eneral Information:_
Erin Glenn Vineyards
www.eringlenn.com

Winery Address:
710 East 2nd Street
The Dalles, OR 97058
(541) 296-4707

Open to Public

Tasting Room:
Hours: Thursdays & Sundays noon-5; Fridays & Saturdays Noon-9

Tours Available:
Frequently

Varieties/Wine Styles:
Cabernet Sauvignon, Dolcetto, Gewürztraminer, Late Harvest/Dessert/Ice Wine, Sauvignon Blanc, Syrah, Tempranillo, Viognier and Bordeaux Blends.

Winery Features:
Tasting Room, Reception Facilities, Picnic Area, Bus/RV Parking, Wheelchair Accessible and Retail Sales.

Large Picture Right: *Wine cellar and barrel room at Erin Glenn's The Mint. Dinners and other events are also held in the atmosfilled cellar. Tours are available.* **Inserted Picture:** *Some of Erin Glenn's young vines.*

Next Page: *A harvest picture at Willamette Valley Vineyards.*

Some Grape Varieties in Oregon

This section highlights the most common varieties in Oregon. There are a total of 72 varieties within the state; however, I will only address 18 of these as the remaining varieties are only produced in very small volumes. First of all, I begin with the two most important grapes: Pinot Noir and Pinot Gris, thereafter they are presented in alphabetical order.

The presentation of each grape variety will include some information about the grape's background, its origin, the various styles and whether or not it is used in a blend as well as the grape's phenology and wine-tasting characteristics for Oregon red and white wines. A character summary is also provided along with a tactile sensory ratio guide that helps you identify the variety, decide on storage potential, grape typicity and how to match it with food or cheese.

Each of the grapes discussed have their own unique characteristics, which I call 'trademark characters or grape typicity.' These grape typical characteristics are an integral part of wine quality and should be present, in some form, in most varietals. However, adverse climate conditions and/or individual winemaking styles can and will affect typicity.

The aim is to show the benefits of each variety. This understanding will increase your appreciation for the grape and serve as a tool to guide you in combining wine and food appropriately and to different social environments.

Oregon Grapes

Pinot Noir -	Red
Pinot Gris -	White
Barbera -	Red
Cabernet Franc -	Red
Cabernet Sauvignon -	Red
Chardonnay -	White
Gewürztraminer -	White
Grenache -	Red
Merlot -	Red
Muscat à Petits Grains -	White
Müller-Thurgau -	White
Pinot Blanc -	White
Riesling -	White
Sauvignon Blanc -	White
Semillon -	White
Syrah/Shiraz -	Red
Tempranillo -	Red
Viognier -	White

Pinot Noir

General characteristics:

Assumed to be one of the oldest grape varieties, Pinot Noir is one of the most challenging grapes to grow. It can produce up to 30 hectoliters per hectare and responds well to being planted in cool climate conditions on well-drained and calcareous soils.

In Oregon the most commonly planted clones are the Pommard, Wadensvil, and Dijon 113, 114, 115, 114 and 777. However, there are hundreds of Pinot Noir clones that exist in the world today. Even Pinot Blanc, Pinot Gris and Gamay are clones. I would not be surprised if both Negro Amaro (Apulia, Italy) and Tempranillo (Spain) are old clones too.

Synonyms:

Pineau, Franc Pineau, Savagnin Noir, Morillon, (France); Spätburgunder, Blauburgunder, Klevener (Germany); Pinot Nero, Pignola (Italy); Nagyburgundi (Hungary).

Areas:

The grape is at its best in Burgundy, Oregon and Alsace but has even established itself in many other wine countries. Good wines are now being produced in Washington State, northern California and South Africa, Australia, New Zealand, Austria and Germany, not to forget Chile.

Wine Styles and Blends:

This grape variety is found both as a single estate, varietal and in blends. In the Willamette Valley great care is taken to ferment in small lots so as not to mix the terroir and style of the various lots within an estate.

In Champagne, France, it is grown to a greater extent than in the whole of Burgundy as it is one of the varieties in Champagne, where it is blended with Pinot Meunier and Chardonnay.

Grape Physiology:

Vigour: Moderate.

Phenology:

Ripens in early season, so it is a good grape for cold weather climates, where summers are relatively short. At full maturity the average sugar content is from 23º to 24º Brix / Balling (total, dissolved compounds in grape juice and sugar concentration) and total titratable acid of 6 to 7 g/l.

Berries:

Small to medium in size with a thin skin. The berry is an off-round shape with a scarlet/violet/ blue color.

Diseases:

Susceptible to downy mildew and weather changes. Low resistance because of its thin skin.

Sensory Characteristics:
Appearance:

In young wines, Pinot Noir has a lighter tone with an extended gradient. In 89/90-point wines it has a light to medium purple/ruby-red hue in young wines and starts to change color already after the 2nd-3rd year. Good mature wines develop an orange brick-colored rim in about their 6th-8th year. However, in Oregon I have seen this change in as many as 12 years.

The Nose:

Pinot Noir has a wonderfully warm, spicy, red berry, strawberry, dark cherry, raspberry and floral character when young. Very good wines display, along with red berries, violets, a nuance of chocolate, vegetables and spices as they age.

Oak characters would be evident in young oak-matured wines. Nevertheless, this will diminish with time and should not be a dominating factor. The signature characteristic trait for Oregon Pinot Noir from the Willamette Valley are still the floral, red and dark cherries, strawberries and some spices.

Other old world styles can show more oxidation or animalistic characteristics. Other modern world styles show more darker fruit, are more viscous and have higher alcohol level.

The Palate:

In Oregon and northern Burgundy Pinot Noir wines show more finesse and a balanced length. They can have more tannins, although these tannins are finer smother in nature. Sunnier climates usually show coarser tannins "Octagon instead of round" in feel. This is due to the addition of tannin, stems, or heavy oak.

Pinot Noir can produce very delicate and elegant wines with excellent length. Alcohol levels from 12.5% to 15%.

Excellent Food Combinations:

Pinot Noir can be served well with light meats, various bird dishes (goose, duck and chicken) and textured fish dishes like salmon. It is excellent with foie gras, cheese and pâté too.

Although other wine professionals suggest wild deer and darker meats with a Pinot Noir, I tend not to prefer these, as I feel that other wine styles suit them better and that the marked acidity levels of Pinot Noir highlight more delicate dishes very well.

Typical Aroma	
	Red Berries
	Strawberry
	Cherry
	Raspberry
	Floral
	Vetetable
oak -Chocalate	
	Violets
oak -Smoked Meat	
Tannin	5
Acidity	7.5
Sweetness	0
Bitterness	0
Weight	7 to 8
Alcohol	12.5-15%

Pinot Gris

General Characteristics:
Pinot Gris, like Pinot Blanc, is a mutation of the Pinot Noir grape. Gris is French for 'gray'. The color of the grape can vary substantially, producing wines that range from white to slightly pink.

In Oregon the most commonly planted clones are the Dijon 146 and 152. However, there are many other clones that exist in the world today.

Synonyms:
Pinot Beurot, Pinot Burot, Tokay d'Alsace, Malvoisie, Gris Cordelier, Fauvet, Auvernat Gris, Petit Gris, Ruländer, Grauer Burgunder, Graulkevner, Grauer Riesling, Tokayer, Pinot Grigio, Tokayer, Crvena Klevanjka, Rulanda.

Areas:
Originally from Burgundy, it is grown at its best in Oregon and Alsace as well as in Austria, Germany, Hungary, Romania, Washington State and California, Australia, New Zealand, Chile, Argentina, Austria, the Czech Republic and Slovakia.

Wine Styles and Blends:
The wineries in Oregon produce some of the world's most aromatic Pinot Gris. However, judgement on whether the Willamette Valley or Alsace produce the highest quality is still out. Naturally, the styles are slightly different.

In Oregon their aromatics are somewhat subdued in comparison to their archrival in Alsace. Here they are almost perfect due to their rich, dry, delicately perfumed styles offering excellent characteristics from appearance to taste and length.

Grape Physiology:
Vigour: Moderate vigour. Yields about 45 hl/ha. It thrives in chalky soils that run deep and have a high mineral content.

Phenology:
Ripens in early season. At full maturity the average sugar content is from 20º to 24º Brix/Balling and total acid of 6 to 7 g/l.

Berries:
Medium in size and oval. They have a yellowish-red-black hue and are used for white winemaking. Pinot Gris has a medium skin thickness.

Diseases:
Resistant to many insects, pests and diseases.

Sensory Characteristics:
Appearance:
Varies from pale yellow to slightly pink in color. It has a medium gradient. Initial changes in the hue can be detected in the 4th year proceeding to light orange-amber by the 5th to 6th year. When maturated in oak it has a viscous appearance and a slightly darker and more yellow-straw hue.

The Nose:
Trademark characters for an Alsace Pinot Gris are marked by apricot, honey, spicy, nutty-mushroom and smoky-like characters.

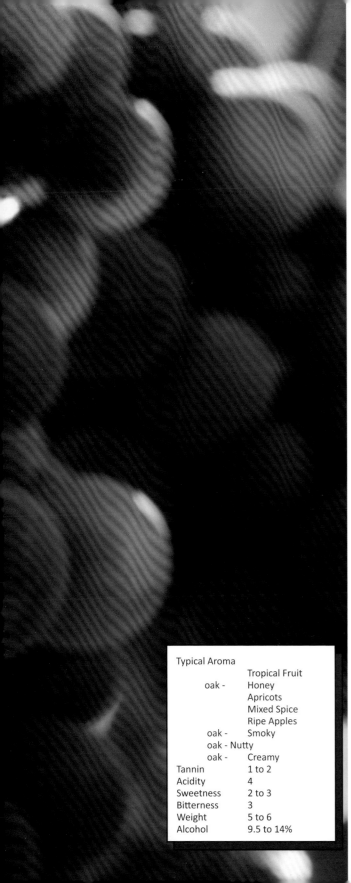

Typical Aroma

		Tropical Fruit
oak -		Honey
		Apricots
		Mixed Spice
		Ripe Apples
oak -		Smoky
oak - Nutty		
oak -		Creamy
Tannin		1 to 2
Acidity		4
Sweetness		2 to 3
Bitterness		3
Weight		5 to 6
Alcohol		9.5 to 14%

In Oregon, most Pinot Gris show more citrus characters such as grapefruit, green apples, and pears. In addition, you might be able to find peaches with some tropical fruit and a touch of spices in the aroma. Oregon's unfiltered wines offer the most competition as they show a lot more characters as they are retained by racking.

Unoaked wines have more citrus and are slightly sharper but display good fruit characters of apricots and dried fruits. Oaked wines have in addition cream, butter and vanilla.

The Palate:
Almost 100% have gone through malolactic fermentation and are softer, creamier that some found in Europe where the tart characters are sometimes desired.

Trademark taste characteristics are everything from a crisp, light and dry wine in northern Italy (Pinot Grigio), to the rich, rustic, viscous, fat, honeyed versions from France's Alsace region, but all Pinot Gris have a slight bitterness in the aftertaste.

Dry no-oak sensory ratios:
Acidity **4**, Fullness **5.5,**
Sweetness **2**, Bitterness **3,**
Abv. 9.5-13.5%

Dry oak aged sensory ratios:
Acidity **4**, Fullness **6**, Sweetness **3,**
Bitterness **3,** Abv. 12.5-14.5%

Excellent Food Combinations:
Pinot Gris is a perfect match to goose liver, pâté, poultry and light wild dishes. Also complements artisan cheeses with some age (±18 months of storage). Salads of various sorts can also benefit from a good Pinot Gris.

Barbera

General Characteristics:

Barbera is the most widely planted grape variety in the world. Regarded as a valued grape in both Italy and California, it thrives in warm climates but also, and more importantly, produces high acidic wines with low tannin content. Being usually a good complement to food, it is considered a good average table wine.

Synonyms:

Barbera Sards, Perricone and Pignatello on Sardinia.

Areas:

Found in Walla Walla and southern Oregon; however, Barbera has its roots in northern Italy, in Barbera d'Alba, Barbera d'Asti and Barbera del Monferrato. It is also found in Argentina, South Africa, California's San Joaquin Valley, where it is responsible for about 13% of the state's total grape production. Barbera is grown throughout southern Italy as well and is the most planted grape variety, closely followed by Sangiovese.

Wine Styles and Blends:

Although used as a single varietal, it is today very often found in blends, in particular in warmer climates, where the grape's high acidity helps to lift other heavier varieties that tend to suffer from poor acidity if picked too late.

Grape Physiology:

Vigour: Very vigorous. It produces high yields of about 70 hl/ha. Grows well on sandy, fine and poor soils.

Phenology:

Ripens in late-season, so it is a good grape for warm weather climates were summers are relatively hot. At full maturity the average sugar content is from 22º to 23.5º Brix / Balling (total dissolved compounds in grape juice and sugar concentration) and total titratable acid of 6 to 7.5 g/l.

Berries:

Medium in size and a thin skin. The berry has an off-round shape with a bluish / violet / pink-red color.

Diseases:

Susceptible to leafroll, rot and Pierce's disease.

Sensory Characteristics:

Appearance:

In young wines, Barbera has a deep purple hue with some pink towards the rim-proper. In warmer climates, such as in southern Italy and central California, it has a tighter gradient but changes hue more rapidly. In 85-point wines it has a light to medium purple/ruby-red hue when young and starts to change color after the 2nd to 3rd year. Good, mature wines develop an orange brick-colored rim already around their 5th to 6th year.

The Nose:

Barbera has a fruity acid character of cherry, strawberry and even some blackcurrant and raspberry when young. Can be aged in oak.

The Palate:

High acid content and usually very little but soft 'fine tannins', balanced as per the ratio chart (3/10 for tannin and 8/10 for acid). Alcohol levels range from 12,5% to 15%. A volatile aroma of plums is usually evident in the aftertaste.

Excellent Food Combinations:

Barbera combines perfectly with fatty or creamy foods. It can also be served with light meat dishes and even a variety of shell-fish, fish and chicken, pâté and quiche plates.

Typical Characteristics	
Red Berry	
	Cherry
	Strawberry
	Blackcurrant
	Raspberry
	Acidic charc.
	Plums
Tannin	3
Acidity	8
Sweetness	0
Bitterness	
Weight	4
Alcohol	12.5-15%

Cabernet Franc

General Characteristics:
There are not too many wines bottled using 100% Cabernet Franc, the most famous being Château Haut-Brion and Château Cheval Blanc in St. Emilion, which is one of the five first growths from Bordeaux.

Synonyms:
Breton, Carmenet, Bouchet, Gross-Bouchet, Grosse-Vidure, Bouchy, Noir-Dur, Méssange Rouge, Trouchet Noir, Bordo and Cabernet Frank.

Areas:
Cabernet Franc is mostly found in Southern Oregon but a few plantings have emerged in the Willamette Valley. Also found in Washington State and California; neverhtless, it is the third most popular grape variety in the Bordeaux region but is also grown in the Loire Valley in France.

Other countries like South Africa, Australia, New Zealand, Chile, Argentina and in some isolated areas of Spain and Italy also have Cabernet Franc.

Wine Styles and Blends:
It comprises about 6-8% of the Bordeaux blend and its major purpose is aromatics and softness. It is mainly a blended variety of Cabernet Sauvignon, Merlot and Petit Verdot.

Grape Physiology:
Vigour: Very productive with good yields exceeding that of its cousin Cabernet Sauvignon.

Phenology:
Ripens in early late-season and prior to Cabernet Sauvignon. At full maturity the average sugar content is from 23º to 24.5º Brix and total titratable acid of 5.5 to 7 g/l.

Berries:
Larger than Cabernet Sauvignon in size, with a thick skin and good tannin (pigments). The berries are round in shape with a blue-black color. They have cylindrical and conical cluster bunches.

Diseases: Susceptible to powdery mildew.

Sensory Characteristics:
Appearance:
A young wine has a deep blue to almost black color but tends to change color early. In very good wines this change starts at about its 5th year and before Cabernet Sauvignon. Excellent first class wines and blends will only start to change color after the 6th to 7th years but will develop an orange brick-colored rim in about their 8th to 10th year.

The Nose:
Cabernet Franc is full of blackberries, mint, green olives, nutmeg, ripe plums and violets. You may even find some strawberry-like characteristics. Trademark characters are violets, mint and ripe plums.

The Palate:
The acidity and balance as per ratio chart (5.2/10 for tannin and 6/10 for acid). Cabernet Franc can produce wines with a complex and elegant balance and competes with the best wines. It has good fruit, and more acidity than tannin under normal fermentation conditions. The alcohol levels range from 12.5% to 14.5%.

Excellent Food Combinations:
From colder climates like Oregon and the Loire Valley, it is best suited to lighter meat dishes, quiches, smoked or fried fish dishes and even salads. A full-bodied Cabernet Franc is good with beef, lamb or even a cheese variety plate.

Typical Characteristics	
	Blackberries
	Cherries
	Mint
	Green Olives
	Nutmeg
	Ripe Plums
	Violets
	Strawberry
Tannin	5.2
Acidity	6.5
Sweetness	0
Bitterness	0
Weight	5
Alcohol	12.5-14.5%

Cabernet Sauvignon

General Characteristics:
Originally from Bordeaux and the most popular red grape in the world, Cabernet Sauvignon, the 'King' of grapes, is found in vineyards and stores throughout the world.

Synonyms:
Petit-Cabernet, Vidure, Petite-Vidure, Bouchet, Bouche, Petit-Bouchet, Sauvignon Rouge.

Areas:
Mainly in south & east Oregon and the Columbia River basin. Cabernet Sauvignon can be found in most wine-growing regions of the world.

Wine Styles and Blends:
As a single varietal wine or in a blend. The Classic Bordeaux blend includes Cabernet Franc, Merlot, Petit Verdot and even Malbec. Other varieties blended with Cabernet Sauvignon are Sangiovese, Nebbiolo, Shiraz, Tempranillo, Tinto Barocca, Zinfandel, Mourvèdre and even Pinot Noir.

Grape Physiology:
Vigour:
Excellent vigour, but if the soil is too fertile uneven berry growth can be found.

Phenology:
Ripens in late season, so it can be prone to weather fluctuations. At full maturity the average sugar content is from 23.5º to 28º Brix / Balling (total dissolved compounds in grape juice and sugar concentration) and a total titratable acid of 6 to 7 g/l.

Berries:
Small, round and very dark. The skin is tough and thick, producing lots of phenols and deeply colored wines. The pips are rather large.

Diseases:
Susceptible to downy and powdery mildew. Because of its thick skin it has a strong resistance to botrytis infection. This is not to say that it cannot be infected with botrytis.

Sensory Characteristics:
Appearance:
Young wines display a dark, deep tone with a tight gradient from the bowl to rim. Its bluish-purple-red hue starts to change around the 3rd -4th year. The wines develop an orange brick-colored rim in about their 6th to 8th year. Classic wines begin to change color only around the 8th year and obtain a brick-red hue at about their 12th to 15th year.

The Nose:
Young wines display ripe blackcurrants and other dark berries, cedar wood, pencil shavings. As the wine matures, so do the aromas. Oak-maturing adds cigar box, vanilla and tobacco. New world styles often present a mint/eucalyptus nose as well.

The Palate:
The taste has a substantial backbone of tannin and acid in young wines but is usually balanced as per the ratio chart. The variety can produce complex wines with a lingering length. When young, they are mouth-puckering, but with enough fruit to allow the tannins to mellow in time. A lesser wine can be a little stalky. Alcohol levels range from 12.5% to 16%.

Excellent Food Combinations:
Various meat dishes with reduced sauces. Young fruit-driven wines should be served with heavier meat dishes, while mature wines go better with gourmet cooking, beef or wild dishes.

Typical Characteristics:

	Blackcurrant	
	Blue Berries	
	Dark Berries	
	Mint	
oak - Cedar wood		
oak - Tobacco		
oak -	Coffee	
Tannin	5 to 8	
Acidity	5 to 8	
Sweetness	0	
Bitterness	0 to 2	
Weight	4 to 9	
Alcohol	12.5-16%	

Chardonnay

General Characteristics:
If the 'King' of red grapes in Oregon is Pinot Noir then the 'King' of white grapes is without a doubt Pinot Gris.

Synonyms:
Pinot Chardonnay, Chardennet, Chaudenay, Pinot Blanc à Cramant, Epinette, Arnaison, Rousseau, Rousssot, Mâconnais, Petite Sainte-Marie, Melon d'Arbois, Petit Chatey, Aubaine, Gelber Weissburgunder, Weisser Clevner.

Areas:
Chardonnay, like Cabernet is found in most wine-growing regions in the world. In Oregon, it is found in all the regions.In france, it is Burgundy's major white grape. There are literally hundreds of other areas that produce very good Chardonnays.

Wine Styles and Blends:
Chardonnay is almost always a single blend, unless you consider Champagne, where it is blended with Pinot Meunier and Pinot Noir. It makes a range of wines from sweet to bone-dry with and without oak.

Grape Physiology:
Vigour: Moderate. Chardonnay yields about 55 hl/ha. Chardonnay is very versatile and+ grows on many soil types but not wet and too fertile. It thrives on calcareous soils and in both warm and cold climates.

Phenology:
Ripens in early mid-season. At full maturity its average sugar content is 19º–26º Brix / Balling (total dissolved compounds in grape juice and sugar concentration) and TA of 5 to 7 g/l.

Berries:
Small, round pale green/yellow berries; thin, tough and transparent skins.

Diseases: Susceptible to powdery mildew and botrytis.

Sensory Characteristics:
Appearance:
Good, young and oaked 88-point Chardonnays should display an oily golden-yellow, greenish tint hue, with a deeper tone and a semi-tight gradient. Good, mature wines develop an amber-orange hue after about their 8th to 10th year. Unoaked wines are usually not as viscous.

The Nose:
Planted worldwide and adapting to various climate conditions and vinification techniques, it is quite difficult to pinpoint. Unoaked it gives sharper acidity, spicy, citrus nose with underlying butter from the oak. Oaked (in warm climates), Chardonnay displays a richer, exotic fruity nose with pineapples, mangoes, leeches and a marked buttery nutty character.

The Palate: When young, it is easy to drink as it has an instant appeal of fruit with a marked steely acidity, if Chablis or Washington State. In warmer climates, Chardonnay will be full, ripe and rounder in character, but always having a viscous flavor of buttery Chardonnay. The flavor can sometimes be lost as the high alcohol overpowers the wine's fruitiness. Oaked; rich with creamy vanilla, oak and spice characters.

Sweet Botrytis (Austria)
Acidity **7.5**, Fullness **8**, Sweetness **8**. Abv. 12.8%

Excellent Food Combinations:
Chardonnay is great with fish, spicy foods, chicken, pork chops, lamb and a good barbeque.

Typical Characteristics

	Dried Fruit
oak -	Spice
	Apples
	Pineapples
	Mangoes
	Leeches
oak -	Butter
oak -	Nutty
Tannin	1 to 2
Acidity	6
Sweetness	1 to 9
Bitterness	0
Weight	5.5 to 9
Alcohol	12.5 to 15.5%

Gewürztraminer

General Characteristics:
Gewürztraminer or Traminer is a variety originally from Germany where 'Gewürz' means spice.

Synonyms: Traminer, Rotclevner, Savagnin Rosé, Gris Rouge, Clevner, Tramini, Heida and others.

Areas:
Originally from the Pfalz region in Germany, the Gewürztraminer was introduced into Alsace after 1871 and is now found in South Africa, Australia, New Zealand, Austria, California, Hungary, The Czech Republic, Romania, Italy and Switzerland. Now growing well in most regions of Oregon too. The wineries in Alsace produce the quality that all Gewürztraminers should be judged against.

Wine Styles and Blends:
Very aromatic wines, often described as spicy, but their complex bouquet can range from grapey-muskiness to a pungency like pepper. Although at its best in Alsace, the Austrians also make excellent sweet botrytis, which can last for 50 years or more. In Alsace they are rich and complex, dry, sweet and aromatic. Usually only found as a single variety.

Grape Physiology:
Vigour: Moderate vigour. Yields about 50 hl/ha. It thrives on deep loam, clay type soils with a good mineral content.

Phenology:
Ripens in mid-season. At maturity the average sugar is 20º-26º Brix/Balling and TA of 5-7.5 g/l.

Berries:
Medium in size and oval. They have a pinkish-red-copper hue and are used for white winemaking. Gewürztraminer has a medium skin thickness.

Diseases: Susceptible to noble rot (Botrytis cinerea).

Sensory Characteristics:
Appearance:
Can range from a light copper to a deep yellow hue and very viscous. It has a medium to tight gradient. Initial changes in the hue are from the 3rd year proceeding to a darker copper -orange-amber hue by the 5th to 6th year. When matured in oak it appears to be even more viscous and has a slightly darker gradient.

The Nose:
Weighty wines with exotic flavors of leeches, roses, orange blossom, mixed spice and perfume, a hit of marmalade-toffee, apricot, honey and smoky characters. Oaked wines display the same characteristics but with cream and vanilla.

The Palate:
Both dry and sweet wines. High alcohol, full-bodied palate, sweet with spices. Low acidity. Dry wines are honeyed and powerful. Impressive in concentration, but sometimes too heavy; potent wines lacking in acidity, sluggish and clinging on the palate, rather sipped than drunk.

Dry with oak sensory ratios: Acidity **5.5**, Fullness **6**, Sweetness **1**, Bitterness **3**, Abv. 12.5-14%

Sweet with oak aged sensory ratios:Acidity **5.8**, Fullness **6.8**, Sweetness **7**, Bitterness **3**, Abv. 12.5-14.5%

Excellent Food Combinations:
Perfect match for smoked salmon, grilled fish, spicy foods and even curry. A Munster or Epoisses cheese or some smoked meats is just wonderful with Gewürztraminer.

Typical Characteristics	
	Honey
	Exotic Fruit
	Mixed Spice
	Leeches
	Roses
	Orange Blossom
	Orange Peel
	Perfume
oak -	Marmalade-toffee
Tannin	1
Acidity	5 to 6
Sweetness	1 to 7
Bitterness	3
Weight	6 to 7
Alcohol	12.5 to 14.5%

Grenache

General Characteristics:
Grenache, the work horse of blends in Spain and the Rhône Valley, is one of the most widely planted grapes in the world and responsible for a large proportion of production. Both red and white varieties exist. The white is called Grenache Blanc and the red Grenache Noir or simply Grenache.

Synonyms:
'Garnacho' exists as a name primarily in Navarra, but 'Garnacha' is normally used in the rest of Spain. Other synonyms: Lladoner, Tinto, Tinto Aragones, Granaccia, Carignan Rosso, Rousillon Tinto, Grenacha, Alicante, Carignane Rousse.

Areas:
Grenache is found in the southern and north eastern appellations of Oregon. It is also found in most growing regions from Chile, Argentina, South Africa, Australia, US, Algeria, Spain, France, Italy to Hungary.

Wine Styles and Blends:
Usually blended but also found as a single variety. In Rhône it can represent as much as 60% of a blend and in Rioja and Navarra up to 80%. Usually blended with Tempranillo, Syrah, Cabernet Sauvignon, Nebbiolo and others.

Grape Physiology:
Vigour: Very productive. Grenache grows well in warm climatic conditions and various soil types. The long growing season produces high sugar levels with low acid and tannin.

Phenology:
Ripens in late season but buds early. At full maturity the average sugar content is 24º–27º Brix / Balling (total dissolved compounds in grape juice and sugar concentration) and total titratable acid of 4.5 to 6 g/l.

Berries:
Small in size, with a medium to thick skin with lower anthocyan (pigments) levels resulting in poorer hues. The berry has an off-round, oval shape grape with a blackish color.

Diseases:
Susceptible to downy mildew, botrytis, moths, insects and birds because of the overly fruity grape with high sugar levels, low acid and tannin.

Sensory Characteristics:
Appearance:
The wines start to change color after the 3rd year. In blends with Syrah from Rhône with 89/90 points the wines are almost black, but a rim color of blue-purple-red can be found. The wines start to change color after the 5th year in southern Rhône. Good mature wines develop an orange brick-colored rim in about their 8th to 10th year.

The Nose:
Grenache is responsible for the fruitiness and 'flesh' in the wine. It has lots of ripe dark berries with lavender, rosemary, red berries, plums and rosemary.

The Palate:
The acidity and balance as per the ratio chart (3.3/10 for tannin and 5/10 for acid). Rich wines often with some of the highest alcohol levels possible, with normal yeast and under normal fermentation conditions. Alcohol levels range from 12.5% to as high as 16%.

Excellent Food Combinations:
Everything from salads to meat dishes as it depends on the style, blend and the area. Grenache can be found as a rosé, white or red.

Typical Characteristics	
	Fruity
	Dark Berries
	Light Berries
	Floral
	Lavender
	Rosemary
	Plums
	Spice
Tannin	3.3
Acidity	5
Sweetness	0
Bitterness	0
Weight	5
Alcohol	12.5-16%

Merlot

General Characteristics:
If Cabernet Sauvignon is the 'King' of grapes, Merlot must be the 'Queen'. Most Bordeaux Châteaux feel that a quality harvest is optimized at around 35-39 hl/ha.

Synonyms:
Crabutet, Bigney, Vitraille, Merlau, Sémillon Rouge and Médoc Noir.

Areas:
Mainly found in south Oregon and the Walla Walla area. Originally from Bordeaux the grape is grown around the world and in almost all wine-producing regions. It is the most planted variety in the Bordeaux region and the third largest variety in France. Château Pétrus in Pomerol can demand the highest prices in the world for a Merlot-wine.

Wine Styles and Blends:
The Classic Bordeaux blend includes Merlot with Cabernet Sauvignon, Cabernet Franc, Petit Verdot and even Malbec. Other varieties known to be blended with Merlot are Grenache, Sangiovese, Shiraz and Tempranillo.

Grape Physiology:
Vigour: Medium to good but Merlot is sensitive to both dry weather and rain. Moderate to high yields.

Phenology:
Ripens in mid-season so can be prone to weather fluctuations. At full maturity the sugar is from 23º to 24.5º Brix / Balling and total titratable acid of 6 to 7 g/l.

Berries:
Medium size, round, blackish color and thin skinned.

Diseases:
Susceptible to botrytis and downy mildew. Low resistance to botrytis infection if planted in fertile soils and if temperature and humidity conditions are less advantageous.

Sensory Characteristics:
Appearance:
In young 89/90-point wines it has a dark bluish-purple-red hue with a tight gradient from bowl to rim and starts to change color gradually around the 3rd to 4th year. Good mature wines develop an orange brick-colored rim in about their 8th to 10th year. Classic wines only begin to change color around the 8th year and get a brick-red hue at about their 12th to 15th year.

The Nose:
Fruitcake and more fruitcake is typical for Merlot. It has a smooth, heavy nose of mixed spices with plums, currants and raisins. With some ageing you'll find vegetables, barnyard, mushrooms and hay tones. Oak-maturing adds cigar box, vanilla, chocolate and tobacco. Plums still remain a major component. New world styles have a mint/eucalyptus nose as well.

The Palate:
In Bordeaux wines, the taste has a substantial backbone of tannin when young and high acid, usually balanced as per the ratio chart above (5/10 for tannin and 6.5/10 for acid). Merlot has softer, sweeter, warmer characters on the palate.

Excellent Food Combinations:
Goes well with dark meat but also with duck, goose and turkey. Young fruit-driven wines should be served with meat dishes, while mature wines go better with gourmet cooking, heavier meats or wild dishes.

Typical Characteristics	
	Dark Berries
	Plums
	Heavy Fruit
	Mixed Spices
oak -	Tobacco
oak -	Cedar
	Raspberry
	Cherry
	Currants
Tannin	5
Acidity	6.5
Sweetness	0
Bitterness	Can be burnt
Weight	7 to 9
Alcohol	11-15%

Muscat à Petits Grains

General Characteristics:

Muscat is a group (commonly known as a family), used to describe many varieties. The five best known are Muscat Blanc à Petits Grains (top quality sweet wines), Muscat d'Alexandrie (table grapes and wines), Muscat Ottonel (usually dry whites), Muscat Hamburg (mainly used as table grapes) and Orange Muscat (sweet wines).

Synonyms:

Muscat Blanc, Frontignac, Moscato, Moscato Bianco, Moscato d'Asti, Muscat Canelli, Muscat Frontignac, White Muscat, White Frontignac, Brown Muscat and many other synonyms. Muscat d'Alexandrie is called Hanepoot in South Africa.

Areas:

Found n southern Oregon and Walla Walla. The Muscat family may be the oldest grape variety known. It is planted in most wine-growing regions.

Wine Styles and Blends:

Muscat Blanc à Petits Grains is easily recognized with its perfumed aromatics. Often sweet and fortified from 3-5% up to 15% abv, especially from the Mediterranean and Australia. In Alsace and Languedoc-Roussillon a dry style is also produced. Also used in Italy to make sparkling wine. Usually a single variety.

Grape Physiology:

Vigour: Varies depending on climate and soil types. Yields vary from 30-55 hl/ha. Thrives on fertile soils.

Phenology:

Ripens in mid-season. At maturity the sugar content is 22º-26º Brix/Balling and TA is 5-7.5 g/l.

Berries:

Small in size and off-round. They have a straw to golden-yellow hue and are used for white winemaking.

Diseases:

Susceptible to sunburn, most diseases and pests. It seems everyone and everything like these grapes.

Sensory Characteristics:
Appearance:

Varies from pale, pinkish-yellow-gold to deep golden-yellow with a slight greenish tint when young. It has a medium to tight gradient. Initial changes detected in the 4th year proceed to darker golden-orange-amber hues by the 7th to 8th year.

The Nose:

A fortified Muscat de Beaumes-de-Venise from southern Rhône would offer a distinctive musky aroma combined with hits of grape orange and marmalade.

The Palate:

Less body than for a botrytis wine from Sauternes or Austria. High alcohol around 15% abv. compensates for low acidity in fortified wines. Dry wines are honeyed and complex.

Dry sensory ratios: Acidity **5.5**, Fullness **3.5**, Sweetness **2**, Abv. 12.5-13%

Sweet with sensory ratios: Acidity **5.5**, Fullness **5.5**, Sweetness **7**, Abv. 10-15%

Excellent Food Combinations:

A great wine by itself or with some hard matured cow or sheep-cheeses like Comté (cow), Gruyère (cow), Parmigiano Reggiano (cow) or Pecorino Sardo (ewe). Matches well with delicate desserts including chocolate.

Typical Characteristics	
	Yeasty
	Gooseberry
oak -	Almonds
	Nettles
oak -	Smoky
	Earthy
	Mineral
	Citrus
Sur Lie - Lees	
Tannin	1 to 4
Acidity	9
Sweetness	1
Bitterness	0
Weight	2 to 4
Alcohol	10 to 15%

Müller-Thurgau

General Characteristics:
Originally assumed to be a crossing between Riesling and Silvaner (or Chasselas), DNA-testing in 1996 has shown that it is a crossing between Riesling and Madeleine Royale[1]. It is named in 1882 after its founder Dr. Müller from Thurgau in Switzerland.

Synonyms:
Riesling-Sylvaner (Switzerland and New Zealand), Rivaner (Luxembourg and Yugoslavia) and Rizlingszilvani (Hungary).

Areas:
Found in south Oregon. Originally the best examples came from Germany where it represented the largest acreage of any single variety, but its popularity has dwindled (today about 13%). It is also found in Oregon, New Zealand, South Africa, Italy, Hungary and Switzerland.

Wine Styles and Blends:
Traditionally unoaked with mainly citrus characters, but some flowery and mineral tones are evident in very good wines. Varying in style from dry to sweet wines with a moderate acidity level, it can be blended with Chardonnay or Sauvignon Blanc.

Grape Physiology:
Vigour: Extremely vigorous. Yields about 150-200 hl/ha. It is most comfortable in deep, cool, moist soils but can also thrive in heavy chalk and loam. It does not produce well in gravel, rocky or sand soils.

Phenology:
Ripens in early-season. At full maturity the average sugar content of 23º-26º Brix / Balling and TA of 6.5 – 7,5 g/l.

Berries:
Large, oval, rich, green hue with medium skins.

Diseases:
Very susceptible to botrytis infection.

Sensory Characteristics:
Appearance:
A light, pale, green-yellow-golden color when young, with and without carbonation. It has a wide gradient with initial change in hue in the 2nd year, proceeding to light amber by the 4th year. Oaked Müller-Thurgau wines are more viscous and show a greenish straw-yellow hue when young and change color in their 3rd to 4th year. Good mature wines develop a light amber hue after their 5th to 6th year.

The Nose:
Fresh pears, citrus, some grassy and mineral characters (if picked early) are found in dry wines, whereas the sweet wines offer pear, honey and/or apricot characters.

The Palate:
Unoaked-dry wines have medium to medium-high acidity levels, whereas, oaked wines have a slightly softer acidity masked by their presence in oak. Sweet or botrytis wines show a more apricot/honey combination.

Excellent Food Combinations:
Pasta, fish and light meats.

[1]. Dettweiler, E., Jung, A., Zyprian, E., Töpfer, R.: "Grapevine cultivar Müller-Thurgau and its true to type descent", Vitis 39(2): 63-65, 2000

Typical Characteristics	
	Pear
	Citrus
	Melon
	Floral
oak -	honey
	Grassy
Tannin	0
Acidity	7
Sweetness	1-8
Bitterness	0
Weight	3-5
Alcohol	12-15%

Pinot Blanc

General Characteristics:
Pinot Blanc is not related to Chardonnay as once believed but part of the Pinot Noir group. What is called Pinot Blanc in Australia is often Chardonnay and some Pinot Blanc vines in California have been identified as Melon de Bourgogne. Pinot Blanc is being used more and more in sparkling wines.

Synonyms:
Beli Pinot, Clevner, Pinot Bianco, Pineau Blanc, Borgogno Bianco, Weissburgunder, Weiser Klevner, Weisser Ruländer and Klevanjka.

Areas:
In all regions of Oregon. Originally from Burgundy, the variety has spread to Italy, South Africa, Australia, New Zealand, Chile, Argentina, US, Austria, Germany, Hungary, the Czech Republic and Slovakia.

Wine Styles and Blends:
Pinot Blanc is normally a single variety and matured in steel but on occasion it meets some oak. It is at its best in northeast Italy, Alsace and California. Usually vinified dry but sometimes blended into sparkling wines. Medium-bodied with good acidity.

Grape Physiology:
Vigour: Average. Yields about 70 hl/ha. It thrives on chalky soils that run deep and that are damp.

Phenology:
Ripens in late early season. At full maturity the average sugar content is from 20º to 24º Brix/Balling and total acid of 6 to 7.5 g/l.

Berries:
Small to medium in size but tend to be rather compact. The berries are round with a medium pale green. They have a medium to thick skin.

Diseases:
Resistant to many insects but tend to rot due to the compactness of the berries on a bunch.

Sensory Characteristics:
Appearance: Varies from pale to straw in color when young, with and without carbonation. It has a wide gradient. Initial changes in the hue can be detected in the 3rd year, proceeding to light amber by the 5th to 6th year. Usually fermented and aged in steel but. In oak it is viscous and slightly more straw-yellow in color.

The Nose: Tree fruit, floral and a slight spiciness in character. Unoaked it has usually more citrus and is slightly sharper with apple and floral characters. Oaked wines are richer and buttery. They have a light fresh apple aroma with a spicy touch, some yeast and honey with the addition of vanilla of oak.

The Palate: Unoaked wines are dry and similar to a light medium-bodied Chardonnay. Usually crispy acidity but also a honeyed version in the US.

Dry no-oak sensory ratios:
Acidity **6**, Fullness **8,** Sweetness **2,** Abv. 12.5-14.5%

Dry oak aged sensory ratios:
Acidity **6**, Fullness **8.5**, Sweetness **2**, Abv. 12.5-14.5%

Sparkling sensory ratios:
Acidity **7**, Fullness **6**, Sweetness **1**, Abv. 12.5-13.5%

Excellent Food Combinations:
A perfect table wine, Pinot Blanc can complement the majority of fish dishes, light meat and mild cheeses.

Typical Characteristics	
	Light Citrus
	Fresh Apples
	Honey
	Spice
	Floral
Tannin	0
Acidity	6 to 7
Sweetness	1 to 2
Bitterness	0
Weight	6 to 8
Alcohol	9.5 to 14.5%

Riesling

General Characteristics:
Like Chenin Blanc, this is both a very versatile grape and one of the great noble varieties.

Synonyms:
Johannisberg Riesling, Rhine Riesling, Petit Rhin Riesling, Petit Riesling, Riesling Blanc, Rizling, Weisser Riesling and White Riesling. Note that Cape Riesling is not a Riesling clone but instead Cruchen Blanc responsible for table wines.

Areas:
Found in south Oregon, the Willamette Valley and the Walla Walla. The 2nd largest variety in Germany. Grown in Alsace in France, Oregon and the US, South Africa, Australia, New Zealand, Chile, Argentina, Canada.

Wine Styles and Blends:
These crisp wines range from bone-dry to lusciously sweet. Called White or Johannisberg Riesling in USA. Usually fermented dry in Alsace. In the best years the richer Vendange Tardive and Sélection de Grains Nobles are produced. In Germany there are Trocken, Halbtrocken, Kabinett, Spätlese, Auslese, Beerenauslese and the sweetest Trockenbeerenauslese as well as Eiswein.

Grape Physiology:
Vigour: Moderate. Very versatile but thrives on sandy loam, slate and well-drained, less fertile areas.

Phenology:
Ripens in late mid-season. At maturity the sugar is 20º-23º Brix/Balling and TA of 7-9 g/l.

Berries:
Small, medium in size, round with a rich, green, golden yellow hue and medium to thick skin.

Diseases:
Resistant to many infections. Survive well in very low temperatures.

.

Sensory Characteristics:
Appearance:
Pale, greenish yellow when young, wide gradient if dry and tighter if sweet. Initial changes of hue in the 4th year, towards light amber by the 7th year. Oaked wines are viscous and change color in the 4th to 5th year. Light amber hue after 10 years.

The Nose:
Aromatic, floral, acidic gradually developing into a unique 'petroleum' type aroma. Unoaked wines have sharper citrus, apple and floral characters, while oaked are richer and more viscous.

The Palate:
Unoaked Alsace Riesling is dry, steely and medium-bodied. German wines are lighter and more honeyed, with delicate flavors of peaches, apricots and minerals. Fine balance between fruit, sweetness and acidity. Very high acidity whether dry or sweet. Dry wines are clean and uncomplicated. Sweet botrytis wines are fruity with apricot, honey, peach and spice.

Dry no-oak sensory ratios:
Acidity **10**, Fullness **3**, Sweetness **1**, Abv. 9.5-12.5%
Dry oak aged sensory ratios:
Acidity **10**, Fullness **4**, Sweetness **2**, Abv. 12.5-14%
Sweet botrytis/Ice wine oak aged sensory ratios:
Acidity **10**, Fullness **7**, Sweetness **8**, Abv. 11.5-13%

Excellent Food Combinations:
Various fish dishes including grilled or baked Salmon. Artisan style cheese plate made from goat, cow or ewe are perfect.

Typical Characteristics

Petroleum
Fruity
Citrus
Apples
Minerally
oak - Honey
Pears
Lime

Tannin	0 to 2
Acidity	10
Sweetness	1 to 8
Bitterness	0
Weight	3 to 7
Alcohol	9.5 to 14%

Sauvignon Blanc

General Characteristics:
Sauvignon Blanc is an aromatic variety that is generally better from cool climate vineyards. Grassy and grapefruity in cool climates; often blandly exotic in warmer climates.

Synonyms:
Sauvignon Jaune, Blance Fumé, Surin, Punechon, Muskat-Silvaner and Fumé Blanc.

Areas:
Found in south Oregon and a few planting in the Willamette Valley. Well-known in the Loire Valley including Sancerre in France. New Zealand, South Africa, Australia, California, Oregon and Washington State produce excellent examples. Also found in Argentina, Chile and Italy.

Wine Styles and Blends:
One of the most important white grapes of Bordeaux, it is found as a single variety and in blends together with Muscadelle and Sémillon. Dry and sweet wines. Fermented and matured in steel and/or oak.

Grape Physiology:
Vigour:
Very vigorous. Sauvignon Blanc yields about 60 hl/ha. It is a very versatile in cool climates and thrives on soil types like chalk, gravel and sandy loam.

Phenology:
Ripens in early mid-season. At full maturity its average sugar content is 21º–24º Brix / Balling and TA of 6 to 7 g/l.

Berries:
Medium-small in size and oval with a distinctive grassy-herbaceous aroma. The grape has a pale, green-yellowish hue and medium tough skin.

Diseases:
Susceptible to black rot and botrytis infection in fertile areas. Sauvignon Blanc is also susceptible to Powdery mildew and Downey mildew.

Sensory Characteristics:
Appearance:
Unoaked wines are pale, green-yellow to golden-yellow, the latter typical in Loire and Bordeaux. Warmer climate wines are darker. Young, unoaked wines show a greenish, pale, yellow hue with a light tight, gradient changing color only in their 3rd year and into light amber in the 7th year. Sauvignon Blanc wines are viscous and with a greenish-straw-yellow hue when young and change their color in their 4th to 5th year. Good mature wines develop a light-amber color hue after about their 8th to 10th year.

The Nose:
Aromatic with a grassy, gooseberry, blackcurrant bush and flinty tones. Aged it becomes vegetal, musk-like or 'catty', as in cat's pee (blackcurrant bush). Unoaked wines are sharper and with underlying mineral characters. Oaked wines are richer with more body and vanilla.

The Palate:
Young, oaked wines are fresh, crisp, uncomplicated and aromatic. In warm climates they are rich and velvety.

Unoaked wines: Acidity **8**, Fullness **3.5**, Sweetness **2,** Abv. 11.5-12.5%.
Oak aged wines: Acidity **8**, Fullness **4.5-6**, Sweetness **2-8**, Abv. 12.5-14%

Excellent Food Combinations:
Shell fish, fried fish and poultry dishes. Cheese plates with French country cheeses like Munster and Epoisses are perfect.

Typical Characteristics

	Cassis
	(cat's Pee)
	Gooseberry
	Grassy
	Flint
	Vegetal
	Musk-like
	Aromatic
Tannin	1 to 3
Acidity	8
Sweetness	2 to 8
Bitterness	0
Weight	3.5 to 6
Alcohol	11.5 to 14%

Sémillon

General Characteristics:

A golden grape from southwest France, Sémillon is one of the unsung heroes of white grape production. As a single variety it is not the most elegant wine but in blends it is just fantastic.

Synonyms:

Sémillon Blanc, Sémillon Muscat, Sémillon Roux, Chevrier, Colombier (not Colombar in South Africa) and Hunter River Riesling.

Areas:

Found in southern Oregon. A classical grape of Bordeaux. Also found in the Hunter Valley in Australia, California, Oregon, Washington, South Africa, Chile and east Europe.

Wine Styles and Blends:

Usually blended with Sauvignon Blanc and Muscadelle, this is the key variety of Sauternes and some of the world's longest living 'unfortified' whites. Excellent varietal dry Sémillon in the Hunter Valley, but otherwise best in blends. In Sauternes combined with Sauvignon Blanc for its high acidity.

Grape Physiology:

Vigour: Very vigorous. Yields about 50 hl/ha.

It thrives in heavy soils and over-cropping.

Phenology:

Ripens in early mid-season. At full maturity the average sugar content is from 20º to 26º Brix/Balling and total acid of 5 to 7 g/l.

Berries:

Medium in size and oval. Yellowish-green hue and an excellent, grassy aroma when smelt. Medium skin thickness.

Diseases:

Susceptible to grey and noble rot (Botrytis cinerea, as shown in the background).

Sensory Characteristics
Appearance:

Greenish yellow-golden hue and very viscous in young wines. It has a medium to tight gradient. Initial changes in hue are detectable in the 5th year proceeding to light-amber hue by the 8th to 10th year if a blend from Bordeaux. Oaked wines are very viscous and slightly more straw-golden-yellow in color than those without oak.

The Nose:

Apricot, honey, nuts, dried fruit and ripe citrus characters. In young dry wines a grassy citrus character is found, but with age they develop a waxy, raisin, lanolin-type character. Sweet wines are complex, smooth and filled with a honey-nutty character. Older, sweet wines develop a softer, fuller, rounder, velvety apricot-raisin nose. Unoaked wines display apple and citrus characters with a touch of pineapple. Oaked wines add cream, butter, vanilla and some smokiness.

The Palate:

Grassy with low acidity levels and lemony in the aftertaste.

Dry unoaked sensory ratios: Acidity **4**, Fullness **7**, Sweetness **1**, Alcohol Levels. 10-12.5%.

Dry oak-aged sensory ratios: Acidity **5.5**, Fullness **6**, Sweetness **2**, Abv. 12.5-13.5%.

Sweet oak-aged sensory ratios: Acidity **7**, Fullness **8**, Sweetness **8**, Abv. 11.5-14%.

Excellent Food Combinations:

A dry Sémillon is wonderful with fish and poultry such as Confit de Canard. A sweet Sémillon can be served with dessert, cheese, goose liver and Terrine.

Typical Characteristics	
	Apricots
	Aromatic
oak -Honey	
oak -Nuts	
	Dried Fruit
	Citrus
oak -Lanolin	
	Raisin
	Velvety
Tannin	1 to 2
Acidity	4 to 7
Sweetness	1 to 8
Bitterness	0
Weight	6 to 8
Alcohol	10 to 14%

Syrah / Shiraz

General Characteristics:

One of the oldest and noblest of grape varieties. Grows best in poor soil, gravel, granite and even high temperatures. Full-bodied, powerful wines in high demand throughout the world.

Synonyms:

Shiraz is almost as common as Syrah. Shiras, Sirac, Syra, Syrac, Sirah, Marsanne Noir, Serine, and Balsamnina.

Areas:

Found in all regions of Oregon. Syrah has its origin in Persia some 14,000 years ago and is one of the oldest grapes known. High quality wines gained their reputation from northern Rhône in France with Côte-Rôtie, Hermitage among others. Australia, South Africa and the USA also have many fine vintages. Also produced in Argentina, Chile and New Zealand.

Wine Styles and Blends:

Found as a single varietal or can be blended. If not a single variety it is usually blended with Grenache, Cinsault, Cabernet Sauvignon, Merlot and in Southern Rhône twelve other grapes which make up the typical Châteauneuf-du-Pape.

Grape Physiology:

Vigour: Very Good. Grows well in various climates and soil types.

Phenology:

Ripens in mid-season and a good grape for cold climates. At full maturity the average sugar content is from 24º to 25º Brix / Balling (total dissolved compounds in grape juice and sugar concentration) and total titratable acid of 6 to 7 g/l.

Berries:

Small to medium in size, with a thick skin. The berry is off-round to oval shape with a blue-black color.

Diseases:

Thick skin and an unusually high resistance to diseases.

Sensory Characteristics:

Appearance:

In young wines, Syrah has a very dark to black tone with a very tight gradient. In 89/90-point wines it is almost black but a rim color of blue-purple-red can be found. The wines start to change color after the 5th year, but in Rhône this can take another 2 to 3 years. Good mature wines develop an orange brick-colored rim in about their 12th year.

The Nose:

Gamy, meaty, leather, mixed spices, black-pepper (trademark), dark berries, tar, rubber, blackcurrants and earthy are some characters found in young wines. In mature 90-point wines they blend together to form an elegance of power and finesse.

The Palate:

In northern Rhône, Syrah wines can have more of a heavy backbone of tannin. Wines from southern Rhône, Australia, South Africa are usually softer 'fine tannins' and good underlying acidity balanced as in the ratio chart. Alcoholic, rich wines with unusual elegance and very good length. Alcohol levels range from 12.5% to 16%.

Excellent Food Combinations:

Syrah demands a rich powerful dish of beef or wild meat, such as venison, boar or Chateaubriand with reduced sauces. Excellent with aromatic cheeses.

Typical Characteristics	
	Gamy
	Meaty
	Leather
	Mixed Spice
	Blackpepper
	Dark Berries
oak -Tar	
	Diesel
	Currants
Tannin	8.5
Acidity	6
Sweetness	0
Bitterness	0
Weight	7 to 9
Alcohol	12.5-16%

Tempranillo

General Characteristics:
Tempranillo is Spain's most grown grape variety, producing high quality wines. It is the major grape in the Rioja blend and has many similarities to Pinot Noir and Cabernet Franc.

Synonyms:
Ull de Llebre, Ojo de Liebe, Cencibel, Tinto Fino, Tinto Madrid, Tempranilla, Tempranillo de la Rioga, Grenache de Logrono, Tinto del Pais, Tinot Roriz and Tinot de Toro.

Areas:
Found in south Oregon and the Walla Walla AVA. Originally brought to Santiago de Compostela, Spain, by French pilgrims. Tempranillo's home is Rioja, but it is also grown in Portugal, where it is known as Tinto Roriz. Used in Port and also found in Argentina, Chile and even South Africa.

Wine Styles and Blends:
Found as a single varietal and often in a blend. A 100% Tempranillo is similar to Pinot Noir. Usually blended with Garnacha or Cabernet Sauvignon in Rioja. Well-made Rioja wines containing Tempranillo can be aged for well over 30 years. The use of American oak barrels is standard in Rioja and French in Penedes.

Grape Physiology:
Vigour: Low vigour and yields about 35 hl/ha. Thrives on calcareous soils.

Phenology:
Ripens in mid-season, so it is a good grape for cold climates. At full maturity the average sugar content is from 21º to 24º Brix / Balling (total dissolved compounds in grape juice and sugar concentration) and TA of 6 to 7 g/l.

Berries:
Medium in size with thin to medium skins. The berry has a slight off-round shape with a bluish to black color.

Diseases:
Susceptible to powdery and downy mildew.

Sensory Characteristics:
Appearance:
Young wines have a tight gradient almost identical to heavy macerated Pinot Noir wines. Tempranillo tends to hold its tone and hue for at least 5 to 6 years. 89/90-point wines have a deep to dark, bluish-ruby-red hue, starting to change in their 5th to 6th year. Good mature wines develop an orange brick-colored rim in about their 10th to 12th year.

The Nose:
If in Rioja and aged in American oak, the wine is warm, fruity and creamy with hints of strawberry, dill, cherry, butter and spice. Aged in French oak the creaminess. Trademark characteristics are vanilla and dill.

The Palate:
Tempranillo usually produces more acid than tannin, i. e. medium 'fine tannins' with good acidity and balanced as per ratio chart. Very delicate and elegant wines with very good length. Alcohol levels range from 12.5% to 14.5%.

Excellent Food Combinations:
Aged Tempranillo should be served with elegant dishes as aged Bordeaux and Burgundy. Young wines go well with beef and lamb.

Typical Characteristics
Red Berries

	Strawberry
	Dill
	Cherry
oak -Butter	
	Spice
	Warm fruit
Tannin	5
Acidity	7
Sweetness	0
Bitterness	0
Weight	6 to 7
Alcohol	12.5-14.5%

Viognier

General Characteristics:
An esteemed white-wine grape considered very rare because of the limited acreage planted throughout the world. With its low yield and high susceptibility to vineyard diseases few wine farmers try to grow it. Viognier is well known in the northern Rhône-wines of Château Grillet, Condrieu and Côte-Rôtie.

Synonyms: Vionnier.

Areas Found:
Found in south Oregon and Walla Walla. About 38 ha in the Rhône Valley in France where some of the finest Viognier can be found. In addition there are some excellent examples coming from California namely Joseph Phelps Vineyards amongst others. Other good examples of Viognier can now be found in Australia, South Africa and Languedoc-Roussillon in the south-west of France.

Wine Styles and Blends:
Viognier is found as both a varietal and as a blend in both red and white wines. Used for its aromatics and as a color stabilizer in red. As a varietal it is a very aromatic and floral dry white wine. As a blend it is vinified together with the Syrah, a red grape, in Côte-Rôtie where it is prized for its addition of weight and violets. Viognier produces excellent wines with a long length and balance.

Grape Physiology:
Vigour: Less than average vigour. Yields only about 25 hl/ha. Thrives in sandy limestone soils with a good mineral content. Unreliable ripening.

Phenology:
Ripens in midseason. At full maturity average sugar content is 20º–23º Brix/Balling and total acid of 5 to 7 g/l.

Berries:
Medium in size and oval. They have a yellowish-red-black hue and are used for white winemaking. Viognier has a medium skin thickness.

Diseases:
Resistant to insects and pests.

Sensory Characteristics:
Appearance: Varies from pale straw to a rich, golden oily color. It has a medium to tight gradient. Initial changes in the hue can be detected in the 3rd year proceeding to golden-orange-amber by the 5th to 6th year.

Nose: Very aromatic displaying violets, peaches, apricots, apples, pears, musk and spice. Unoaked wines have more citrus and are slightly sharper but with good floral and fruit characters (peach, apricot). Oaked wines also have creamy, buttery, smoky and vanilla characters.

Palate: Full-bodied, rich, rustic, viscous, fat, with good 'volatile aroma' characteristics. A marked bitterness with low acidity.

Dry no-oak sensory ratios:
Acidity **3.8**, Fullness **7**, Sweetness **2.5**, Bitterness **4**, Abv. 12-12.5%

Dry oak aged sensory ratios:
Acidity **4**, Fullness **8**, Sweetness **3**, Bitterness **4**, Abv. 12.5-14%

Excellent Food Combinations:
Best matched with charismatic, powerful fish dishes and a creamy wine sauce. Food with some character.

Typical Characteristics	
	Aromatic
	Peachy
	Floral
	Pears
	Musk
	Tropical Fruit
	Spice
Tannin	1 to 3
Acidity	3 to 4.5
Sweetness	2.5 to 3
Bitterness	3 to 4
Weight	7 to 8
Alcohol	12 14%

Zinfandel

General Characteristics:

Of uncertain origin, Zinfandel is a winemaker's dream, it is very versatile grape and one which can produce many different styles from white and light roses to sparkling, full-bodied red wines and even Port. Zinfandel is also affectionately called just Zin.

Synonyms:

Primitivo, Primativo (Italy).

Areas: Found in south Oregon. South Africa, Chile, Argentina and Australia and in larger use in Puglia, Italy and California.

Wine Styles and Blends:

Single varietal or blended with Syrah, Cabernet Sauvignon, Merlot and Grenache. White Zinfandel is fruity. Sparkling wine varying in residual sugar. A port style fortified wine of usually very good quality. Light, medium and full-bodied red wines.

Grape Physiology:

Vigour: Very Good. Zinfandel grows well in warm but not too hot climatic conditions and various soil types.

Phenology:

Ripens in mid to late-season, although unevenly, which can cause problems during harvesting. At full maturity the average sugar content is from 24º to 26º Brix / Balling (total dissolved compounds in grape juice and sugar concentration) and total titratable acid of 5.5 to 7 g/l.

Berries:

Small in size, with a medium to thick skin. The berry is off-round to oval in shape with a blue-black color.

Diseases:

Susceptible to bunch rot if irrigated. Otherwise, due to its thick skin, it has high resistance to diseases.

Sensory Characteristics:
Appearance:

Very dark to black tone and tight gradient in young quality wines, almost black with a blue-purple rim. Its color changes after the 3rd year in central California, in Napa and Sonoma Valleys after another 2-3 years. Good mature wines develop an orange brick-colored rim in about their 8th year.

The Nose:

Blackberries, black cherries, ginger, rose-hip, cloves, mixed spices, dark berries, tar, rubber, black-currants are some of the typical characters found in good quality zinfandels. Trademark characters are ginger and cloves with a slight greenstick aroma. In mature 90-point wines they blend into elegance of power and finesse.

The Palate:

In northern California the wines can have slightly more tannin and acidity than in the central region. The acidity is in balance with tannin as per the ratio chart above (6/10 for tannin and 7/10 for acid). High alcohol wines with unusual elegance and very good length. The alcohol levels range from 12.5% to 18%.

Excellent Food Combinations:

The spread of wine styles available from Zinfandel provide good possibilities for combining Zinfandel with various foods. Top class red wines need to be consumed with red or wild meats.

Next Page: *An orchard in Yamhil County*

Typical Characteristics

Blackberries
Black-cherries
Tar
Rubber
Cloves
Mixed Spice
Ginger
Greenstick

Tannin	6
Acidity	7
Sweetness	
Bitterness	Slight
Weight	6 to 9
Alcohol	12.5 - 18%

Directory

Willamette Valley Wineries

Abiqua Wind Vineyard
www.paradiswine.com
Winery Address:
19822 McKillop Lp Rd NE
Scotts Mills, OR 97375
(503) 874-9818
Open to Public
Tasting Room:
Hours: Call for appointment
Tasting Fee: $3.00 (Refundable with purchase)
Tours Available:
By Appointment Only
Varieties/Wine Styles:
Gewürztraminer, Muller-Thurgau, Muscat,
Pinot Gris and Pinot Noir.
Winery Features:
Tasting Room, Picnic Area and Retail Sales.
****

ADEA
www.adeawine.com
Winery Address:
26421 NW Hwy 47
Gaston, OR 97119
(503) 662-4509
Open to Public by Appointment Only
Tasting Room:
Hours: By Appointment Only
Tasting Fee: $10
Tours Available:

By Appointment Only
Varieties/Wine Styles:
Chardonnay, Pinot Gris and Pinot Noir.
Winery Features:
Tasting Room, Picnic Area, Bus/RV Parking,
Wheelchair Accessible and Retail Sales.
****

Adelsheim Vineyard
www.adelshiem.com
(see pages 70-75)

Winery Address:
16800 NE Calkins Lane
Newberg, OR 97132
(503) 538-3652
Open to Public
Tasting Room:
Hours: Wed-Sun, 11am - 4pm
Tasting Fee: $10.00
Tours Available:
By Appointment Only
Varieties/Wine Styles:
Auxerrois, Chardonnay, Late Harvest/Dessert/
Ice Wine, Pinot Blanc, Pinot Gris, Pinot Noir,
Syrah and Tocai Friulano.
Winery Features:
Tasting Room, Wheelchair Accessible and
Retail Sales.
****

Airlie Winery & Dunn Forest Vineyard
www.airliewinery.com
Winery Address:
15305 Dunn Forest Drive
Monmouth, 97361
(503) 838-6013
Open to Public
Tasting Room:
Hours: March-December Sat-Sun, 12pm - 5pm

Varieties/Wine Styles:
Pinot noir, Pinot gris, Chardonnay, Maréchal
Foch, Gewürztraminer, Riesling, and Müller
Thurgau.
Winery Features:
Tasting Room, Wedding Facilities, Reception
Facilities, Picnic Area, Bus/RV Parking and
Retail Sales.
****

Alloro Vineyard
www.allorovineyard.com
Winery Address:
22075 SW Lebeau Road
Sherwood, OR 97140
(503) 625-1978
Open to Public by Appointment Only
Tours Available:
By Appointment Only
Varieties/Wine Styles:
Chardonnay, Pinot Noir, Vino Nettare and a
Muscat/Riesling dessert wine .
Certificates:
Certified Sustainable
Winery Features:
Wheelchair Accessible and Retail Sales.
****

Amalie Robert Estate
www.amalierobert.com
Winery Address:
13531 Bursell Road
Dallas, OR 97338
(503) 831-4703

*Picture Right: Map showing the different
wine regions of Oregon. Picture Following Page: The striated rock formations and
sand dunes of Pacific City on the Oregon
coast line.*

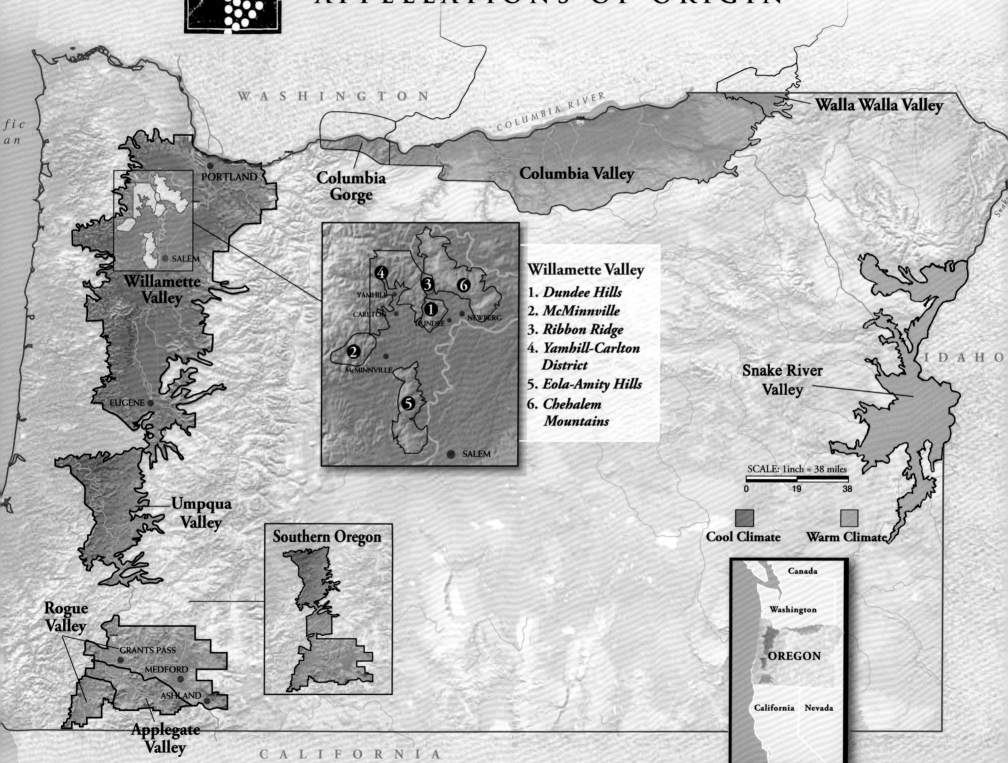

OREGON WINE REGIONS
APPELLATIONS OF ORIGIN

OREGON WINE

WASHINGTON

COLUMBIA RIVER

Walla Walla Valley

PORTLAND

Columbia Gorge

Columbia Valley

SALEM

Willamette Valley

Willamette Valley

1. *Dundee Hills*
2. *McMinnville*
3. *Ribbon Ridge*
4. *Yamhill-Carlton District*
5. *Eola-Amity Hills*
6. *Chehalem Mountains*

YAMHILL

CARLTON

DUNDEE

NEWBERG

McMINNVILLE

SALEM

EUGENE

Snake River Valley

IDAHO

SCALE: 1inch = 38 miles

0   19   38

Cool Climate   **Warm Climate**

Umpqua Valley

Southern Oregon

Canada

Washington

Rogue Valley

GRANTS PASS

MEDFORD

ASHLAND

OREGON

Applegate Valley

California   Nevada

CALIFORNIA

Willamette Valley Wineries, continued

Open to Public by Appointment Only
Tours Available:
By Appointment Only
Varieties/Wine Styles:
Chardonnay, Pinot Meunier, Pinot Noir, Syrah and Viognier.
Winery Features:
Retail Sales

****

Amity Vineyards
www.amityvineyards.com
Winery Address:
18150 Amity Vineyards Rd
Amity, OR 97101
(503) 835-2362
Open to Public
Tasting Room:
Hours: Daily, June-October, 11am - 5pm
November-May, 12pm - 5pm
Tasting Fee: $7.00
Additional Tasting Room:
Oregon Wine Tasting Room 19690 SW Highway 18, McMinnville, OR 97128
Tours Available:
By Appointment Only
Varieties/Wine Styles:
Gamay Noir, Gewürztraminer, Pinot Blanc, Pinot Noir and Riesling.
Certificates:
Certified Organic and Certified Sustainable.
Winery Features:
Tasting Room, Second Tasting Room, Picnic Area and Bus/RV Parking.

****

Anam Cara Cellars
www.anamcaracellars.com
Winery Address:
Twelfth & Maple Wine Co, 1242 SE Maple St., Dundee, OR 97115
(503) 537-9150
Tours Available:
By Appointment Only
Varieties/Wine Styles:
Gewürztraminer, Pinot Noir and Riesling.

****

Anderson Family Vineyard
www.dundeehills.org/anderson.htm
Winery Address:
20120 NE Herring Ln
Newberg, OR 97132
(503) 554-5541
Open to Public by Appointment Only
 Varieties/Wine Styles:
Chardonnay, Pinot Gris and Pinot Noir.
Winery Features:
Picnic Area, Wheelchair Accessible and Retail Sales.

****

Andrew Rich Wines
www.andrewrichwines.com
Winery Address:
Carlton Winemakers Studio 801 N. Scott St.
Carlton, OR 97111
(503) 284-6622
Open to Public by Appointment Only
Tasting Room:
Hours: Daily 11am - 5pm
Varieties/Wine Styles:
Cabernet Franc, Gewürztraminer, Grenache, Late Harvest/Dessert/Ice Wine, Malbec, Pinot Noir, Sauvignon Blanc, Syrah, Mourvedre and Counoise.
Winery Features:
Tasting Room, Picnic Area, Wheelchair Accessible and Retail Sales

****

Ankeny Vineyard Winery
www.ankenyvineyard.com
Winery Adress:
2565 Riverside Dr. South
Salem, Oregon 97306
(503) 378-1498
Open to Public
Tasting Room:
Hours: Daily 11am - 5pm
Varieties/Wine Styles:
Pinot Noir, Pinot Noir Rosé and Pinot Gris.
Winery Features:
Retail Sales and Tasting Room.

****

Anne Amie Vineyards
www.anneamie.com
Winery Address:
6580 NE Mineral Springs Rd
Carlton, OR 97111
(503) 864-2991
Open to Public
Tasting Room:
Hours: March-December, daily 10am - 5pm
Januari-DFebruari, Mon-Thu by appointment only, Fri-Sun 10am-5pm
Tasting Fee: $5
Varieties/Wine Styles:
Pinot Blanc, Pinot Gris, Pinot Noir, Riesling.

Picture Right: *A view of the rolling hills at Elk Cove vineyards in the Willamette Valley.*

Willamette Valley Wineries, continued

Winery Features:
Tasting Room, Picnic Area, Bus/RV Parking, Wheelchair Accessible and Retail Sales.
****

Antica Terra
www.anticaterra.com
Winery Address:
PO Box, 19406
Portland, 97280
(503) 244-1748
Tasting Room:
Hours: By Appointment Only
Varieties and/or Wine Styles:
Pinot Noir
Winery Features:
Tasting Room and Retail Sales.
****

Apolloni Vineyards
www.apolloni.com
Winery Address:
14135 NW Timmerman Road Forest Grove
Oregonn, 97116
(503) 330-5946
Open to Public
Tasting Room:
Hours: Fri-Sun, 12pm - 5pm
Varieties and/or Wine Styles:
Pinot Noir, Pinot Gris, Pinot Blanc, Chardonnay

Picture Left: *A Lama. One of literally hundreds maby even thousands found throughout Oregon. Why? You might ask, well, I have not idea.*

and Viognier.
Winery Features:
Tasting Room, Restaurant and Retail Sales.
****

Aramenta Cellars
www.aramentacellars.com
Winery Address:
17979 N.E. Lewis Rogers Ln.
Newberg, Oregon 97132
(503) 538-7230
Visitors Welcome Daily 10.30am - 5pm
Groups by appointment
Tasting Room:
Hours: 10.30am - 5pm
Varieties and/or Wine Styles:
Pinot Noir
Winery Features:
Tasting Room and Retail Sales.
****

ArborBrook Vineyards
www.arborbrookwines.com
Winery Address:
17770 NE Calkins Lane
Newberg, OR 97132
(503) 538-0959
Open to Public by Appointment Only
Tasting Room:
Hours: By Appointment Only
Tasting Fee: $7.00
Varieties and/or Wine Styles:
Pinot Gris, Pinot Noir and Semillon.
Winery Features:
Tasting Room, Picnic Area, Wheelchair Accessible and Retail Sales.
****

Archery Summit
www. archerysummit.com
(see pages 94-99)

Winery Address:
18599 NE Archery Summit Rd
Dayton, OR 97114
(503) 864-4300
Open to Public
Tasting Room:
Tasting Fee: $15.00
Tours Available:
By Appointment Only
Varieties/Wine Styles:
Pinot Noir
Winery Features:
Tasting Room and Retail Sales.
****

Argyle Winery
www.argylewinery.com
Winery Address:
691 Highway 99W
Dundee, OR 97115
(503) 538-8520
Open to Public
Tasting Room:
Tasting Fee: $
Hours: Daily 11am - 5pm, except major holidays.
Tours Available:
By Appointment Only
Varieties/Wine Styles:
Chardonnay, Merlot, Pinot Noir, Riesling and Sparkling.
Winery Features:
Tasting Room, Picnic Area, Wheelchair Accessible and Retail Sales.
****

August Cellars
www.augustcellars.com
Winery Address:
14000 NE Quarry Rd

Willamette Valley Wineries,
continued

Newberg, OR 97132
(503) 554-6766
Open to Public
Tasting Room:
Hours: Daily 11am - 5pm
Tasting Fee: $ (Refundable with purchase)
Tours Available:
Frequently
Varieties/Wine Styles:
Chardonnay, Gewürztraminer, Maréchal Foch,
Pinot Gris, Pinot Noir and Riesling.
Winery Features:
Tasting Room, Picnic Area, Bus/RV Parking,
Wheelchair Accessible and Retail Sales.
****

Ayoub Vineyard
www.ayoubwines.com
Winery Address:
9650 NE Keyes Lane
Dundee, 97115
(503) 554-9583
Tasting Room:
Hours: By appointment only
Tasting Fee: 10$
Varieties/Wine Styles:
Pinot Noir
Winery Features:
Tasting Room, Retail Sales.
****

Beaux Frères Winery
www.beauxfreres.com
(see pages 112-117)
Winery Address:

15155 NE North Valley Rd.
Newberg, Oregon 97132
Tel: 503.537.1137
Call for an Appointment
Tasting Room:
Visiting hours: Thanksgiving and Memorial Day
weekends
Tours Available:
By appointment for mailing list customers,
only
Varieties/Wine Styles:
Pinot Noir
Certificates:
Certified Biodynamic & Organic
Winery Features:
Tasting Room, Picnic Area, Bus/RV Parking, and
Wheelchair Accessible.
****

Bella Vida Vineyard
www.bellavida.com
Winery Address:
9380 NE Worden Hill Rd
Dundee, OR 97115
(503) 538-9821
Open to Public
Tasting Room:
Hours: Memorial Day Weekend - Thanksgiving
Weekend
Tasting Fee: $2.00
Tours Available:
Frequently
Varieties/Wine Styles:
Pinot Gris, Pinot Noir and Riesling.
Certificates:
Certified Sustainable
Winery Features:
Tasting Room, Picnic Area, Wheelchair Acces-
sible and Retail Sales.

****

Bella Pente Vineyards and Winery
www.bellepente.com
Winery Address:
12470 NE Rowland Rd
Carlton, OR 97111
(503) 852-9500
Open to Public by Appointment Only
Tours Available:
By Appointment Only
Varieties/Wine Styles:
Chardonnay, Gamay Noir, Gewürztraminer,
Late Harvest/Dessert/Ice Wine, Muscat, Pinot
Gris, Pinot Noir and Riesling.
Winery Features:
Picnic Area and Retail Sales.
****

Beran Vineyards
www.beranvineyards.com
Winery Address:
30088 SW Egger Road
Hillsboro, 97123
(503) 628-1298
Tasting Room:
By Appointment Only. Please call to arrange
your visit.
Varieties/Wine Styles:
Pinot Noir
Winery Features:
Retail Sales.
****

Bergström Winery
www.bergstromwines.com
(see pages 106-111)
Winery Address:
18215 NE Calkins Lane
Newberg, Oregon 97132
(503) 544-0468

Willamette Valley Wineries, continued

Open to Public
Tasting Room:
Hours: Tastings will be offered 4 times daily at: 10:00, 11:30, 2:00 and 3:30.
RESERVATIONS ARE REQUIRED.
Wine club members receive complimentary tastings for up to four people.
Tasting Fee: $25
Tours Available:
Frequently
Varieties/Wine Styles:
Chardonnay, Riesling, Pinot Noir, Sauvignon Blanc, Pinot Girs, and a Bordeaux Blend.
Certificates:
Certified Biodynamic & Organic
Winery Features:
Tasting Room, Picnic Area, Bus/RV Parking, Wheelchair Accessible and Retail Sales.
****

Bethel Heights Vineyard
www.bethelheights.com
Winery Address:
6060 Bethel Heights Rd NW
Salem, OR 97304
(503) 581-2262
Open to Public
Tasting Room:
Hours: Varies by season
Tasting Fee: $
Tours Available:
Frequently
Varieties/Wine Styles:
Chardonnay, Pinot Blanc, Pinot Gris and Pinot

Noir.
Certificates:
Certified Sustainable
Winery Features:
Tasting Room, Picnic Area, Bus/RV Parking, Wheelchair Accessible and Retail Sales.
****

Bishop Creek Cellars
www.bishopcreekcellars.com
Winery Address:
700 E First Street, #200
Newberg, OR 97132
(503) 476-8686
Tasting Room:
Hours: Tuesday-Sunday 12pm - 6pm and 12pm - 9pm on First Fridays.
Varieties/Wine Styles:
Pinot Noir and Pinot Gris.
Winery Features:
Retail Sales.
****

Black Cap of Oregon
www.blackcapwine.com
Winery Address:
935 NE 10th Avenue
McMinnville, OR 97128
(971) 237-0626
Open to Public by Appointment Only
Varieties/Wine Styles:
Chardonnay and Pinot Noir.
Winery Features:
Retail Sales.
****

Boedecker Cellars
www.boedeckercellars.com
Winery Address:
801 N. Scott St.
Carlton, OR 97111

(503) 288-7752
Tasting Room:
Hours: Daily 11am - 5pm, Closed in January.
Varieties/Wine Styles:
Chardonnay, Pinot Noir and Pinot Noir Rosé.
Winery Features:
Retail Sales.
****

Brick House Wine Company
www.brickhousewines.com
Winery Address:
18200 Lewis Rogers Ln
Newberg, OR 97132
(503) 538-5136
Open to Public by Appointment Only.
Tasting Room:
Hours: Thursdays, Fridays and Saturdays by appointment April-August.
Tasting Fee: $10.00
Varieties/Wine Styles:
Pinot Noir and Gamay Noir.
Certificates:
Certified Organic and Certified Biodynamic.
Winery Features:
Tasting Room, Wheelchair Accessible and Retail Sales.
****

Broadley Vineyards
www.broadleyvineyards.com
Winery Address:
25158 Orchard Tract Road
Monroe, OR 97456
(541) 847-5934
Tasting Room:
Tasting Room Open by Appointment, 265 South Fifth (Hwy 99).
Varieties/Wine Styles:
Pinot Noir

Willamette Valley Wineries, continued

Winery Features:
Tasting Room and Retail Sales.
****

Brooks Wines
www.brookswines.com
Winery Address:
2803 Orchard Avenue
McMinnville, OR 97128
(503) 435-1278
Tasting Room:
By appointment only
Varieties/Wine Styles:
Pinot Noir and Riesling.
Winery Features:
Tasting Room and Retail Sales.
****

Bryce Vineyard
www.brycevineyard.com
Winery Address:
801 N. Scott St
Carlton, OR 97111
(503) 554-9816
Open to Public
Tasting Room:
Hours: Daily February-December, 11am - 5pm
Varieties/Wine Styles:
Pinot Noir and Viognier.

Picture Left: *A drive up the west coast of Oregon will provide you with diverse weather conditions. Here, at midday, the mountains were literally covered in fog.*

Winery Features:
Tasting Room, Picnic Area, Bus/RV Parking,
Wheelchair Accessible and Retail Sales.
****

Bryn Mawr Vineyards
www.brynmawrvineyards.com
Winery Address:
5955 Bethel Heights Rd NW
Salem, OR 97304
(503) 581-4286
Open to Public
Tasting Room:
Hours: 12pm - 5pm
Tours Available:
Frequently
Varieties/Wine Styles:
Chardonnay, Pinot Noir and Tempranillo.
Winery Features:
Tasting Room, Picnic Area, Bus/RV Parking,
Wheelchair Accessible and Retail Sales.
****

Carabella Vineyard
www.carabellawine.com
Winery Address:
P.O. Box 2180, Wilsonville
OR 97070
(503) 699-1829
Tasting Room:
Not open to public
Tours Available:
Summer vineyard tours for distributors.
Varieties/Wine Styles:
Pinot Noir, Pinot Gris and Chardonnay.
Winery Features:
Tasting Room and Retail Sales.
****

Willamette Valley Wineries, continued

Carlo & Julian

Winery Address:
1000 E Main Street
Carlton, OR 97111
(503) 852-7432
Tasting Room:
Hours: By appointment only
Varieties/Wine Styles:
Pinot Noir, Tempranillo and Nebbiolo.
Winery Features:
Retail Sales.
****

Carlton Winemakers Studio

www.winemakersstudio.com
Winery Address:
801 N Scott St
Carlton, OR 97111
(503) 852-6100
Open to Public
Tasting Room:
Hours: Please call
Tasting Fee: $varies
Varieties/Wine Styles:
Cabernet Franc, Chardonnay, Gewürztraminer, Late Harvest/Dessert/Ice Wine, Muscat, Pinot Gris, Pinot Noir, Riesling, Sauvignon Blanc, Sparkling, Syrah, Tempranillo and Viognier.
Winery Features:
Tasting Room, Picnic Area, Bus/RV Parking, Wheelchair Accessible and Retail Sales.
****

Champoeg Wine Cellars

www.champoegwine.com
Winery Address:
10375 Champoeg Rd NE
Aurora, OR 97002
(503) 678-2144
Open to Public
Tasting Room:
Hours: Thu-Mon, 11am - 5pm Fridays, 11am - 7pm
Tours Available:
Frequently
Varieties/Wine Styles:
Chardonnay, Late Harvest/Dessert/Ice Wine, Pinot Gris, Pinot Noir, Riesling, Port and Petite Riesling.
Certificates:
Certified Sustainable
Winery Features:
Tasting Room, Picnic Area, Bus/RV Parking and Retail Sales.
****

Chateau Bianca Winery

www.chateaubianca.com
Winery Address:
17485 Hwy 22
Dallas, OR 97338
(503) 623-6181
Open to Public
Tasting Room:
Hours: Daily Oct-May, 11am - 5pm June-Sept, 10am - 6pm. Closed in January.
Tasting Fee: $Yes (Refundable with purchase)
Tours Available:
By Appointment Only
Varieties/Wine Styles:
Chardonnay, Gewürztraminer, Late Harvest/Dessert/Ice Wine, Maréchal Foch, Muscat, Pinot Blanc, Pinot Gris, Pinot Noir, Riesling and Sparkling.
Winery Features:
Tasting Room, Wedding Facilities, Reception Facilities, Bed & Breakfast, Picnic Area, Bus/RV Parking, Wheelchair Accessible and Retail Sales.
****

Chehalem

www.chehalemwines.com
Winery Address:
31190 NE Veritas Lane
Newberg, OR 97132
(503) 538-4700
Open to Public by Appointment Only
Tasting Room:
Hours: By Appointment Only
Tours Available:
By Appointment Only
Varieties/Wine Styles:
Chardonnay, Gamay Noir, Pinot Blanc, Pinot Gris, Pinot Noir and Riesling.
Certificates:
Certified Sustainable
Winery Features:
Tasting Room, Wheelchair Accessible and Retail Sales.
****

Cherry Hill Winery

www.cherryhillwinery.com
Winery Address:
7867 Crowley Rd
Rickreall, OR 97371
(503) 623-7867
Open to Public
Tasting Room:
7867 Crowley Road
Rickreall, OR 97371

Willamette Valley Wineries, continued

Tasting Fee: $10.00 (Refundable with purchase)
Hours: May1st-Oct15th, Sat-Sun, 11am - 5pm
Tours Available:
Frequently
Varieties/Wine Styles:
Pinot Gris and Pinot Noir.
Winery Features:
Tasting Room, Wedding Facilities, Reception Facilities, Picnic Area, Wheelchair Accessible and Retail Sales.
****

Christopher Bridge Cellars and Satori Vineyard

www.christopherbridgewines.com
Winery Address:
12770 S Casto Rd
Oregon City, OR 97045
(503) 263-6267
Open to Public by Appointment Only
Tours Available:
By Appointment Only
Varieties/Wine Styles:
Pinot Gris and Pinot Noir.
Winery Features:
Tasting Room and Retail Sales.
****

Picture Right: *A view from Cape Lookout State Park in the Coastal Range.***Picture Following Page:** *A spectacular picture of Domaine Serene.*

Willamette Valley Wineries,
continued

Cloudrest Vineyards
www.gardenaesthetics.com/grapeharvest.htm
Winery Address:
34780 SW Cloudrest Ln
Hillsboro, OR 97123
(503) 628-2552
Open to Public by Appointment Only
Tours Available:
By Appointment Only
Varieties/Wine Styles:
Pinot Gris
Winery Features:
Picnic Area.
****

Coelho Winery of Amity
www.coelhowinery.com
Winery Address:
111 5th St
Amity, OR 97101
(503) 835-9305
Open to Public
Tasting Room:
Hours: Jan-Apr, Fri-Sun 11am - 5pm
May-Dec, Daily, 11am - 5pm
Tasting Fee: $5
Tours Available:
Frequently
Varieties/Wine Styles:
Chardonnay, Maréchal Foch, Pinot Gris, Pinot Noir and Riesling.
Winery Features:
Tasting Room, Wedding Facilities, Reception Facilities, Picnic Area, Bus/RV Parking, Wheel-chair Accessible and Retail Sales.
****

Coleman Vineyard
www.colemanwine.com
Winery Address:
22734 SW Latham Rd
McMinnville, OR 97128
(503) 843-2707
Open to Public by Appointment Only.
Tasting Room:
(at Redhawk)
Hours: By Appointment Only
Tasting Fee: $8.00 (Refundable with purchase)
Tours Available:
By Appointment Only
Varieties/Wine Styles:
Late Harvest/Dessert/Ice Wine , Pinot Blanc , Pinot Gris and Pinot Noir.
Winery Features:
Tasting Room, Picnic Area, Bus/RV Parking, Wheelchair Accessible and Retail Sales.
****

Cristom Vineyards
www.cristomwines.com
(see pages 82-87)
Winery Address:
6905 Spring Valley Road NW
Salem, OR 97304 * Tel:(503) 375-3068
Open to Public
Tasting Room:
Hours: Thu-Sun, 11am - 4pm
Tasting Fee: $15.00 (Refundable with purchase)
Tours Available:
By Appointment Only
Varieties/Wine Styles:
Chardonnay, Pinot Gris, Pinot Noir, Syrah, and Viognier.

Winery Features:
Tasting Room, Wheelchair Accessible, Retail Sales, and Wine Club.
****

Cubanisimo Vineyards
www.cubanisimovineyards.com
Winery Address:
1754 Best Rd. NW
Salem, OR 97304
(503) 588-1763
Open to Public
Tasting Room:
Hours:April-Labor Day, Fri-Sun, 11am - 5pm
Tours Available:
By Appointment Only
Varieties/Wine Styles:
Pinot Noir and Rosado of Pinot Noir.
Winery Features:
Tasting Room, Wedding Facilities, Reception Facilities, Picnic Area, Bus/RV Parking, Wheel-chair Accessible and Retail Sales.
****

Dalla Vina Wines
www.dallavinawines.com
Winery Address:
33750 Sw Ladd Hill Road
Wilsonville, OR 97070
(503) 925-0712
Varieties/Wine Styles:
Cabernet Franc , Cabernet Sauvignon, Chardonnay, Late Harvest/Dessert/Ice Wine, Pinot Noir, Riesling, Syrah and Red Blend.
****

David Hill and Winery
www.davidhillwinery.com
Winery Address:
46350 NW David Hill Rd

Willamette Valley Wineries, continued

Forest Grove, OR 97116
(503) 992-8545
Open to Public
Tasting Room:
Hours: Daily 12 - 5pm
Tours Available:
By Appointment Only
Varieties/Wine Styles:
Chardonnay, Gewürztraminer, Late Harvest/Dessert/Ice Wine, Muscat, Pinot Blanc, Pinot Gris, Pinot Noir, Riesling, Semillon and Sylvaner.
Certificates:
Certified Sustainable
Winery Features:
Tasting Room, Wedding Facilities, Reception Facilities, Picnic Area, Bus/RV Parking, Wheelchair Accessible and Retail Sales.
****

De Ponte Cellars
www.depontecellars.com
Winery Address:
17545 Archery Summit Rd
Dayton, OR 97114
(503) 864-3698
Open to Public
Tasting Room:
Tasting Fee: $7.00 (Refundable with purchase)
Tours Available:
Frequently
Varieties/Wine Styles:
Melon de Bourgogne (Muscadet) and Pinot Noir

Certificates:
Certified Sustainable
Winery Features:
Tasting Room, Picnic Area, Wheelchair Accessible and Retail Sales.
****

Dobbes Family Estate & Wine By Joe
www.dobbesfamilyestate.com
Winery Address:
240 SE 5th Street
Dundee, OR 97115
(503) 538-1141
Open to Public by Appointment Only
Tours Available:
By Appointment Only
Varieties/Wine Styles:
Late Harvest/Dessert/Ice Wine, Pinot Blanc, Pinot Gris, Pinot Noir, Syrah and Viognier.
Certificates:
Certified Sustainable
Winery Features:
Picnic Area, Bus/RV Parking, Wheelchair Accessible and Retail Sales.
****

Domaine Coteau
www.domainecoteau.com
Winery Address:
258 N. Kutch St
Carlton, OR 97111
(503) 697-7319
Open to Public
Tasting Room:
Tasting Fee: $5.00
Hours: Sat-Sun, 12pm - 5pm
Tours Available:
By Appointment Only
Varieties/Wine Styles:
Pinot Noir

Winery Features:
Tasting Room and Retail Sales.
****

Domaine Serene
www.domaineserene.com

(see pages 76-81)

Winery Address:
6555 NE Hilltop Lane
Dayton, OR 97114
(503) 864-4600
Open to Public
Tasting Room:
Tasting Fee: $15.00 (Refundable with purchase)
Hours: Thu-Sun, 11am - 4pm
Tours Available:
By Appointment Only
Varieties/Wine Styles:
Chardonnay, Pinot Noir and Syrah.
Winery Features:
Tasting Room, Wheelchair Accessible and Retail Sales.
****

Duck Pond Cellars
www.duckpondcellars.com
Winery Address:
23145 Hwy 99W S
Dundee, OR 97115
(503) 538-3199
Open to Public
Tasting Room:
Hours: Mon - Sun, 11am - 5pm
Tours Available:
By Appointment Only
Varieties/Wine Styles:
Cabernet Sauvignon, Chardonnay, Gewürztraminer, Late Harvest/Dessert/Ice Wine, Merlot,

Willamette Valley Wineries,
continued

Pinot Gris, Pinot Noir, Riesling, Sangiovese,
Semillon, Sparkling, Syrah and Viognier.
Winery Features:
Tasting Room, Picnic Area, Bus/RV Parking,
Wheelchair Accessible and Retail Sales.
****

Elk Cove Vineyards
www.elkcove.com
Winery Address:
27751 NW Olson Rd
Gaston, OR 97119
(503) 985-7760
Open to Public
Tasting Room:
Hours: Daily 10am - 5pm
Tours Available:
By Appointment Only
Varieties/Wine Styles:
Gewürztraminer,Grenache, Late Harvest/Dessert/Ice Wine, Pinot Blanc, Pinot Gris, Pinot
Noir, Riesling, Sparkling, Syrah and Viognier.
Winery Features:
Tasting Room, Wedding Facilities, Reception
Facilities, Picnic Area, Bus/RV Parking, Wheelchair Accessible and Retail Sales.
****

Picture Left: *Harvest at Torri Mor.*
Picture Preceding Page: *Views of the
Pacific Ocean in July.*

Willamette **V**alley **W**ineries,
continued

Elkhorn Ridge Vineyards & Winery
www.elkhornridgevineyards.com
Winery Address:
10895 Brateng Rd
Monmouth, OR 97361
(208) 720-3062
Tours Available:
By Appointment Only
Varieties/Wine Styles:
Pinot Blanc, Pinot Gris and Pinot Noir.
Winery Features:
Retail Sales.
****

Emerson Vineyards
www.emersonvineyards.com
Winery Address:
11665 Airlie Rd
Monmouth, OR 97361
(503) 838-0944
Open to Public
Tasting Room:
Hours: By Appointment Only and Saturdays
12pm - 5pm
Tasting Fee: $5.00
Tours Available:
By Appointment Only
Varieties/Wine Styles:
Chardonnay, Pinot Gris, Pinot Noir and Syrah.
Winery Features:
Tasting Room, Bus/RV Parking, Wheelchair Accessible and Retail Sales.
****

Eola Hilla Wine Cellars
www.eolahillswinery.com
Winery Address:
501 S Pacific Highway
Rickreall, OR 97371
(503) 623-2405
Open to Public
Tasting Room:
Hours: 11am - 5pm, excluding Thanksgiving & Christmas day.
Tours Available:
Frequently
Varieties/Wine Styles:
Cabernet Sauvignon, Chardonnay, Gewürztraminer, Late Harvest/Dessert/Ice Wine, Maréchal Foch, Merlot, Pinot Gris, Pinot Noir, Sangiovese, Viognier, White Zinfandel and Zinfandel.
Winery Features:
Tasting Room, Wedding Facilities, Reception Facilities, Picnic Area, Bus/RV Parking, Wheelchair Accessible and Retail Sales.
****

Erath Vineyards
www.erath.com
Winery Address:
9409 NE Worden Hill Rd
Dundee, OR 97115
(503) 538-3318
Open to Public
Tasting Room:
Hours: Daily 11am - 5pm
Tours Available:
By Appointment Only
Varieties/Wine Styles:
Dolcetto, Gewürztraminer, Pinot Blanc, Pinot Gris, Pinot Noir and Riesling.

Winery Features:
Tasting Room, Picnic Area, Bus/RV Parking, Wheelchair Accessible and Retail Sales.
****

Et Fille Wines
www.etfillewines.com
Winery Address:
c/o August Cellars, 14000 NE Quarry Road
Newberg, OR 97132
(503) 449-5030
Open to Public
Tours Available:
By Appointment Only
Varieties/Wine Styles:
Pinot Noir
Winery Features:
Picnic Area, Wheelchair Accessible and Retail Sales.
****

Ferraro Cellar
www.ferrarocellar.com
Winery Address:
28005 NE Bell Road
Newberg, OR 97132
(503) 645-0627
Open to Public by Appointment Only.
Tasting Room:
1505 Portland RD
Newberg, OR 97132
Hours: Fri-Sat, 11am - 5pm
Tasting Fee: $4.00 (Refundable with purchase)
Tours Available:
By Appointment Only
Varieties/Wine Styles:
Cabernet Sauvignon and Merlot.
Winery Features:
Tasting Room and Retail Sales.
****

Willamette Valley Wineries, continued

Greenwood Vineyard
Winery Address:
3935 Oak Knoll Rd NW
Salem, OR 97304
(503) 399-1092
Varieties/Wine Styles:
Pinot Noir
Winery Features:
Retail Sales.
****

Hamacher Wines
www.hamacherwines.com
Winery Address:
801 North Scott St
Carlton, OR 97111
(503) 852-7200
Open to Public
Tasting Room:
Hours: 11am - 5pm
Tasting Fee: $3
Tours Available:
Frequently
Varieties/Wine Styles:
Chardonnay, Pinot Noir, Rosé of Pinot Noir and Port.
Winery Features:
Tasting Room, Picnic Area, Wheelchair Accessible and Retail Sales.
****

Hawks View Vineyards
www.hawksviesvinyard.com
(see pages 88-93)

Vineyard Address:
20175 SW Edy Road
Sherwood, OR 97140
Tel:(503) 710-1408
By Appointment Only
Tasting Room:
Hours: By appointment only.
Tasting Fee: $15.00 (Refundable with purchase)
Tours Available:
By Appointment Only
Varieties/Wine Styles:
Pinot Noir and Pinot Gris.
New Winery Features:
Tasting Room, Conference Center, Wheelchair Accessible, Retail Sales, and Wine Club.
****

Hip Chicks do Wine
www.hipchicksdowine.com
Winery Address:
4510 SE 23rd Avenue
Portland, OR 97202
(503) 234-3790
Open to Public
Tasting Room:
Hours: Daily 11am - 6pm
Tours Available:
Frequently
Varieties/Wine Styles:
Cabernet Sauvignon, Chardonnay, Gewürz-

Picture Right: *A typical lake view in western Oregon.*

Willamette Valley Wineries, continued

traminer, Merlot, Muller-Thurgau, Pinot Gris, Pinot Noir, Riesling, Syrah and Zinfandel.
Winery Features:
Tasting Room, Reception Facilities, Picnic Area, Bus/RV Parking, Wheelchair Accessible and Retail Sales.
****

J.K. Carriere Wines
www.jkcarriere.com
Winery Address:
30295 Hwy 99W
Newberg, OR 97132
(503) 554-0721
Open to Public by Appointment Only
Tours Available:
By Appointment Only
Varieties/Wine Styles:
Pinot Noir and Rosé of Pinot Noir.
Winery Features:
Bed & Breakfast, Wheelchair Accessible and Retail Sales.
****

Kramer Vineyards
www.kramerwine.com
Winery Address:
26830 NW Olson Rd
Gaston, OR 97119
(503) 662-4545
Open to Public
Tasting Room:
26830 NW Olson Road
Gaston, OR 97119
Hours: Mar-April, Fri-Sun 12pm - 5pm

Nov-Dec, Daily
Tours Available:
Frequently
Varieties/Wine Styles:
Chardonnay, Late Harvest/Dessert/Ice Wine, Merlot, Muller-Thurgau, Pinot Gris, Pinot Noir, Sparkling, Syrah, Carmine, Pinot Port and Rosé.
Certificates:
Certified Sustainable
Winery Features:
Tasting Room, Wedding Facilities, Reception Facilities, Picnic Area, Bus/RV Parking and Retail Sales.
****

Kristin Hill Winery
Winery Address:
3330 SE Amity Dayton Highway
Amity, OR 97101
(503) 835-0850
Open to Public
Tasting Room:
Hours: Daily 12pm - 5pm
Tours Available:
By Appointment Only
Varieties/Wine Styles:
Chardonnay, Gewürztraminer, Maréchal Foch, Muller-Thurgau, Pinot Gris, Pinot Noir and Sparkling.
Winery Features:
Tasting Room, Picnic Area, Bus/RV Parking and Retail Sales.
****

Lachini Vineyards
www.lachinivineyards.com
Winery Address:
18225 Calkins Lane
Newberg, OR 97132
(503) 864-4553

Open to Public by Appointment Only
Tours Available:
By Appointment Only
Varieties/Wine Styles:
Cabernet Sauvignon, Merlot, Pinot Gris and Pinot Noir.
Certificates:
Certified Sustainable
Winery Features:
Bus/RV Parking and Retail Sales.
****

Lange Estate Winery and Vineyards
www.langewinery.com
Winery Address:
18380 NE Buena Vista Drive
Dundee, OR 97115
(503) 538-6476
Open to Public
Tasting Room:
Hours: Daily 11am - 5pm
Tasting Fee: $5
Tours Available:
Frequently
Varieties/Wine Styles:
Chardonnay, Pinot Blanc, Pinot Gris and Pinot Noir.
Winery Features:
Tasting Roo, Picnic Area, Wheelchair Accessible and Retail Sales.
****

Laura Volkman Vineyards
www.volkmanvineyards.com
Winery Address:
14000 NE Quarry Rd
Newberg, OR 97132
(503) 806-4047
Open to Public by Appointment Only.
Tasting Room:

Willamette Valley Wineries,
continued

Hours: By Appointment Mon-Sat 10am - 2pm
Tasting Fee: $5 (Refundable with purchase)
Tours Available:
By Appointment Only
Varieties/Wine Styles:
Pinot Noir
Winery Features:
Tasting Room, Picnic Area, Wheelchair Accessible and Retail Sales.
****

Laurel Hood
Winery Address:
17755 N.E. Calkins Lane
Newberg, OR 97132
(503) 436-1666
Tasting Room:
263 N. Hemlock
Cannon Beach, Or 97110
Tasting Fee: $1 (Refundable with purchase)
Varieties/Wine Styles:
Pinot Gris, Pinot Noir, Tempranillo, Tinto del Pais and Tempranillo.
Winery Features:
Tasting Room and Retail Sales.
****

Lawton Winery
www.lawtonwinery.com
Winery Address:
20990 NE Kings Grade
Newberg, OR 97132
(503) 538-6509
Open to Public by Appointment Only
Tasting Room:

Hours: By Appointment Only
Tours Available:
By Appointment Only
Varieties/Wine Styles:
Pinot Noir and Riesling.
Winery Features:
Tasting Room, Picnic Area and Retail Sales.
****

Lemelson Vineyards
www.lemelsonvineyards.com
Winery Address:
12020 Ne Stag Hollow Rd
Carlton, OR 97111
503-852-6619
Open to Public by Appointment Only
Tasting Room:
Hours: By Appointment Only
Tasting Fee: $15 (Refundable with purchase)
Tours Available:
By Appointment Only
Varieties/Wine Styles:
Chardonnay, Pinot Gris, Pinot Noir and Riesling.
Certificates:
Certified Organic and Certified Sustainable
Winery Features:
Tasting Room, Wheelchair Accessible and Retail Sales.
****

Marquam Hill Vineyards
www.marquamhillvineyards.biz
Winery Address:
35803 S. Hwy 213
Molalla, OR 97038
(503) 829-6677
Open to Public
Tasting Room:
Hours: 11am - 6pm

Tasting Fee: $2.00 (Refundable with purchase)
Tours Available:
Frequently
Varieties/Wine Styles:
Cabernet Sauvignon, Chardonnay, Gewürztraminer, Late Harvest/Dessert/Ice Wine, Muller-Thurgau, Pinot Gris, Pinot Noir, Riesling, Sangiovese, Sparkling and Pinot Port.
Certificates:
Certified Sustainable
Winery Features:
Tasting Room, Wedding Facilities, Reception Facilities, Picnic Area, Bus/RV Parking, Wheelchair Accessible and Retail Sales.
****

Maysara Winery
www.maysara.com
Winery Address:
15765 SW Muddy Valley Rd
McMinnville, OR 97128
(503) 843-1234
Open to Public
Tasting Room:
Hours: Tue-Sat, 12pm - 5pm
Tasting Fee: $5 (Refundable with purchase)
Tours Available:
By Appointment Only
Varieties/Wine Styles:
Pinot Blanc, Pinot Gris and Pinot Noir.
Certificates:
Certified Biodynamic
Winery Features:
Tasting Room, Wedding Facilities, Reception Facilities, Picnic Area, Bus/RV Parking, Wheelchair Accessible and Retail Sales.
****

Picture Following Page: *Willamette Valley in the fall.*

Willamette Valley Wineries,
continued

Medici Vineyards
Winery Address:
28005 NE Bell Rd
Newberg, OR 97132
(503) 538-9668
Open to Public by Appointment Only
Tasting Room:
1505 Portland RD
Newberg, OR 97132
Hours: Thu-Sat, 11am - 5pm
Tasting Fee: $4 (Refundable with purchase)
Tours Available:
By Appointment Only
Varieties/Wine Styles:
Pinot Noir and Riesling.
Winery Features:
Tasting Room and Retail Sales.
****

Monks Gate
www.monksgate.com
Winery Address:
9500 NE Oak Springs Farm Rd
Carlton, OR 97111
(503) 852-6521
Open to Public by Appointment Only
Tasting Room:
Hours: By Appointment Only
Tasting Fee: $8 (Refundable with purchase)
Tours Available:
By Appointment Only
Varieties/Wine Styles:
Pinot Noir
Winery Features:

Tasting Room, Picnic Area, Wheelchair Accessible and Retail Sales.
****

Montinore Estate
www.montinore.com
Winery Address:
3663 SW Dilley RD
Forest Grove, OR 97116
(503) 359-5012
Open to Public
Tours Available:
By Appointment Only
Varieties/Wine Styles:
Gewürztraminer, Late Harvest/Dessert/Ice Wine, Muller-Thurgau, Pinot Gris, Pinot Noir and Riesling.
Winery Features:
Tasting Room, Picnic Area, Bus/RV Parking, Wheelchair Accessible and Retail Sales.
****

Natalie's Estate Winery
www.nataliesestatewinery.com
Winery Address:
16825 N.E. Chehalem Drive
Newberg, OR 97132
(503) 554-9350
Open to Public by Appointment Only
Tasting Room:
Hours: By Appointment Only
Tours Available:
Frequently
Varieties/Wine Styles:
Cabernet Sauvignon, Chardonnay, Merlot, Pinot Noir, Syrah, Viognier and Zinfandel.
Winery Features:
Tasting Room, Reception Facilities and Retail Sales.
****

Oak Knoll Winery
www.oakknollwinery.com
Winery Address:
29700 SW Burkhalter Rd
Hillsboro, OR 97123
(503) 648-8198
Open to Public
Tasting Room:
Hours: Fall,Winter, Daily 11am - 5pm
Springer,Summer, Mon-Fri 11am - 6pm, Sat-Sun 11am - 5pm
Tours Available:
By Appointment Only
Varieties/Wine Styles:
Chardonnay, Fruit, Gewürztraminer, Muller-Thurgau, Pinot Gris, Pinot Noir, Riesling, Niagara and Twilight Blush.
Winery Features:
Tasting Room, Wedding Facilities, Reception Faculties, Picnic Area, Bus/RV Parking, Wheelchair Accessible and Retail Sales.
****

Panther Creek
www.panthercreekcellars.com
Winery Address:
455 NE Irvine
McMinnville, OR 97128
(503) 472-8080
Open to Public
Tasting Room:
Hours: Wen-Sun 12pm - 5pm
Tasting Fee: $5 (Refundable with purchase)
Tours Available:
Frequently
Varieties/Wine Styles:
Melon de Bourgogne (Muscadet), Pinot Gris and Pinot Noir.
Winery Features:

Willamette Valley Wineries,
continued

Tasting Room, Bus/RV Parking, Wheelchair Accessible and Retail Sales.
****

Paradis Family Vineyards
www.paradiswine.com
Winery Address:
17267 Abiqua Rd NE
Silverton, OR 97381
(503) 873-8475
Open to Public by Appointment Only
Tasting Room:
Hours: 2nd Saturday each month, varies.
Tours Available:
By Appointment Only
Varieties/Wine Styles:
Muscat, Pinot Gris and Pinot Noir.
Certificates:
Certified Sustainable
Winery Features:
Tasting Room, Picnic Area, Bus/RV Parking, Wheelchair Accessible and Retail Sales.
****

Penner-Ash Wine Cellars
www.pennerash.com
Winery Address:
15771 NE Ribbon Ridge Rd
Newberg, OR 97132
(503) 554-5545
Open to Public
Tasting Room:
Hours: Fri-Sun, 11am - 5pm
Tasting Fee: $5 (Refundable with purchase)
Tours Available:

By Appointment Only
Varieties/Wine Styles:
Pinot Noir, Syrah and Viognier.
Certificates:
Certified Sustainable
Winery Features:
Tasting Room, Picnic Area, Wheelchair Accessible and Retail Sales.
****

Ponzi Vineyards
www.ponziwines.com
Winery Address:
14665 SW Winery Lane
Beaverton, OR 97007
(503) 628-1227
Open to Public
Tasting Room:
Hours: 11am - 5pm
Tasting Fee: $Varies
Additional Tasting Room:
100 SW Seventh Street
Dundee, OR 97115
Tours Available:
Frequently
Varieties/Wine Styles:
Arneis, Chardonnay, Dolcetto, Late Harvest/Dessert/Ice Wine, Pinot Blanc, Pinot Gris, Pinot Noir and Riesling.
Certificates:
Certified Sustainable
Winery Features:
Tasting Room, Second Tasting Room, Wedding Facilities, Reception Facilities, Picnic Area, Bus/RV Parking, Wheelchair Accessible and Retail Sales.
****

R. Stuart & Co.
www.rstuartandco.com
Winery Address:
845 NE Fifth St
McMinnville, OR 97128
(503) 472-6990
Open to Public
Tasting Room:
Hours: Daily, 11am - 5pm
Tours Available:
By Appointment Only
Varieties/Wine Styles:
Pinot Gris, Pinot Noir and Sparkling.
Winery Features:
Tasting Room, Bus/RV Parking, Wheelchair Accessible and Retail Sales.
****

Redhawk Winery
www.redhawkwine.com
Winery Address:
2995 Michigan City Ln NW
Salem, OR 97304
(503) 362-1596
Open to Public
Tasting Room:
Hours: Daily 11am - 5pm
Tours Available:
By Appointment Only
Varieties/Wine Styles:
Cabernet Sauvignon, Chardonnay, Dolcetto, Merlot, Pinot Gris, Pinot Noir, Riesling and Syrah.
Winery Features:
Tasting Room, Wedding Facilities, Reception Facilities, Picnic Area, Bus/RV Parking, Wheelchair Accessible and Retail Sales.
****

Willamette Valley Wineries,
continued

Rex Hill Vineyards
www.rexhill.com

Winery Address:
30835 N Hwy 99W
Newberg, OR 97132
(503) 538-0666
Open to Public
Tasting Room:
Hours: 11am - 5pm, Summer 10am - 5pm
Tasting Fee: $10
Tours Available:
By Appointment Only
Varieties/Wine Styles:
Chardonnay , Pinot Gris and Pinot Noir.
Certificates:
Certified Sustainable
Winery Features:
Tasting Room, Picnic Area, Wheelchair Accessible and Retail Sales.
****

Ribbon Ridge Vineyard
www.ribbonridge.com

Winery Address:
801 N Scott St
Carlton, OR 97111
(503) 502-5255
Open to Public
Tasting Room:
Carlton Winemakers Studio
Carlton, OR 97111
Hours: 11am - 5pm
Tasting Fee: $
Tours Available:

Frequently
Varieties/Wine Styles:
Muscat, Pinot Gris and Pinot Noir.
Winery Features:
Tasting Room, Bus/RV Parking, Wheelchair Accessible and Retail Sales.
****

Ruby Carbiener
www.rcvineyards.com

Winery Address:
14135 NW Timmerman Rd
Forest Grove, OR 97116
(503) 524-5663
Open to Public
Tasting Room:
Hours: Fri-Sun, 12am - 5pm
Tours Available:
By Appointment Only
Varieties/Wine Styles:
Chardonnay, Pinot Gris, Pinot Noir and Maréchal Foch.
Certificates:
Certified Sustainable
Winery Features:
Tasting Room, Wedding Facilities, Reception Facilities, Picnic Area, Bus/RV Parking, Wheelchair Accessible and Retail Sales.
****

SakéOne
www.sakeone.com

Winery Address:
820 Elm St
Forest Grove, OR 97116
(503) 357-7056
Open to Public
Tasting Room:
Hours: Daily, 12am - 5pm
Tasting Fee: $3

Tours Available:
Frequently
Varieties/Wine Styles:
Nigori Genshu, Nama, Genshu and Fruit Flavor Infused.
Winery Features:
Tasting Room, Wedding Facilities, Reception Facilities, Picnic Area, Bus/RV Parking, Wheelchair Accessible and Retail Sales.
****

Sass Winery / Wild Winds Winery

Winery Address:
9092 Jackson Hill Rd SE
Salem, OR 97306
(503) 391-9991
Open to Public by Appointment Only
Tours Available:
By Appointment Only
Varieties/Wine Styles:
Chardonnay, Gewürztraminer, Pinot Blanc, Pinot Gris and Pinot Noir.
Winery Features:
Wedding Facilities, Bus/RV Parking, Wheelchair Accessible and Retail Sales.
****

Scott Paul Wines
www.scottpaul.com

Winery Address:
128 S. Pine St.
Carlton, OR 97111
(503) 852-7300
Open to Public
Tasting Room:
Hours: Wen-Sun, 11am - 4pm
Tasting Fee: $5 (Refundable with purchase)
Tours Available:
By Appointment Only
Varieties/Wine Styles:

Willamette Valley Wineries, continued

Pinot Noir
Winery Features:
Tasting Room, Wheelchair Accessible and
Retail Sales.
****

Shafer Vineyard Cellars
www.shafervineyardcellars.com
Winery Address:
6200 NW Gales Creek Rd
Forest Grove, OR 97116
(503) 357-6604
Open to Public
Tasting Room:
Hours: April-Dec, Daily 11am - 5pm
Tours Available:
By Appointment Only
Varieties/Wine Styles:
Chardonnay, Gewürztraminer, Late Harvest/
Dessert/Ice Wine, Muller-Thurgau, Pinot Gris,
Pinot Noir, Riesling, Sauvignon Blanc and
Sparkling.
Winery Features:
Tasting Room, Wedding Facilities, Reception
Facilities, Picnic Area, Bus/RV Parking, Wheel-
chair Accessible and Retail Sales.
****

Sokol Blosser Winery
www.sokolblosser.com
(see pages 100-105)
Winery Address:
5000 NE Sokol Blosser Ln
Dayton, OR 97114
(503) 864-2282

Open to Public
Tasting Room:
Hours: 10am - 4pm
Tasting Fee: $5-15
Tours Available:
By Appointment Only
Varieties/Wine Styles:
Late Harvest/Dessert/Ice Wine, Muller-Thur-
gau, Pinot Gris, Pinot Noir and Late Harvest
Riesling.
Certificates:
Certified Organic and Certified Sustainable
Winery Features:
Tasting Room, Picnic Area, Bus/RV Parking,
Wheelchair Accessible and Retail Sales.
****

Solena Cellars
www.solenacellars.com
Winery Address:
2803 Orchard Avenue
McMinnville, OR 97128
(503) 852-0082
Open to Public by Appointment Only
Tasting Room:
213 South Pine Street
Carlton, OR 97111
Hours: Thu-Sun, 12pm - 5pm; Daily by appoint-
ment.
Tours Available:
By Appointment Only
Varieties/Wine Styles:
Cabernet Sauvignon, Merlot, Pinot Gris, Pinot
Noir, Syrah and Zinfandel.
Winery Features:
Tasting Room, Wheelchair Accessible and
Retail Sales.
****

Soter Vineyards
www.sotervineyards.com
Winery Address:
10880 Mineral Springs Rd
Carlton, OR 97111
(503) 662-5600
Open to Public by Appointment Only.
Tasting Room:
Tasting Fee: $20 (Refundable with purchase)
Hours: Weekdays, by advance appointment
only
Tours Available:
By Appointment Only
Varieties/Wine Styles:
Cabernet Franc, Pinot Noir and Sparkling.
Certificates:
Certified Sustainable
Winery Features:
Tasting Room and Retail Sales.
****

St. Innocent Winery
www.stinnocentwine.com
Winery Address:
1360 Tandem Ave. NE
Salem, OR 97303
(503) 378-1526
Open to Public
Tasting Room:
Hours: Weekends, 12pm - 5pm
Tours Available:
By Appointment Only
Varieties/Wine Styles:
Chardonnay, Pinot Blanc, Pinot Gris and Pinot
Noir.
Certificates:
Certified Biodynamic and Certified Sustainable
Winery Features:
Tasting Room, Bus/RV Parking, Wheelchair Ac-

cessible and Retail Sales.
****

Stag Hollow Wines
www.staghollow.com
Winery Address:
7930 NE Blackburn Rd
Yamhill, OR 97148
(503) 662-5609
Open to Public by Appointment Only.
Tasting Room:
Hours: By Appointment Only
Tasting Fee: $5 (Refundable with purchase)
Tours Available:
By Appointment Only
Varieties/Wine Styles:
Chardonnay, Dolcetto, Lemberger, Muscat, Pinot Noir and Tempranillo.
Winery Features:
Tasting Room, Wheelchair Accessible and Retail Sales.
****

Stoller
www.stollervineyards.com
Winery Address:
16161 NE McDougall Rd.
Dayton, OR 97114
(503) 864-3404
Open to Public by Appointment Only
Tasting Room:
Hours: By Appointment Only

Picture Left: *Rolling hills of the Willamette Valley.* **Preceding Picture:** *Landscape shot from west Oregon.*

Tasting Fee: $10
Varieties/Wine Styles:
Chardonnay and Pinot Noir.
Winery Features:
Tasting Room, Picnic Area, Bus/RV Parking, Wheelchair Accessible and Retail Sales.
****

Stone Wolf Vineyards and Mystic Mountain Vineyards
www.stonewolfvineyards.com
Winery Address:
2155 NE Lafayette Ave
McMinnville, OR 97128
(503) 434-9025
Open to Public
Tasting Room:
Hours: Daily, 2pm - 5pm
Tasting Fee: $2 (Refundable with purchase)
Tours Available:
By Appointment Only
Varieties/Wine Styles:
Chardonnay, Muller-Thurgau, Pinot Gris and Pinot Noir.
Winery Features:
Tasting Room, Picnic Area, Bus/RV Parking, Wheelchair Accessible and Retail.
****

The Coastal Vineyard
www.thecostvineyard.com
Winery Address:
5917 Orchard Heights Rd NW
Salem, OR 97304
(503) 922-3549
Varieties/Wine Styles:
Pinot Noir
Winery Features:
Retail Sales.
****

The Eyrie Vineyards
www.eyrievineyards.com
Winery Address:
935 NE 10th Ave.
McMinnville, OR 97128
(503) 472-6315
Open to Public
Tasting Room:
Hours: Tue-Sat 11am - 4pm
Tasting Fee: $5
Tours Available:
By Appointment Only
Varieties/Wine Styles:
Chardonnay, Pinot Blanc, Pinot Gris, Pinot Meunier, Pinot Noir and Muscat Ottonel.
Winery Features:
Tasting Room, Wheelchair Accessible and Retail Sales.
****

The Four Graces
www.thefourgraces.com
Winery Address:
9605 NE Fox Farm Road
Dundee, OR 97115
(503) 554-8000
Open to Public
Tasting Room:
Hours: Wen-Sun 11am - 5pm
Tasting Fee: $10
Tours Available:
By Appointment Only
Varieties/Wine Styles:
Pinot Blanc, Pinot Gris and Pinot Noir.
Winery Features:
Tasting Room, Picnic Area, Bus/RV Parking, Wheelchair Accessible and Retail Sales.
****

Willamette **V**alley **W**ineries, continued

Torii Mor Vineyard & Winery
www.toriimorwinery.com
(see pages 58-63)

Winery Address:
18325 NE Fairview Dr
Dundee, OR 97115
(503) 554-0105
Open to Public
Tasting Room:
Hours: Daily 11am - 5pm
Tasting Fee: $5
Varieties/Wine Styles:
Chardonnay, Pinot Blanc, Pinot Gris, Pinot Noir, Port and Late Harvest Gewürztraminer.
Winery Features:
Tasting Room, Picnic Area, Wheelchair Accessible and Retail Sales.
****

Twelve Wine
www.twelvewine.com
Winery Address:
12401 NW Fir Crest Rd
Carlton, OR 97111
(503) 358-6707
Open to Public by Appointment Only
Tours Available:
By Appointment Only
Varieties/Wine Styles:
Pinot Blanc and Pinot Noir.
Winery Features:
Retail Sales.
****

Van Duzer Vineyards
www.vanduzer.com
Winery Address:
11975 Smithfield Rd
Dallas, OR 97338
(800) 884-1927
Open to Public
Tasting Room:
Hours: March-Dec, Daily, 11am - 5pm
Tours Available:
By Appointment Only
Varieties/Wine Styles:
Pinot Gris and Pinot Noir.
Certificates:
Certified Sustainable
Winery Features:
Tasting Room, Picnic Area, Wheelchair Accessible and Retail Sales.
****

Vidon Vineyard
www.vidonvineyard.com
Winery Address:
17425 NE Hillside Drive
Newberg, OR 97132
(503) 538-4092
Open to Public by Appointment Only
Tasting Room:
Hours: By Appointment Only
Tasting Fee: $5 (Refundable with purchase)
Tours Available:
By Appointment Only
Varieties/Wine Styles:
Pinot Noir
Winery Features:
Tasting Room, Picnic Area, Wheelchair Accessible and Retail Sales.
****

Walnut City Wineworks
www.walnutcitywineworks.com
Winery Address:
475 NE 17th Street
McMinnville, OR 97128
(503) 472-3215
Open to Public by Appointment Only
Tasting Room:
Hours: Thu-Sun, 11am - 4.30pm
Tasting Fee: $5 (Refundable with purchase)
Tours Available:
By Appointment Only
Varieties/Wine Styles:
Cabernet Sauvignon, Late Harvest/Dessert/Ice Wine, Pinot Gris, Pinot Noir and Viognier.
Winery Features:
Tasting Room, Wheelchair Accessible and Retail Sales.
****

WildAire Cellars
www.wildairecellars.com
Winery Address:
14000 NE Quarry Rd (inside August Cellars)
Newberg, OR 97132
(503) 851-3689
Open to Public
Tours Available:
By Appointment Only
Varieties/Wine Styles:
Pinot Noir
Winery Features:
Picnic Area, Bus/RV Parking, Wheelchair Accessible and Retail Sales.
****

Picture Right: *Winter falls in the Willamette Valley.*
Picture Following Page: *A view from Torii Mor's terrace over looking their estate vineyard and the Willamette Valley.*

Willamette Valley Wineries, continued

Willakenzie Estate
www.willakenzie.com
Winery Address:
19143 NE Laughlin Road
Yamhill, OR 97148
(503) 662-3280
Open to Public
Tasting Room:
Hours: May-Oct, Daily 12pm - 5pm
Nov-Apr, Fri-Sun 12pm - 5pm or by appointment.
Tours Available:
By Appointment Only
Varieties/Wine Styles:
Gamay Noir, Late Harvest/Dessert/Ice Wine, Pinot Blanc, Pinot Gris, Pinot Meunier and Pinot Noir.
Certificates:
Certified Sustainable
Winery Features:
Tasting Room, Picnic Area, Bus/RV Parking, Wheelchair Accessible and Retail Sales.
****

Willamette Valley Vineyards
www.willamettevalleyvineyards.com
(see pages 64-69)
Winery Address:
8800 Enchanted Way SE
Turner, OR 97392
(503) 588-9463
Open to Public
Tasting Room:
Tasting Fee: Complimentary Tasting & $5 Re-

serve includes free Riedel wine glas.
Hours: Daily, 11am - 6pm, except major holidays.
Additional Tasting Room:
Tualatin Estates, 10850 NW Seavey Road
Forest Grove, OR 97392
Tours Available:
By Appointment Only
Varieties/Wine Styles:
Cabernet Franc, Cabernet Sauvignon, Chardonnay, Gewürztraminer, Late Harvest/Dessert/Ice Wine, Malbec, Merlot, Muscat, Pinot Blanc, Pinot Gris, Pinot Noir, Riesling, Sauvignon Blanc, Syrah, Tempranillo and Viognier.
Certificates:
Certified Sustainable
Winery Features:
Tasting Room, Second Tasting Room, Wedding Facilities, Reception Facilities, Picnic Area, Bus/RV Parking, Wheelchair Accessible and Retail Sales.
****

Wine Country Farm Cellars
www.winecountryfarm.com
Winery Address:
6855 Breyman Orchards Road
Dayton, OR 97114
(503) 864-3446
Open to Public
Tasting Room:
Hours: Daily, 11am - 5pm
Tours Available:
Frequently
Varieties/Wine Styles:
Chardonnay, Merlot, Muller-Thurgau, Pinot Noir, Riesling and Sauvignon Blanc.
Winery Features:
Tasting Room, Wedding Facilities, Reception

Facilities, Bed & Breakfast, Picnic Area, Bus/RV Parking, Wheelchair Accessible and Retail Sales.
****

Winter's Hill Vineyard
www.wintershillwine.com
Winery Address:
6451 NE Hilltop Road
Dayton, OR 97114
(503) 864-4610
Open to Public
Tasting Room:
Hours: Daily, 12am - 5pm
Tours Available:
By Appointment Only
Varieties/Wine Styles:
Late Harvest/Dessert/Ice Wine, Muscat, Pinot Blanc, Pinot Gris and Pinot Noir.
Certificates:
Certified Sustainable
Winery Features:
Tasting Room, Picnic Area, Bus/RV Parking, Wheelchair Accessible and Retail Sales.
****

Witness Tree Vineyard
www.witnesstreevineyard.com
Winery Address:
7111 Spring Valley Road NW
Salem, OR 97304
(503) 585-7874
Open to Public
Tasting Room:
Hours: Summer, Tue-Sun 11am - 5pm and all weekends all year long.
Tours Available:
Frequently
Varieties/Wine Styles:
Chardonnay, Dolcetto, Late Harvest/Dessert/

Ice Wine, Pinot Blanc, Pinot Noir and Viognier.
Certificates:
Certified Sustainable
Winery Features:
Tasting Room, Picnic Area, Wheelchair Accessible and Retail Sales.
****

Belle Vallee Cellars
www.bellevallee.com

Winery Address:
804 NW Buchanan Ave
Corvallis, OR 97330
(541) 757-9463
Open to Public by Appointment Only
Tours Available:
By Appointment Only
Varieties/Wine Styles:
Cabernet Franc, Cabernet Sauvignon, Merlot, Pinot Gris, Pinot Noir, Syrah and Carmenere.
Winery Features:
Bus/RV Parking, Wheelchair Accessible and Retail.
****

Benton-Lane Winery
www.benton-lane.com

Winery Address:
23924 Territorial Hwy
Monroe, OR 97456
(541) 847-5792
Tasting Room:
Hours: Weekdays 12pm - 4.30pm, Weekends March-Nov 11am - 5pm
Tours Available:
By Appointment Only
Varieties/Wine Styles:
Pinot Blanc, Pinot Gris, Pinot Noir and Pinot Noir Rosé.
Certificates:

Certified Sustainable
Winery Features:
Tasting Room, Picnic Area, Bus/RV Parking, Wheelchair Accessible and Retail Sales.
****

Bishop Creek Cellars
www.urbanwineworks.com

Winery Address:
100 S. College St.
Newberg, OR 97132
(503) 550-7700
Open to Public
Tasting Room:
407 NW 16th
Portland, OR 97209
Tasting Fee: average of $7
Hours: Daily 12pm - 8.30pm, Sun to 6pm
Additional Tasting Room:
777 MLK Jr. Blvd (Oregon Convention Center)
Portland, OR 97232
Tours Available:
Frequently
Varieties/Wine Styles:
Pinot Gris and Pinot Noir
Certificates:
Certified Organic and Certified Sustainable.
Winery Features:
Tasting Room, Second Tasting Room, Wedding Facilities, Reception Facilities, Wheelchair Accessible and Retail.
****

Chateau Lorane
www.chateaulorane.com

Winery Address:
27415 Siuslaw River Road
Lorane, OR 97451
(541) 942-8028
Open to Public

Tasting Room:
Hours: Daily 12pm - 5pm
Varieties/Wine Styles:
Baco Noir (hybrid), Cabernet Franc, Cabernet Sauvignon, Chardonnay, Gamay Noir, Gewürztraminer, Late Harvest/Dessert/Ice Wine, Malbec, Maréchal Foch, Melon de Bourgogne (Muscadet), Merlot, Pinot Blanc, Pinot Gris, Pinot Meunier, Pinot Noir, Riesling, Sauvignon Blanc, Syrah, Tempranillo, Viognier, Zinfandel, Huxelrebe (crossing between Chasselas and Courtillier Musque), Niagara (crossing between Concord and Cassady), Grand Noir, Leon Millot, Durif and fruit meads.
Winery Features:
Tasting Room, Wedding Facilities, Reception Facilities, Picnic Area, Bus/RV Parking, Wheelchair Accessible and Retail.
****

Eugene Wine Cellars
www.eugenewinecellars.com

Winery Address:
255 Madison St
Eugene, OR 97402
(541) 342-2600
Open to Public by Appointment Only
Tasting Room:
Hours: By Appointment Only
Tours Available:
By Appointment Only
Varieties/Wine Styles:
Chardonnay, Pinot Gris, Pinot Noir and Viognier.
Winery Features:
Tasting Room, Wedding Facilities, Reception Facilities, Bus/RV Parking and Retail Sales.
****

Willamette Valley Wineries,
continued

Harris Bridge Vineyard
www.harrisbridgevineyard.com
Winery Address:
22937 Harris Rd
Philomath, OR 97370
(541) 929-3053
Open to Public
Tasting Room:
Tasting Fee: $
Tours Available:
Frequently
Varieties/Wine Styles:
Late Harvest/Dessert/Ice Wine, Pinot Gris and
Pinot Noir.
Winery Features:
Tasting Room, Wedding Facilities, Reception
Facilities, Picnic Area, Wheelchair Accessible
and Retail Sales.
****

Iris Hill Winery
www.irishill.com
Winery Address:
82110 Territorial Road
Eugene, OR 97405
(541) 345-1617
Open to Public
Tasting Room:
Tasting Fee: $5 (Refundable with purchase)
Hours: Thu-Sun, 12pm - 5pm
Tours Available:
Frequently
Varieties/Wine Styles:
Chardonnay, Pinot Gris and Pinot Noir.

Certificates:
Certified Sustainable
Winery Features:
Tasting Room, Wedding Facilities, Reception
Facilities, Picnic Area, Bus/RV Parking, Wheel-
chair Accessible and Retail Sales.
****

King Estate
www.kingestate.com
(see pages 118-125)
Winery Address:
80854 Territorial Rd
Eugene, OR 97405
(541) 942-9874
Open to Public
Tasting Room:
Tasting Fee: $Varies (Refundable with pur-
chase)
Hours: Sun-Thu 11am - 7pm, Fri-Sat 11am
- 8pm
Tours Available:
Frequently
Varieties/Wine Styles:
Chardonnay, Late Harvest/Dessert/Ice Wine ,
Pinot Gris and Pinot Noir.
Certificates:
Certified Organic
Winery Features:
Tasting Room, Picnic Area, Bus/RV Parking,
Wheelchair Accessible and Retail.
****

LaVelle Vineyards
www.lavelle-vineyards.com
Winery Address:
89697 Sheffler Rd
Elmira, OR 97437

Picture Right: *Fall in the Willamette Valley.*

Willamette Valley Wineries,

Open to Public
Tasting Room:
Hours: Daily 12pm - 5pm
Tours Available:
By Appointment Only
Varieties/Wine Styles:
Cabernet Sauvignon, Chardonnay, Gamay Noir,
Merlot , Pinot Gris, Pinot Noir, Riesling and
Sparkling.
Winery Features:
Tasting Room, Second Tasting Room Wedding
Facilities, Reception Facilities, Picnic Area,
Wheelchair Accessible and Retail.
****

Pfeiffer Vineyards
www.villaevenings.com
Winery Address:
25040 Jaeg Rd
Junction City, OR 97448
(541) 998-2828
Open to Public
Tasting Room:
Hours: Weekends, 12pm - 5pm
Tours Available:
Frequently
Varieties/Wine Styles:
Chardonnay, Merlot, Pinot Gris and Pinot Noir.
Winery Features:
Tasting Room, Wedding Facilities, Reception
Facilities Picnic Area, Bus/RV Parking, Wheel-
chair Accessible and Retail.
****

Picture Left: *Harvest time.*

Willamette **V**alley **W**ineries,
continued

Pheasant Court Winery
www.pheasantcourtwinery.com
Winery Address:
1301 Main Street
Philomath, OR 97370
(541) 929-7715
Open to Public by Appointment Only
Tasting Room:
Hours: Sat-Sun 12pm - 6pm
Tours Available:
By Appointment Only
Varieties/Wine Styles:
Chardonnay, Maréchal Foch, Merlot, Pinot Gris, Pinot Noir, Viognier, Maréchal Foch and Port.
Winery Features:
Tasting Room and Retail.
****

Saginaw Vineyard
www.saginawvineyard.com
Winery Address:
80247 Delight Valley School Rd
Cottage Grove, OR 97424
(541) 942-1364
Open to Public
Tasting Room:
Hours: Wed-Sun, 11am - 5pm
Tours Available:
By Appointment Only
Varieties/Wine Styles:
Chardonnay, Maréchal Foch, Pinot Gris and Pinot Noir.
Winery Features:

Tasting Room, Reception Facilities, Picnic Area, Bus/RV Parking, Wheelchair Accessible and Retail Sales.
****

Secret House Winery
www.secrethousewinery.com
Winery Address:
88324 Vineyard Lane
Veneta, OR 97487
(541) 935-3774
Open to Public
Tasting Room:
Hours: 11am - 5pm, Call for winter hours.
Varieties/Wine Styles:
Cabernet Sauvignon, Muller-Thurgau, Pinot Gris, Pinot Noir, Riesling, Sparkling and White Pinot Noir (Blush).
Winery Features:
Tasting Room, Wedding Facilities, Reception Facilities, Picnic Area, Bus/RV Parking, Wheelchair Accessible and Retail Sales.
****

Silvan Ridge-Hinman Vineyards
www.silvanridge.com
Winery Address:
27012 Briggs Hill Rd
Eugene, OR 97405
(541) 345-1945
Open to Public
Tasting Room:
Hours: Daily, 12pm - 5pm
Tasting Fee: $some (Refundable with purchase)
Varieties/Wine Styles:
Cabernet Sauvignon, Chardonnay, Merlot, Muscat , Pinot Gris, Pinot Noir, Riesling, Syrah, Viognier and Early Muscat Semi-Sparkling.
Winery Features:

Tasting Room, Wedding Facilities, Reception Facilities, Picnic Area, Bus/RV Parking, Wheelchair Accessible and Retail Sales.
****

Spindrift Cellars
www.spindriftcellars.com
Winery Address:
810 Applegate St
Philomath, OR 97370
(541) 929-6555
Open to Public
Tasting Room:
Hours: Saturdays 12pm - 5pm
Tours Available:
Frequently
Varieties/Wine Styles:
Chardonnay, Pinot Blanc, Pinot Gris and Pinot Noir.
Certificates:
Certified Sustainable
Winery Features:
Tasting Room, Wedding Facilities, Reception Facilities, Picnic Area, Bus/RV Parking, Wheelchair Accessible and Retail Sales.
****

Sweet Cheeks Winery
www.sweetcheekswinery.com
Winery Address:
27007 Briggs Hill Rd
Eugene, OR 97405
(541) 349-9463
Open to Public
Tasting Room:
Hours: Daily, 12pm - 6pm
Tours Available:
Frequently
Varieties/Wine Styles:
Chardonnay, Pinot Gris, Pinot Noir, Riesling

and Sparkling.
Winery Features:
Tasting Room, Wedding Facilities, Reception Facilities, Picnic Area, Bus/RV Parking, Wheelchair Accessible and Retail.
****

Tyee Wine Cellars
www.tyeewine.com
Winery Address:
26335 Greenberry Road
Corvallis, OR 97333
(541) 753-8754
Open to Public
Tasting Room:
Hours: Weekends, Apr-Dec, Daily in Summer, 12pm - 5pm
Tours Available:
By Appointment Only
Varieties/Wine Styles:
Chardonnay, Gewürztraminer, Pinot Blanc, Pinot Gris and Pinot Noir.
Certificates:
Certified Sustainable
Winery Features:
Tasting Room, Wedding Facilities, Reception Facilities, Picnic Area, Bus/RV Parking, Wheelchair Accessible and Retail Sales.
****

Agate Ridge Vineyard
www.agateridgevineyard.com
Winery Address:
1098 Nick Young Rd.
Eagle Point, OR 97524

(541) 830-3050
Open to Public
Tasting Room:
Hours: Tue-Sun 11am - 5pm
Varieties/Wine Styles:
Cabernet Franc, Cabernet Sauvignon, Chardonnay, Grenache, Malbec, Pinot Gris, Pinot Noir, Semillon, Sauvignon Blanc, Syrah, Viognier, Zinfandel, Marsanne and Roussanne.
Winery Features:
Tasting Room, Picnic Area, Bus/RV Parking and Retail Sales.
****

Bridgeview Vineyards
www.bridgeviewwine.com
Winery Address:
4210 Holland Loop Road
Cave Junction, OR 97523
(541) 592-4688
Open to Public
Additional Tasting Room:
16995 N. Applegate Road
Grants Pass, OR 97527
Tours Available:
By Appointment Only
Varieties/Wine Styles:
Cabernet Franc, Cabernet Sauvignon, Chardonnay, Gewürztraminer, Late Harvest/Dessert/Ice Wine, Merlot, Muller-Thurgau, Muscat, Pinot Gris, Pinot Noir, Riesling and Syrah.
Winery Features:
Tasting Room, Second Tasting Room, Picnic Area, Bus/RV Parking, Wheelchair Accessible and Retail Sales.
****

Cricket Hill Winery
www.crickethillwinery.com
Winery Address:

2131 little Applegate Rd
Jacksonville, OR 97530
(541) 899-7264
Open to Public by Appointment Only
Tours Available:
By Appointment Only
Varieties/Wine Styles:
Cabernet Franc, Claret and Merlot.
Winery Features:
Retail Sales.
****

Del Rio Vineyards
www.delriovineyards.com
(see pages 130-135)
Winery Address:
52 N. River Road
Gold Hill, OR 97525
(541) 855-1212
Open to Public
Tasting Room:
Tasting Fee: $5
Hours: Daily, 11am - 5pm. Summer; 11am - 6pm
Tours Available:
By Appointment Only
Varieties/Wine Styles:
Cabernet Franc, Cabernet Sauvignon, Chardonnay, Claret, Merlot, Muscat, Pinot Gris, Syrah and Viognier.
Winery Features:
Tasting Room, Wedding Facilities, Reception Facilities, Picnic Area, Bus/RV Parking, Wheelchair Accessible and Retail Sales.

Picture Preceding Page: A view of Mt. Hood from Columbia Gorge.
Picture Right: Climatic condition in the Willamette Valley.

Willamette Valley Wineries, <br> continued

****

Devitt Winery
www.devittwinery.com

(see pages 136-141)

Winery Address:
11412 Hwy 238
Jacksonville, OR 97530
(541) 899-7511
Open to Public
Tasting Room:
Hours: Daily 11am - 5pm
Tours Available:
Frequently
Varieties/Wine Styles:
Cabernet Franc, Cabernet Sauvignon, Chardonnay, Merlot, Pinot Noir, Sangiovese, Syrah, Tempranillo, Viognier and Zinfandel.
Certificates:
Certified Sustainable
Winery Features:
Tasting Room, Picnic Area, Bus/RV Parking, Wheelchair Accessible and Retail Sales.

****

Folin Cellars
www.folincellars.com

Winery Address:
9468 Ramsey Rd
Gold Hill, OR 97525

Picture Left: *A fall sunset in the Willamette Valley.*

(541) 855-1838
Open to Public by Appointment Only
Tours Available:
By Appointment Only
Varieties/Wine Styles:
Grenache, Syrah, Tempranillo, Viognier,
Mourvedre and Petite Sirah.
Winery Features:
Retail Sales.
****

Foris Vineyards Winery
www.foriswine.com
Winery Address:
654 Kendall Rd
Cave Junction, OR 97523
(541) 592-3752
Open to Public
Tours Available:
Frequently
Varieties/Wine Styles:
Cabernet Franc, Cabernet Sauvignon, Chardonnay, Claret, Gewürztraminer, Grenache,
Merlot, Muscat, Pinot Blanc, Pinot Gris, Pinot
Noir and Sparkling.
Winery Features:
Tasting Room, Picnic Area, Wheelchair Accessible and Retail.
****

LongSword Vineyard
www.longswordvineyard.com
Winery Address:
8555 Hwy 238
Jacksonville, OR 97530

(541) 899-1746
Open to Public
Tasting Room:
Hours: 12pm - 5pm
Tours Available:
Frequently
Varieties/Wine Styles:
Chardonnay
Winery Features:
Tasting Room, Picnic Area, Wheelchair Accessible and Retail Sales.
****

Mardrone Mountain
www.madronemountain.com
Winery Address:
540 Tumbleweed Trail
Jacksonville, OR 97530
(541) 899-9642
Open to Public by Appointment Only
Varieties/Wine Styles:
Late Harvest/Dessert/Ice Wine
Winery Feature:
Retail Sales.
****

Naked Winery
www.nakedwinery.com
Winery Address:
2260 Riverdale Road
Hood River, OR 97031
(800) 666-9303
Open to Public by Appointment Only
Tours Available:
By Appointment Only
Varieties/Wine Styles:
Cabernet Sauvignon, Chardonnay, Merlot,
Pinot Gris, Sangiovese and Syrah.
****

RoxyAnn Winery
www.roxyann.com
Winery Address:
3285 Hillcrest Rd
Medford, OR 97504
(541) 776-2315
Open to Public
Tasting Room:
Tasting Fee: $3 (Refundable with purchase)
Hours: 11am - 6pm
Varieties/Wine Styles:
Cabernet Franc, Cabernet Sauvignon, Claret,
Grenache, Malbec, Merlot, Pinot Gris, Sangiovese, Syrah, Tempranillo, Viognier, Roussanne,
Petite Verdot and Carmenere.
Certificates:
Certified Sustainable
Winery Features:
Tasting Room, Wedding Facilities, Reception
Facilities, Picnic Area, Bus/RV Parking, Wheelchair Accessible and Retail.
****

Slagle Creek Vineyards
www.slaglecreek.com
Winery Address:
1629 Slagle Creek Rd
Grants Pass, OR 97527
(541) 846-6176
Varieties/Wine Styles:
Chardonnay, Merlot and Syrah.
Winery Features:
Retail Sales.
****

Trium
www.riumwine.com
Winery Address:
7112 Rapp Ln
Talent, OR 97540

Willamette Valley Wineries,
continued

(541) 535-4015
Open to Public by Appointment Only
Tasting Room:
Tasting Fee: $ (Refundable with purchase)
Hours: By appointment Only
Tours Available:
By Appointment Only
Varieties/Wine Styles:
Cabernet Franc, Cabernet Sauvignon, Claret, Grenache, Malbec, Merlot, Pinot Gris, Tempranillo and Viognier.
Certificates:
Certified Sustainable
Winery Features:
Tasting Room, Wheelchair Accessible and Retail.
****

Weisinger's of Ashland
www.weisingers.com

Winery Address:
3150 Siskiyou Blvd.
Ashland, OR 97520
(541) 488-5989
Open to Public
Tasting Room:
Tasting Fee: $3-5 (Refundable with purchase)
Tours Available:
By Appointment Only
Varieties/Wine Styles:
Cabernet Franc, Cabernet Sauvignon, Chardonnay, Claret, Gewürztraminer, Merlot, Pinot Noir, Semillon, Syrah and Tempranillo.

Winery Features:
Tasting Room, Bed & Breakfast, Picnic Area, Bus/RV Parking, Wheelchair Accessible and Retail Sales.
****

Wooldridge Creek Vineyard & Winery
www.wcwinery.com

Winery Address:
818 Slagle Creek Rd
Grants Pass, OR 97527
(541) 846-6364
Open to Public
Tasting Room:
Hours: Sat-Sun, 11am - 5pm
Tours Available:
By Appointment Only
Varieties/Wine Styles:
Cabernet Franc, Cabernet Sauvignon, Chardonnay, Gewürztraminer, Late Harvest/Dessert/Ice Wine, Malbec, Merlot, Pinot Noir, Sangiovese, Sparkling, Syrah, Tempranillo, Viognier and Zinfandel.
Winery Features:
Tasting Room, Picnic Area, Wheelchair Accessible and Retail Sales.
****

Southern Oregon

Abacela Vineyards & Winery
www.abacela.com

Winery Address:
12500 Lookingglass Road
Roséburg, OR 97470
(541) 679-6642
Open to Public
Tasting Room:
Tasting Fee: $5 (Refundable with purchase)
Hours: Daily, 11am - 5pm
Tours Available:
By Appointment Only
Varieties/Wine Styles:
Albarino, Cabernet Franc, Claret, Dolcetto, Grenache, Late Harvest/Dessert/Ice Wine, Malbec, Merlot, Muscat, Nebbiolo, Syrah, Tempranillo, Viognier, Graciano, Bastardo, Tinta Roriz, Tinta Amarela, Tinta Cão, Tourig, Naçional , Tannat and Petit Verdot.
Winery Features:
Tasting Room, Picnic Area, Bus/RV Parking, Wheelchair Accessible and Retail.
****

Delfino Vineyards
www.delfinovineyards.com

Winery Address:
3829 Colonial Rd
Roséburg, OR 97470
(541) 673-7575
Tours Available:
By Appointment Only
Varieties/Wine Styles:
Cabernet Sauvignon, Dolcetto, Merlot, Muller-

Southern Oregon, continued

Thurgau, Syrah, Tempranillo and Zinfandel.
****

Flying Dutchman Winery
www.dutchmanwinery.com

Winery Address:
915 First Street Otter Rock,
OR 97369
(541) 765-2553
Open to Public
Tasting Room:
Hours: June-Sept, 11am - 6pm. Rest of the
year 11am - 5pm. Closed Christmas Day.
Varieties/Wine Styles:
Pinot Noir, Cabernet Sauvignon, Cabernet
Franc, Syrah, Chardonnay and Riesling.
Winery Features:
Tasting Room, Picnic Area, Gift Shop and Retail
Sales.

****

Girardet Wine Cellars
www.girardetwine.com

Winery Address:
895 Reston Rd
Roséburg, OR 97470
(541) 679-7252
Open to Public
Tasting Room:
Hours: Daily, 11am - 5pm
Tours Available:
Frequently

Picture Right: *Fall leaves from a Pinot Noir
vine.*

Southern Oregon, continued

Varieties/Wine Styles:
Baco noir, Cabernet Sauvignon, Chardonnay, Gewürztraminer, Pinot Gris, Pinot Noir, Riesling and White Zinfandel.
Winery Features:
Tasting Room, Picnic Area, Bus/RV Parking, Wheelchair Accessible and Retail Sales.
****

Henry Estate Winery
www.henryestate.com
(see pages 124-129)
Winery Address:
687 Hubbard Creekroad
Umpqua, OR 97486
(541) 459-5120
Open to Public
Tasting Room:
Hours: Daily, 11am - 5pm
Tours Available:
Frequently
Varieties/Wine Styles:
Chardonnay, Gewürztraminer , Merlot, Muller-Thurgau , Pinot Gris, Pinot Noir, Riesling, Sparkling, Syrah and Viognier.
Winery Features:
Tasting Room, Wedding Facilities, Reception Facilities, Picnic Area, Bus/RV Parking, Wheelchair Accessible and Retail Sales.
****

Hillcrest Vineyard
www.hillcrestvineyard.com.au
Winery Address:
240 Vineyard Ln
Roséburg, OR 97470
(541) 673-3709
Open to Public
Tasting Room:
Hours: Daily, 11am - 5pm
Tours Available:
Frequently
Varieties/Wine Styles:
Cabernet Sauvignon, Chardonnay, Grenache, Malbec, Merlot, Pinot Noir, Riesling, Sauvignon Blanc, Syrah, Viognier, Zinfandel and Teroldego.
Certificates:
Certified Sustainable
Winery Features:
Tasting Room, Picnic Area, Bus/RV Parking, Wheelchair Accessible and Retail Sales.
****

Marshanne Landing
Winery Address:
381 Hogan Rd
Oakland, OR 97462
(541) 459-8497
Open to Public
Tasting Room:
Tasting Fee: $
Hours: Summer weekends 11am - 5pm
Tours Available:
By Appointment Only
Varieties/Wine Styles:
Cabernet Franc, Cabernet Sauvignon, Chardonnay, Grenache, Merlot, Pinot Noir, Syrah, Tempranillo, Viognier and Mourvedre.

Winery Features:
Tasting Roomm, Wheelchair Accessible and Retail.
****

MelRosé Vineyards
www.melRosévineyards.com
Winery Address:
885 Melqua Rd
Roséburg, OR 97470
(541) 672-6080
Open to Public
Tasting Room:
Hours: Daily, 11am - 5pm
Tours Available:
Frequently
Varieties/Wine Styles:
Baco noir, Chardonnay, Dolcetto, Merlot, Pinot Gris, Pinot Noir, Riesling, Syrah, Tempranillo and Viognier.
Winery Features:
Tasting Room, Wedding Facilities, Reception Facilities, Picnic Area, Bus/RV Parking, Wheelchair Accessible and Retail Sales.
****

Palotai Vineyard and Winery
www.palotaiwines.com
Winery Address:
272 Capital Ln
Roséburg, OR 97470
(541) 464-0032
Open to Public
Tasting Room:
Hours: Fri-Sun, 11am - 5pm
Tasting Fee: $ (Refundable with purchase)
Tours Available:
By Appointment Only

Southern Oregon, continued

Varieties/Wine Styles:
Baco noir, Chardonnay, Claret, Dolcetto, Merlot, Muscat, Pinot Gris, Pinot Noir, Riesling, Syrah, Zinfandel, Bulls Blood and Bella Bianca.
Winery Features:
Tasting Room, Picnic Area, Bus/RV Parking, Wheelchair Accessible and Retail.
****

Spangler Vineyards
www.spanglervineyards.com
Winery Address:
491 Winery Ln
Roséburg, OR 97470
(541) 679-9654
Open to Public
Tasting Room:
Hours: Daily, 11am - 5pm
Tours Available:
By Appointment Only
Varieties/Wine Styles:
Cabernet Franc, Cabernet Sauvignon, Claret, Late Harvest/Dessert/Ice Wine, Merlot, Pinot Noir, Sparkling, Syrah and Viognier.
Winery Features:
Tasting Room, Wedding Facilities, Reception Facilities, Picnic Area, Bus/RV Parking, Wheelchair Accessible and Retail Sales.
****

Eastern Oregon

Cathedral Ridge Winery
www.cathedralridgewinery.com

(see pages 142-147)

Winery Address:
4200 Post Canyon Drive
Hood River, OR 97031
(541) 386-2882
Open to Public
Tasting Room:
Hours: Daily, 11am - 5pm
Tours Available:
Frequently
Varieties/Wine Styles:
Cabernet Sauvignon, Chardonnay, Merlot, Pinot Gris, Pinot Noir, Riesling, Syrah, Blush, Dry Riesling and Cabernet/Merlot.
Winery Features:
Tasting Room, Wedding Facilities, Reception Facilities, Picnic Area, Bus/RV Parking, Wheelchair Accessible and Retail Sales.
****

Dry Hollow Vineyards
www.dryhollowvineyards.com
Winery Address:
3410 Dry Hollow Lane The Dalles,
OR 97058
(541) 296-2953
Tasting Room:
Hours: President's Day Weekend; Memorial Day-Thanksgiving Sat-Sun 12pm - 5pm, Third Friday every month 4pm - 8pm.
Varieties/Wine Styles:
Merlot, Syrah, Chardonnay and Cabernet

Sauvignon.
Winery Features:
Tasting Room, Picnic Area and Retail Sales.
****

Erin Glenn Vineyards
www.eringlenn.com

(see pages 148-153)

Winery Address:
710 East 2nd Street
The Dalles, OR 97058
(541) 296-4707
Open to Public
Tasting Room:
Hours: Thu and Sun 12pm - 5pm, Fri and Sat 12pm - 9pm
Tours Available:
Frequently
Varieties/Wine Styles:
Cabernet Sauvignon, Dolcetto, Gewürztraminer, Late Harvest/Dessert/Ice Wine, Sauvignon Blanc, Syrah, Tempranillo, Viognier and Bordeaux Blends.
Winery Features:
Tasting Room, Reception Facilities, Picnic Area, Bus/RV Parking, Wheelchair Accessible and Retail Sales.
****

Hood River Vineyards
www.hoodrivervineyards.us
Winery Address:
4693 Westwood Drive
Hood River, OR 97031
(541) 386-3772
Open to Public
Tasting Room:
Hours: Daily, 11am - 5pm
Varieties/Wine Styles:
Cabernet Sauvignon, Chardonnay, Fruit,

Gewürztraminer, Merlot, Pinot Gris, Pinot Noir, Riesling, Sangiovese, Syrah, White Zinfandel, Zinfandel, Black Muscat, Barbera other red blends, Rosé, Sherry and Port.
Winery Features:
Tasting Room, Picnic Area, Wheelchair Accessible and Retail Sales.
****

Mt. Hood Winery
www.mthoodwinery.com
Winery Address:
3189 Highway 35
Hood River, OR 97031
(541) 386-8333
Open to Public
Tasting Room:
Hours: 12pm - 5pm
Tours Available:
By Appointment Only
Varieties/Wine Styles:
Chardonnay, Merlot, Pinot Gris and Pinot Noir.
Winery Features
Tasting Room, Wedding Facilities, Reception Facilities, Picnic Area, Bus/RV Parking, Wheelchair Accessible and Retail Sales.
****

Pheasant Valley Winery
www.pheasantvalleywinery.com
Winery Address:
3890 Acree Drive Hood River,
Oregon 97031
(541) 387-3040
Open to Public

Tasting Room:
Hours: Seasonal Hours: April-Oct 11am - 6pm. Winter Hours: Nov-March 11am - 5pm. Closed in January.
Varieties/Wine Styles:
Chardonnay, Pinot Noir, Gewürztraminer, Syrah, Pinot Gris, Cabernet Sauvignon, Riesling,
Winery Features:
Tasting Room, Gift Shop, Picnic Area, Bus/RV Parking and Retail Sales.
****

Phelps Creek Vineyards
www.phelpscreekvineyards.com
Winery Address:
1850 Country Club Rd
Hood River, OR 97031
(541) 386-2607
Open to Public
Tasting Room:
Hours: May-Oct, Wen-Sun 11am - 5pm
Tours Available:
Frequently
Varieties/Wine Styles:
Chardonnay and Pinot Noir.
Winery Features:
Tasting Room, Wedding Facilities, Reception Facilities, Picnic Area, Bus/RV Parking, Wheelchair Accessible and Retail Sales.
****

The Pines
www.thepinesvineyard.com
Winery Address:
202 State St. Hood River,
OR 97031
(541) 993-8301
Open to public
Tasting Room:
Hours: Feb-Dec, Wen-Sun. May-Sep, Wed-Fri

1pm - 7pm, Sat-Sun 12pm - 6pm
Tours Available:
Frequently
Varieties/Wine Styles:
Pinot Gris, Viognier, Merlot, Zinfandel and Syrah.
Winery Features:
Tasting Room and Retail Sales.
****

Quenett Winery
www.quenett.com
Winery Address:
111 Oak Street Hood River,
OR 97031
(541) 386-2229
Tasting Room:
Hours: Daily 12pm - 6pm, Fri-Sat 12pm - 8pm
Varieties/Wine Styles:
Cabernet Sauvignon, Sangiovese, Zinfandel, Merlot, Syrah, Barbera, Viognier, Pinot Gris and Chardonnay.
Winery Features:
Tasting Room and Retail Sales.
****

Viento
www.vientowines.com
Winery Address:
2449 NW West Hill Rd
McMinnville, OR 97128
(503) 434-9587
Additional Tasting Room:
3890 Acree Drive
Hood River, OR 97031
Varieties/Wine Styles:
Late Harvest/Dessert/Ice Wine, Viognier, Syrah, Sangiovese, Barbera, Riesling, Gewürztraminer and Pinot Noir.
Winery Features:

Second Tasting Room and Retail Sales.
****

Wheatridge in the Nook
www.wheatridgeinthenook.com
Winery Address:
11102 Philippi Canyon Lane
Arlington, OR 97812
(541) 454-2585
Open to Public
Tasting Room:
Hours: Sun-Sat, 11am - 6 pm
Tours Available:
Frequently
Varieties/Wine Styles:
Cabernet Sauvignon, Chenin blanc, Chardonnay, Merlot, Sangiovese, Syrah, Viognier and Barbera.
Winery Features:
Tasting Room, Wedding Facilities, Reception Facilities, Bus/RV Parking, Wheelchair Accessible and Retail Sales.
****

Appellation Oregon

Zerba Cellars
www.zerbacellars.com
Winery Address:
85530 Hwy 11
Milton-Freewater, OR 97862
(541) 938-9463
Open to Public
Tasting Room:
Hours: 12pm - 5pm
Tours Available:
By Appointment Only
Varieties/Wine Styles:
Cabernet Franc, Cabernet Sauvignon, Chardonnay, Dolcetto, Grenache, Late Harvest/Dessert/Ice Wine, Malbec, Merlot, Nebbiolo, Sangiovese, Semillon, Syrah, Tempranillo, Viognier, Barberra, Roussanne and Mouvedre.
Winery Features:
Tasting Room, Bus/RV Parking, Wheelchair Accessible and Retail Sales.
****

12 Ranch Wines
www.12ranchwines.com
Winery Address:
4550 Burgdorf Rd
Bonanza, OR 97623
(541) 545-1204
Open to Public by Appointment Only
Tasting Room:
Hours: By Appointment Only
Varieties/Wine Styles:
Cabernet Sauvignon, Chardonnay, Merlot and Syrah.

Winery Features:
Tasting Room, Picnic Area, Bus/RV Parking and Retail Sales.
****

Urban Wine Works
www.urbanwineworks.com
Winery Address:
777 MLK Jr Blvd
Portland, OR 97209
(503) 226-9797
Open to Public
Tasting Room:
Tasting Fee: $7
Hours: Wen-Sat, 12pm - 6pm
Varieties/Wine Styles:
Chardonnay, Gamay Noir, Muscat, Pinot Blanc, Pinot Gris, Pinot Noir, Riesling and Syrah.
Winery Features:
Tasting Room, Second Tasting Room, Wheelchair Accessible and Retail.

Glossary

Appellation is based on a delimited grape-growing region which, in most cases, serves two purposes. 1) to delimit an area based upon topography and climatic conditions where grapes are grown, 2) a guarantee that the grapes used within a specific wine bearing a certain appellation come from that specific delimited area, or a specified percentage thereof. There are many appellations around the world, such as: **Australia**, Australian Geographical Indications; **Austria**, Districtus Austria; **Canada**, Vintners Quality Alliance; **France**, Appellation d'origine contrôlée; **Germany**, German wine classification; **Italy**, Denominazione di Origine Controllata; **Portugal**, Denominação de Origem Controlada; **South Africa**, Wine of Origin; **Spain**, Denominación de Origen; and in the **United States**, American Viticultural Area. Each of these appellations have sub-appellations.

American Viticultural Area (AVA) is a delimited grape-growing region distinguishable by geographic features, with boundaries defined by the United States government's Alcohol and Tobacco Tax and Trade Bureau (TTB). These boundaries are associated with state boundaries, for example, Oregon and Washington State both share three common AVAs: Columbia Gorge, Columbia Valley and the Walla Walla.

Balance is the combination of tannin, acidity, fruit, salt, umami, alcohol, bitterness, weight and overall structure. Moreover, there is another major factor to consider. Is the wine's taste in balance for that specific variety, blend, style or region? These integral combinations of balance are vital not only to the longevity of the wine, but to the wine's terroir (mineral make-up) and style. The overall balance, in accordance with its varietal or blend characteristics, region, style and length is important when matching wine with food.

Biodynamic® or In-Conversion Biodynamic status is given to farms that are operating according to Demeter Certified Biodynamic® standards with a two-year minimum stewardship requirement.

Carbon-Neutral is a program focused on reducing carbon emissions into the atmosphere. There are three steps: 1) energy audit, measurement of greenhouse gases (basically carbon/CO2), 2) creating a footprint for the winery, and 3) the development of a "Carbon Reduction Plan."

Gravity Flow. Its purpose is to reduce unnecessary pressure on the grapes and wine and by naturally transferring from tank to barrel with the use of gravity.

International Pinot Noir Celebration (IPNC) is an annual event held on the last weekend in July. The venue is held at the Linfield College campus in McMinnville, Oregon. The first celebration was in 1986. Pinot noir producers from all over the world are invited to attend. The event is open to the general public by prior ticket. The three-day event cost $795 in 2006.

LEED® stands for the Leadership in Energy and Environmental Design (LEED) Green Building Rating System™ is a nationally accepted benchmark in the United States for the design, construction, and operation of high performance "Green Buildings." LEED promotes a whole-building approach to sustainability. There are five key areas of environmental and human health (sustainable site development, water savings, energy efficiency, materials selection, and Indoor environmental quality).

Length or aftertaste is one of the overall quality characteristics looked for in well-made wines. Wines without length are usually short, flabby, cloying and simple. Length is attributed to a combination of acids, phenols and fruit present in red wines and acids, residual sugars, fruit and phenols, if on lees or oak-matured, in white wines. Quality wines have very long aftertaste, offering lingering sensations and characteristics reminiscent of the wine just tasted. The longer the aftertaste the better the wine, as long as the wine remains in balance with its style, blend and grape characteristics and that no single element dominates. Length is an important factor in quality wines and especially for the sommelier at a restaurant when matching wines with foods.

LIVE (Low Input Viticulture & Enology) LIVE, Inc. is a sustainable agricultural program.

Terroir is originally a French term that is now widely accepted and used internationally in the wine world. It is used to associate specific natural qualities related to the soil and micro-climate within a common area. Some of these qualitative and quantitative parts are recognized as: the mineral and soil content, drainage capabilities and other vital aspect-related features that can affect and differentiate the quality of a vine's fruit, or its vigor— which in turn, affect the fruit's specific character profile, for instance, its aroma and taste. Terroir can cover an entire appellation, a specific area, vineyard, block or individual section of a vineyard.

Tannin is the total grouping of polyphenols. Polyphenols are also known as flavonoids which are all antioxidants and include anthocyanins (color pigments) and tannins (10+). These are all grouped together and for the purpose of tasting called tannin or the wine's astringency. Tannin is a complex compound, whose structure affects the life and stability of the wine itself. It is extracted from the stems, pips, leaves, grape skin and the oak barrels used for maturation.

These tannins together with the acid make-up and fruit give us the balance required for good wines with storage potential. The tannin to acid and fruit ratio is therefore extremely important and directly reflects the quality of the wine. All wines have some tannin in their structure, but, obviously, red wines using colored grapes receive more contact with the skins during maceration and fermentation, where color and tannins are extracted. The tannin's complex structure begins its life cycle in wine as a young, tough, cloying compound, connecting itself to the saliva in the mouth. This is why red wines with a lot of tannin feel dry. The tannin binds itself to the amino acids in your saliva, leaving the mouth without lubrication, hence dry. Tannins can be described as fine or coarse with additional descriptions such as round, octagony and square used to further illustrate feel.

Tilth Certified Organic was founded in 1974. Oregon Tilth is a non-profit research and education membership organization dedicated to biologically sound and socially equitable agriculture.

Typicity or varietal typicity. Grape or blend typicity is an essential aspect of grape identification. Without the traditional grape characteristics we will get sameness. Imagine all wines tasting the same with exactly the same acidity, sugar, tannin, oak and character. There are almost 3000 grape varieties to choose from, all of which have their own characteristics and technical compositions, we must, without abate, insist on winemakers adhering to the accepted and recognized qualities for grapes or blends. Grape and blend typicity is the wine-taster's key in identifying and matching wine with food. Grape or blend typicity is therefore dependent on the grape variety, blend and terroir:

VINEA – The Winegrowers' Sustainable Trust is a voluntary group of winegrowers that have taken a pledge to produce grapes and wine using environmental, economic and social sustainability practices.

Index

Bibliography

Clive S. Michelsen. "*Tasting & Grading Wine*." Malmö: JAC International AB, 2005. ISBN: 91-975326-0-6

Oregon Wine Board. "*Grower and Winery Resources*." Portland: Oregon Wine Board, 2007.

National Agricultural Statistics Service. "*2006 Oregon Vineyard and Winery Report*." Portland: , USDA. 2007.

Photo Credits

Frank Barnett Photography ©. Pages: 6 C, 7, 66 L1 and 66 L2.

Beaux Frères©. Pages: 113, 115 R2, 116.

Cathedral Ridge Winery©. Pages: 143 insert, 144 L3,

Clive Michelsen©. Pages: 2,9, 10 all, 15, 16, 17, 20, 27, 31, 32, 35, 36, 40, 52, 54, 59, 60, 61, 63, 65, 66 L3, 66 L4, 68, 71, 72, 73, 74, 76, 78 L1 & L2, 79, 80 insert, 83, 84, 85, 86, 89, 90, 91, 92, 93, 95, 96, 97, 98, 101, 102, 103, 104, 108 L1-3, 109, 110, 114, 115 R1 R3 & R4, 121, 125, 126, 127, 128, 131, 133, 134, 135137, 138, 139, 140 insert, 142 144 L1 -2 & L4, 145, 146, 149, 150, 151, 152, 175, 179, 187, 189R, 198, 199, 202, 203, 205, 206, 210, 213, 218, 219, 222, 230, 231, 238, 238, 246, 247.

Del Rio Vineyards & Winery©. Page: 41.

Domaine Serene©. Pages: 78 L3 & L4, 80, and 214.

Janis Miglavs. Pages: 6 L, 12, 25, 39, 42, 51, 56, 57, 67, 68 insert, 140, 154, 155, 157, 158, 160, 162, 165, 167, 169, 171, 173, 177, 181, 183, 189L, 191, 193, 195, 197, 220, 226, 227, 234, 237, 242, 249, 250, 253, and 264.

Josuha Bergström©. Pages: 28, 106, 108 L4, and 244.

King Estate©. Pages: 46, 119, 120, 122, and 123.

Oregon Wine Board©. Pages: 23, 26, and 201.

Sokol Blosser©. Page: 108 R1.

Willamette Valley Vineyards©. Pages: 57, 154, and 220.

Cover Design

Design: Eaterine Bagdavadze
Pictures: Clive Michelsen & Janis Miglavs.

Picture Right: Pinot Noir prior to harvest.